CW00953292

CLASSICAL AUTHORS

500 BCE TO 1100 CE

THE BRITANNICA GUIDE TO AUTHORS

CLASSICAL AUTHORS

500 BCE to 1100 CE

EDITED BY KATHLEEN KUIPER, SENIOR EDITOR, ARTS AND CULTURE

Britannica
Educational Publishing

IN ASSOCIATION WITH

ROSEN
EDUCATIONAL SERVICES

Published in 2014 by Britannica Educational Publishing
(a trademark of Encyclopædia Britannica, Inc.)
in association with Rosen Educational Services, LLC
29 East 21st Street, New York, NY 10010.

Copyright © 2014 Encyclopædia Britannica, Inc. Britannica, Encyclopædia Britannica,
and the Thistle logo are registered trademarks of Encyclopædia Britannica, Inc. All
rights reserved.

Rosen Educational Services materials copyright © 2014 Rosen Educational Services, LLC.
All rights reserved.

Distributed exclusively by Rosen Educational Services.
For a listing of additional Britannica Educational Publishing titles, call toll free (800) 237-9932.

First Edition

Britannica Educational Publishing
J.E. Luebering: Director, Core Reference Group
Adam Augustyn: Assistant Manager, Core Reference Group
Marilyn L. Barton: Senior Coordinator, Production Control
Steven Bosco: Director, Editorial Technologies
Lisa S. Braucher: Senior Producer and Data Editor
Yvette Charboneau: Senior Copy Editor
Kathy Nakamura: Manager, Media Acquisition
Kathleen Kuiper, Senior Editor, Arts and Culture

Rosen Educational Services
Jeanne Nagle: Senior Editor
Nelson Sá: Art Director
Cindy Reiman: Photography Manager
Karen Huang: Photo Researcher
Brian Garvey: Designer
Introduction by Joseph Kampff

Library of Congress Cataloging-in-Publication Data

Classical Authors, 500 BCE to 1100 CE/edited by Kathleen Kuiper—First edition
pages cm.—(The Britannica guide to authors)
"In association with Britannica Educational Publishing, Rosen Educational Services."
Includes bibliographical references and index.
ISBN 978-1-61530-997-9 (library binding)
1. Authorship—History. 2. Creation (Literary, artistic, etc.)—History. I. Kuiper, Kathleen.
879—d23

Manufactured in the United States of America

On the cover, p. iii: Bust of the Greek historian Herodotus, who brought a storyteller's
flair to his recounting of Greek-Persian wars in his multi-volume *History. DEA/G.
Nimatallah/De Agostini/Getty Images*

CONTENTS

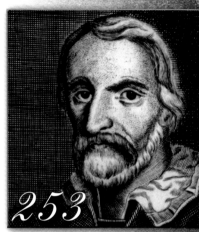

297

INTRODUCTION

Stone carving found in the tomb of Mery, chief scribe of Saqqara royal archives, in Egypt. DEA/G. Dagli Orti/De Agostini Picture Library/Getty Images

Do authors matter? This is perhaps the first question readers of this book, the first volume of the Britannica Guide to Authors series, may wish to ask themselves. Yet, because the answer seems self-evident, casual readers may never get around to formulating this question. Typically one thinks glancingly (if at all) that there is a person behind the telling of a story and then gets on with the business of reading. Nevertheless, the question of an author's significance is not only interesting, but meaningful. What conclusions are drawn can profoundly affect the way in which texts are read and the significance readers are able to derive from those texts.

To fully understand the significance of authorship, one may start by defining the term itself. *Encyclopædia Britannica* defines an *author* as "one who is the source of some form of intellectual or creative work; especially, one who composes a book, article, poem, play, or other literary work intended for publication." *Britannica* adds that the word *author* is derived from the Latin *auctor*, which means "authorizer, responsible agent, originator, or maker." Thus authors may be seen as authorities of sorts; as the creators of literary works they in some way authorize a work's meaning and can be held accountable for its effects.

This connotation of the word *author* may be usefully compared with that of the word *writer*. Descending from the Old English *wrītan*—which means "to scratch, draw, or inscribe"—the word *writer* does not have the metaphysical heft of *author*. Common sense seems to bear out this distinction. While readers often find it quite important to know who authored the novel or poem they are about to read or the play they intend to see, most people are unlikely to concern themselves with who wrote the instruction manual that came with a new cell phone.

In an academic setting, students often find it challenging to read works that were written in another era. Not only are the culture and manners alien, but sometimes it is especially difficult to become comfortable with an author's style. Students often assume that knowledge of the author's life and historical context will help make sense of his or her work. Indeed, this approach to reading probably strikes most people as perfectly natural, sensible, and practical. The mining of the author's biography for inferences about a work's meaning in fact became the standard method of interpretation practiced by literary critics of the 19th and early 20th centuries. In the latter half of the 20th century, however, several prominent literary theorists called this author-based method of interpretation into question; the debate about the significance of authorship in literary interpretation continues today. The arguments against authorship that were advanced by the mid 20th-century New Critics—who asserted that meaning was to be determined strictly by examination of the work itself and not by biography-based suppositions—and by later literary theorists as well are compelling, but they have not, for all their influence, entirely erased the authors. Generally speaking, most thinking people agree that while it is a bad idea to read an author's biography with a strict view to psychological interpretation of that author's work, it sometimes helps a reader to understand the context of the storytelling—how this particular author came to tell this particular story at this particular time.

In fact, authors continue to matter precisely because they provide the basis of the conversation the reader engages in. Reading is a participatory activity. No novel, play, poem, or other literary work exists in a vacuum. An author provides a vision of the world; a reader responds to that vision through a personal filter made from experience and contemplation. The author's personal story and particular circumstances in a sense hold open the door. A sound understanding of a text's provenance will considerably enrich the meanings readers are able to construct. By the same token, a knowledge of the author's own story may deter a reader from examining that individual's perspective. Is the author's experience similar to one's own? Does her style strike a deeper chord? In presenting a wealth of accurate, in-depth biographical, contextual, bibliographical, and critical information on authors of the Classical period, the *Britannica Guide to Authors: 500 BCE to 1100 CE* provides an invaluable tool for those who wish to read with authority.

Perhaps surprisingly, the first author the reader encounters in this book may not be a single author, or even an author at all in the traditional sense of that word. Yet the works attributed to Homer are some of the most influential in Western literature. It would be difficult to overstate the importance of Homer's *Iliad* and *Odyssey*. These epic poems formed an essential component of ancient Greek and Latin education—and, as such, their influence can be detected throughout works of the Classical period, such as in Virgil's *Aeneid*. They also held a more exalted position in the minds of ancient Greeks, who memorized these works and looked to them for insights into lofty subjects such as honour, heroism, leadership, and other aspects of Greek identity and culture, as well as for advice on more practical, day-to-day matters. Thus, the *Iliad* and the *Odyssey* are foundational texts for Western civilization. They have greatly influenced thinkers and writers of the Renaissance in Italy. More recently, the books of Homer's *Odyssey* served as a structural model for James Joyce's *Ulysses*, a work that many critics consider the greatest novel of the 20th century. Homer continues to inspire writers in the 21st century—such as Australian poet and novelist David Malouf (*Ransom*, 2009) and

American novelist and computer programmer Zachery Mason (*The Lost Books of the Odyssey*, 2010).

It is probable that there was a historic figure called Homer who lived in Ionia (now Turkey) in the 9th or 8th centuries BCE and that this figure contributed greatly to the *Iliad* and the *Odyssey* as we know them today. It is less likely that he authored these works. Rather, Homer's involvement with these works may be better compared to the work of a talented editor. Although it is not impossible that he composed both the *Iliad* and the *Odyssey*, it is more likely that Homer—a poet, or *aoidos* ("singer") working in an oral tradition—pieced together the works from many shorter, preexisting poems that he had reformed and developed in the process of memorizing them for recital. Questions concerning the authorship of these poems appear to have emerged among the ancients themselves, and these doubts have lingered since. Modern readers are perhaps too far removed from the origins of these poems to answer the questions of their authorship with any certainty. Nevertheless, important and compelling explanations of the poems' formulaic structures and their impacts on past readers and cultures have resulted from careful analyses of the *Iliad* and the *Odyssey* through the lens of authorship. By familiarizing themselves with the most current information about Homer, his texts and contexts, as well as storytelling and history in Classical times, readers will have at their disposal some of the tools necessary for a rich, and richly rewarding, reading experience.

While the *Iliad* and *Odyssey* are universally recognized as great works of literature, the works of Marcus Tullius Cicero are of a vastly different nature. Cicero was a Roman orator, statesman, philosopher, and writer who lived from 106 BCE to 43 CE. Although he is acknowledged as a minor poet—his technical innovation profoundly influenced Virgil's work—he is known primarily for his speeches, his writings on rhetoric, and his letters. Today, Cicero is largely recognized as the greatest Roman orator and an important politician whose presence in Roman politics toward the end of the Roman Republic cannot be overstated.

Cicero was one of the earliest epistolary authors. More than 900 of Cicero's letters from the year 67 BCE to his death still exist. These are organized into four collections: letters to his friends, to his brother, to Marcus Junius Brutus, and to his publisher and financial advisor Titus Pomponius Atticus, to whom the majority of the letters are addressed. Cicero's vast correspondence has proved invaluable to historians, who would be unable to accurately date many important historical events of the period without it. His letters also provide remarkable access to the man himself. In his letters to Brutus, Cicero candidly describes what he believes are the keys to his success as an orator. Chief among them is his excellent and far-reaching knowledge of literature.

The authors of a number of works treated in this book are unknown; these tales are included because they are foundational to the cultures that produced them. Among these anonymous works is *Beowulf*, a heroic, epic poem considered by scholars to be the greatest extant work of Old English literature. Although it was probably composed in the early part of the 8th century, *Beowulf* did not appear in print until 1815. Not only did the work lack a named author, it originally was printed without a title. The name by which it is known was derived from the later convention of referring to the text by the main protagonist's name. It is a classic of Germanic tradition, and it has remained a compelling read in the hands of such translators as the Irish poet Seamus Heaney.

Another anonymous work that has persisted in the Western tradition is *The Thousand and One Nights*, a collection of stories without a single author or geographic origin. The tales in this collection descend from the long oral traditions of places such as India, Iran, Iraq, Egypt, and Turkey. *The Thousand and One Nights* consists of a diverse assembly of fairy tales, romances, fables, and parables and other genres. Arguably the most famous tales are those of "Aladdin and the Magic Lamp," "Ali Baba and the Forty Thieves," and "Sindbad the Sailor." The collection is unified by a "frame narrative." The stories are presented as being told to King Shahryar.

The king, having been regularly deceived by his wife, seeks revenge for his disgrace by marrying and killing a new wife every day. This cycle of violence ends unexpectedly when he marries Scheherazade. On their first night together, Scheherazade tells the king a story that carries them through the night and into the early morning. Though the king has every intention of killing Scheherazade when her tale is finished, she ends her recitation without concluding the story. The cliffhanger proves irresistible to Shahryar. Because he must hear how the story ends, he puts off the execution until the next night. Scheherazade weaves the conclusion of one story into the next, and, by nightly leaving her story unfinished, she is able to elude her death sentence indefinitely. The tale of Scheherazade and Shahryar provides the frame story that unites the collection.

No matter what they read or how they read it—delving into the electronic version of the latest science fiction novel on a tablet, flipping through the pages of a graphic novel or comic book, or studying the classics for school (or for pleasure)—readers are tethered to what they read. The ways in which readers think about authors and their relationships to the texts they produce are innumerable. As readers read, the works in which they are immersed take on a richness, a meaning far beyond the intentions of the author. They superimpose their own experiences onto an author's storyline. Authors also are tied to their own sources of inspiration. Each of the authors included in this volume was influenced by his or her culture and traditions, as well as by an appreciation of other writers or other sources of inspiration. Most of all, authors and readers share a love of interaction, of the ancient connection between storyteller and audience.

HOMER

(fl. 9th or 8th century BCE?, Ionia? [now in Turkey])

The presumed author of the two great epic poems of ancient Greece—the *Iliad* and the *Odyssey*—is a shadowy figure called Homer. Little is known of him beyond the fact that his was the name attached in antiquity by the Greeks themselves to the poems. That there was an epic poet called Homer and that he played the primary part in shaping the *Iliad* and the *Odyssey*—so much may be said to be probable. If this assumption is accepted, then Homer must assuredly be one of the greatest of the world's literary artists.

He is also one of the most influential authors in the widest sense, for the two epics provided the basis of Greek education and culture throughout the Classical age and formed the backbone of humane education down to the time of the Roman Empire and the spread of Christianity. Indirectly through the medium of Virgil's *Aeneid* (which was loosely molded after the patterns

Statue of Homer, to whom two of literature's greatest works, the Iliad and the Odyssey, are attributed. Gregory Markov/Shutterstock.com

of the *Iliad* and the *Odyssey*), directly through their revival under Byzantine culture from the late 8th century CE onward, and subsequently through their passage into Italy with the Greek scholars who fled westward from the Ottomans, the Homeric epics had a profound impact on the Renaissance culture of Italy. Since then the proliferation of translations has helped to make them the most important poems of the Classical European tradition.

It was probably through their impact on Classical Greek culture itself that the *Iliad* and the *Odyssey* most subtly affected Western standards and ideas. The Greeks regarded the great epics as something more than works of literature; they knew much of them by heart, and they valued them not only as a symbol of Hellenic unity and heroism but also as an ancient source of moral and even practical instruction.

The general belief that Homer was a native of Ionia (the central part of the western seaboard of Asia Minor) seems a reasonable conjecture for the poems themselves are in predominantly Ionic dialect. Although Smyrna and Chios early began competing for the honour (the poet Pindar, early in the 5th century BCE, associated Homer with both), and others joined in, no authenticated local memory survived anywhere of someone who, oral poet or not, must have been remarkable in his time. The absence of hard facts puzzled but did not deter the Greeks; the fictions that had begun even before the 5th century BCE were developed in the Alexandrian era. The longest to have survived purports to be by Herodotus himself; but it is quite devoid of objective truth.

Modern Inferences

Modern scholars agree with the ancient sources only about Homer's general place of activity. The most concrete piece of ancient evidence is that his descendants, the Homeridae, lived on the Ionic island of Chios. Yet an east Aegean environment is suggested for the main author of the *Iliad* by certain local references in the poem; that is, to the peak of Samothrace just appearing over the intervening mass of Imbros when seen from the plain of Troy, to the birds at the mouth of the Cayster near Ephesus, to storms off Icaria and northwest winds from Thrace. East Aegean colouring is fainter in the *Odyssey*, which is set primarily in western Greece.

Admittedly, there is some doubt over whether the *Iliad* and the *Odyssey* were even composed by the same main author. Such doubts began in antiquity itself and depended mainly on the difference of genre (the *Iliad* being martial and heroic, the *Odyssey* picaresque and often fantastic), but they may be reinforced by subtle differences of vocabulary even apart from those imposed by different subjects.

The internal evidence of the poems is of some use in determining when Homer lived. Certain elements of the poetic language, which was an artificial amalgam never exactly reproduced in speech, indicate that the epics were not only post-Mycenaean in composition but also substantially later than the foundation of the first Ionian settlements in Asia Minor of about 1000 BCE. The running together of adjacent short vowels and the disappearance of the semivowel digamma (a letter formerly existing in the Greek alphabet) are the most significant indications of this. At the other end of the time scale the development in the poems of a true definite article, for instance, represents an earlier phase than is exemplified in the poetry of the middle and late 7th century. Both stylistically and metrically, the Homeric poems appear to be earlier than the Hesiodic poems, which many scholars place not long after 700 BCE. A different and perhaps more precise criterion is provided by datable objects and practices mentioned in the poems. Nothing, except for one or two probably Athenian additions, seems from this standpoint to be later than about 700; on the other hand, the role assigned in the *Odyssey* to the Phoenicians as traders, together with one or two other phenomena, suggests a date of composition— for the relevant contexts at least—of sometime after 900. A few passages in the *Iliad* may imply a new form of fighting in close formation, dependent on the development of special armour for foot soldiers (hoplites) after about 750, and references to the Gorgon mask as a decorative motif point in the same direction. It seems plausible to conclude that the period of composition was the 9th or 8th century, with several features pointing more clearly to the 8th. It may be no coincidence that cults of Homeric heroes tended to spring up toward the end of the 8th century, and that scenes from the epic begin to appear on pots at just about the same time.

Homer as an Oral Poet

But even if his name is known and his date and region can be inferred, Homer remains primarily a projection of the great poems themselves. Their qualities are significant of his taste and his view of the world, but they also reveal something more specific about his technique and the kind of poet he was. It has been one of the most important discoveries of Homeric scholarship, associated particularly with the name of an American scholar, Milman Parry, that the Homeric tradition was an oral one—that this was a kind of poetry made and passed down by word of mouth and without the intervention of writing. Indeed Homer's own term for a poet is *aoidos*, "singer." The *Odyssey* describes two such poets in some detail: Phemius, the court singer in the palace of Odysseus in Ithaca, and Demodocus, who lived in the town of the semi-mythical Phaeacians and sang both

4

for the nobles in Alcinous's palace and for the assembled public at the games held for Odysseus. On this occasion he sings of the illicit love affair of Ares and Aphrodite in a version that lasts for exactly 100 Homeric verses. This and the other songs assigned to these singers—for example, that of the Trojan Horse, summarized in the *Odyssey*—suggest that ordinary *aoidoi* in the heroic tradition worked with relatively short poems that could be given completely on a single occasion. That is what one would expect, and it is confirmed by the habits of singers and audiences at other periods and in other parts of the world (the tradition of the poet-singers of Serbia has provided the most fruitful comparison so far). Whatever the favoured occasion for heroic song—whether the aristocratic feast, the religious festival, or popular gatherings in tavern or marketplace—a natural limitation on the length of a poem is imposed by the audience's available time and interest as well as by the singer's own physique and the scope of his repertoire. Such relatively short songs must have provided the backbone of the tradition inherited by Homer, and his portraits of Demodocus and Phemius are likely to be accurate in this respect. What Homer himself seems to have done is to introduce the concept of a quite different style of poetry, in the shape of a monumental poem that required more than a single hour or evening to sing and could achieve new and far more complex effects, in literary and psychological terms, than those attainable in the more anecdotal and episodic songs of his predecessors.

Poetic Techniques

It can be asked how one can be so confident in classing Homer himself as an oral singer, for if he differed from Phemius or Demodocus in terms of length, he may also have differed radically in his poetic techniques. The very nature of his verse may provide a substantial part of the answer. The style of the poems is "formulaic"; that is, they rely heavily on the use not only of stock epithets and repeated verses or groups of verses—which can also be found to a much lesser extent in a literate imitator like Virgil—but also on a multitude of fixed phrases that are employed time and time again to express a similar idea in a similar part of the verse. The clearest and simplest instance is the so-called noun-epithet formulas. These constitute a veritable system, in which every major god or hero possesses a variety of epithets from which the choice is made solely according to how much of the verse, and which part of it, the singer desires to use up. Odysseus is called divine Odysseus, many-counseled Odysseus, or much-enduring divine Odysseus simply in accordance with the amount of material to be fitted into the remainder of the hexameter (six-foot) verse. A ship is described as black, hollow, or symmetrical not to distinguish this particular ship from others but solely in relation to the qualities and demands of the rhythmical context.

The whole noun-epithet system is both extensive and economical—it covers a great variety of subjects with very little exact reduplication or unnecessary overlap. It would seem that so refined and complex a system could not be the invention of a single poet but must have been gradually evolved in a long-standing tradition that needed both the extension and the economy for functional reasons—that depended on these fixed phrase units because of its oral nature, in which memory, practice, and a kind of improvising replace the deliberate, self-correcting, word-by-word progress of the pen-and-paper composer. Admittedly, the rest of Homer's vocabulary is not as markedly formulaic as its noun-epithet aspect (or, another popular example, as its expressions for beginning and ending a speech). Many expressions, many portions of sentences are individually invented for the occasion, or at least so it seems. Even so, there is a strongly formulaic and ready-made component in the artificial language that was used by Homer, including its less conspicuous aspects such as the arrangement of particles, conjunctions, and pronouns.

It looks, therefore, as though Homer must have trained as an ordinary *aoidos*, who began by building up a repertoire of normal-length songs acquired from already established singers. The greatest heroic adventures of the past must already have been prominent in any repertoire, especially the Panhellenic adventures of the Seven Against Thebes, the Argonauts, and the Achaean attack on Troy. Some aspects of the Trojan War might already have been expanded into songs of unusual length, though one that was still manageable on a single occasion. Yet the process was presumably carried much further in the making of the monumental *Iliad*, consisting of more than 16,000 verses, which would take four or five long evenings, and perhaps more, to perform. This breakthrough into the monumental, which made exceptional and almost unreasonable demands of audiences, presupposes a singer of quite exceptional capacity and reputation—one who could impose the new and admittedly difficult form upon his listeners by the sheer unfamiliar genius of his song. The 8th century BCE was in other respects, too, an era of cultural innovation, not least in the direction of monumentality, and huge temples (like the early temple of Hera in Samos) and colossal funerary vases (like the amphorae in the so-called Geometric style from the Dipylon cemetery in Athens) may have found a literary analogue in the idea of a vast poetical treatment of the Trojan War.

But in an important sense Homer was building upon a tendency of all known oral heroic poetry toward elaboration and expansion. Singers do not acquire a song from another singer by simple memorization. They adjust what

7

they hear to an existing store of phrases, typical scenes, and themes, and they tend to replace what is unfamiliar with something they already know, or to expand it by adding familiar material that it happens to lack. Every singer in a living oral tradition tends to develop what is acquired from other singers. There is an element of improvisation, as well as of memory, in the appropriation of fresh material.

Cumulative Poetic Structure

Homer must have decided to elaborate his materials not only in quality but also in length and complexity. All oral poetry is cumulative in essence; the verse is built up by adding phrase upon phrase, the individual description by adding verse upon verse. The whole plot of a song consists of the progressive accumulation of minor motifs and major themes, from simple ideas (such as "the hero sets off on a journey" or "addresses his enemy") through typical scenes (such as assemblies of mortals or gods) to developed but standardized thematic complexes (such as episodes of recognition or reconciliation). Homer seems to have carried this cumulative tendency into new regions of poetry and narrative. In this as in other respects (for example, in his poetical language) he was applying his own individual vision to the fertile raw material of an extensive and well-known tradition.

The result is much more complex than with an ordinary traditional poem. Understanding the origin and essential qualities of the *Iliad* or the *Odyssey* entails trying to sort out not only the separate components of the pre-Homeric tradition but also Homer's own probable contributions, whether distinguishable by their dependence on the monumental idea or by their apparent novelty vis-à-vis the tradition as a whole or by other means. Dialectal and linguistic components must be identified as far as possible—survivals of the Mycenaean language, for example, or words used exclusively in the Aeolian cities of the west coast of Asia Minor, or Athenian dialect forms introduced into the poems after the time of Homer. So, too, must specific references to such elements as armour, clothing, houses, burial customs, and political geography, be assignable to a particular era, the Late Bronze Age, the Early Iron Age, or the period of Homer's own activity—at the very least to be taken as relatively early or late within the whole range of the poetic tradition down to Homer. These are the tasks of modern Homeric scholarship.

Stabilizing the Text

An important and difficult question that affects the accuracy of modern Homeric texts, is that of the date when the epics became "fixed"—which means given authoritative written form, since oral transmission is always to some extent fluid. An alphabetic writing system reached Greece in the 9th or early 8th century BCE. Before that was a gap of 200 or 300 years, following the collapse of Mycenaean culture and the disappearance of Linear B writing (with each sign generally representing a syllable), during which Greece seems to have been nonliterate.

During that interval, certainly, much of the epic tradition was formed. The earliest alphabetic inscriptions to have survived, a few of them containing brief scraps of hexameter verse, date from about 730 BCE. Therefore, if Homer created the *Iliad* at some time after 750 BCE, he could conceivably have used writing to help him. Scholars do not know for certain, but this much can be generally agreed: that the use of writing was ancillary, and that Homer behaved in important ways like a traditional oral poet.

At least it may be accepted that partial texts of the epics were probably being used by the Homeridae and by professional reciters known as rhapsodes by the latter part of the 7th century BCE. The first complete version may well have been that established as a standard for rhapsodic competitions at the great quadrennial festival at Athens, the Panathenaea, at some time during the 6th century BCE. Even that did not permanently fix the text, and from then on the history of the epics was one of periodical distortion followed by progressively more effective acts of stabilization. The widespread dissemination of the poems consequent upon the growth of the Athenian book trade in the 5th century and the proliferation of libraries after the 4th was followed by the critical work of the Alexandrian scholar Aristarchus of Samothrace in the 2nd century BCE, and much later by the propagation of accurate minuscule texts (notably the famous manuscript known as Venetus A of the *Iliad*), incorporating the best results of Greco-Roman scholarship, in the Byzantine world of the Middle Ages. Rare portions of either poem may have been added after, but not long after, the main act of composition. Even so, the overriding impression is one of powerful unity.

The Iliad

The *Iliad* is not merely a distillation of the whole protracted war against Troy but simultaneously an exploration of the heroic ideal in all its self-contradictoriness—its insane and grasping pride, its magnificent but animal strength, its ultimate if obtuse humanity. The poem is, in truth, the story of the wrath of Achilles, the greatest warrior on the Greek side, that is announced in its very first words. Yet for thousands of verses on end Achilles is an unseen presence as he broods among his Myrmidons, waiting for Zeus's promise to be fulfilled—the promise that the Trojans will set fire to the Achaean ships and force King Agamemnon to beg him to return to the fight. Much of the poetry between the first book, in which the quarrel flares up, and the 16th, in which Achilles makes the crucial concession of allowing his friend Patroclus to fight on his behalf, consists of long scenes of battle, in which individual encounters alternate with mass movements of the opposing armies.

The battle poetry is based on typical and frequently recurring elements and motifs, but it is also subtly varied by highly individualized episodes and set pieces: the catalog of troop contingents, the formal duels between Paris and Menelaus and Ajax and Hector, Helen's identifying of the Achaean princes, Agamemnon inspecting his troops, the triumph of Diomedes, Hector's famous meeting back in Troy with his wife Andromache, the building of the Achaean wall, the unsuccessful embassy to Achilles, the night expedition, Hera's seduction of Zeus, and Poseidon's subsequent invigoration of the Achaeans. Patroclus's death two-thirds of the way through the poem brings Achilles back into the fight, although not before the recovery of Patroclus's body, the making of new divine armour for Achilles, and his formal reconciliation with Agamemnon. In book 22 he kills the deluded Hector; next he restores his heroic status by means of the funeral games for Patroclus; and in the concluding book Achilles is compelled by the gods to restore civilized values and his own magnanimity by surrendering Hector's body to King Priam.

The Odyssey

The *Odyssey* tends to be blander in expression and sometimes more diffuse in the progress of its action, but it presents an even more complex and harmonious structure than the *Iliad*. The main elements are the situation in Ithaca, where Penelope, Odysseus's wife, and their young son, Telemachus, are powerless before her arrogant suitors as they despair of Odysseus's return from the siege of Troy; Telemachus's secret journey to the Peloponnese for news of his father, and his encounters there with Nestor, Menelaus, and Helen; Odysseus's dangerous passage, opposed by the sea-god Poseidon himself, from Calypso's island to that of the Phaeacians, and his narrative there (from book 9 to book 12) of his fantastic adventures after leaving Troy, including his escape from the cave of the Cyclops, Polyphemus; his arrival back in Ithaca, solitary and by night, at the poem's halfway point, followed by his meeting with his protector-goddess Athena, his elaborate disguises, his self-revelation to the faithful swineherd Eumaeus and then to Telemachus, their complicated plan for disposing of the suitors, and its gory fulfillment. Finally comes the recognition by his faithful Penelope, his recounting to her of his adventures, his meeting with his aged father, Laertes, and the restitution, with Athena's help, of stability in his island kingdom of Ithaca.

The result of Homer's fusion of formulaic style and brilliant personal vision is an impressive amalgam of literary power and refinement. The *Iliad* and the *Odyssey*, however, owe their preeminence not so much to their antiquity and to their place in Greek culture as a whole but to their timeless success in expressing on a massive scale so much of the triumph and the frustration of human life. Their greatest power lies, perhaps, in their dramatic quality because much of each poem consists of conversation and speeches, in which rhetoric is kept firmly under control and the individual characters emerge as they confront each other and the gods with advice, inquiry, request, resignation, and passion. Achilles, Hector, Menelaus, Ajax, Odysseus, and the others acquire a kind of heroic glow that even Greek tragedy later found hard to emulate.

HESIOD

(fl. *c.* 700 BCE)

Not a great deal is known about the details of Hesiod's life. Hesiodos (Latin Hesiodus) was a native of Boeotia, a district of central Greece to which his father had migrated from Cyme in Asia Minor. Hesiod may at first have been a professional reciter of poetry, learning the technique and vocabulary of the epic by memorizing and reciting heroic songs. He himself attributes his poetic gifts to the Muses, who appeared to him while he was tending his sheep. Giving him a poet's staff and endowing him with a poet's voice, they bade him "sing of the race of the blessed gods immortal."

That his epics won renown during his lifetime is shown by his participation in the contest of songs at the funeral games of Amphidamas at Chalcis on the island of Euboea. This, he says, was the

Hesiod, detail of a 3rd-century mosaic by Monnus; in the Rhenish State Museum, Trier, Germany. Courtesy of the Rheinisches Landesmuseum, Trier, Germany.

only occasion on which he crossed the sea, but it is not likely to have been the only invitation he received from places other than his hometown of Ascra, near Mount Helicon.

Genuine Works

Two of Hesiod's complete epics have survived—the *Theogony*, relating the myths of the gods, and the *Works and Days*, describing rural life. The *Theogony* is clearly the earlier of the two. In it, following the Muses' instructions, Hesiod recounts the history of the gods, beginning with the emergence of Chaos, Gaea (Earth), and Eros. Gaea gives birth to Uranus (Heaven), the Mountains, and Pontus (the Sea); and later, after uniting herself to Uranus, she bears many other deities. One of them is the Titan Cronus, who rebels against Uranus, emasculates him, and afterward rules until he in turn is overpowered by Zeus. This story of crime and revolt, which is the central subject of the *Theogony*, is interrupted by many additional pedigrees of gods. Elsewhere, in addition to mythical family relations, Hesiod presents new ones that are the product of his own speculation. Thus, the names of the 50 sea maidens (the Nereids) fathered by the sea god Nereus indicate various qualities of the Sea. In a different way, the story describing the first woman, Pandora, sent by Zeus to bedevil mortals, brings out Hesiod's firm belief in the supreme and irresistible power of Zeus. This power is most majestically displayed in the Titanomachia, the battle between the Olympian gods, led by Zeus, and the Titans, who support Cronus.

Hesiod's authorship of the *Theogony* once was questioned but is no longer doubted, though the work does include sections inserted by later poets and rhapsodes. The story of Typhoeus's rebellion against Zeus was almost certainly added by someone else, while the somewhat overlapping accounts of Tartarus, the hymn on Hecate, and the progeny of the sea monster Keto are highly suspect. The discovery of a Hurrian (Middle Eastern) theogony similar to Hesiod's seems to indicate that Hesiod's theogony owes significant episodes to Middle Eastern models. Nonetheless, the Uranus-Cronus-Zeus succession as told by Hesiod approximates the pattern of a classical Greek tragic trilogy. Thus, the Erinyes (the Fates, or deities of vengeance) are born when Uranus is overthrown by Cronus, while their own hour for action comes when Cronus is about to be overthrown by Zeus. These and other similar features plausibly represent Hesiod's own contributions to the inherited story.

Hesiod's other epic poem, the *Works and Days*, has a more personal character. It is addressed to his brother Perses, who by guile and bribery has already secured for himself an excessive share of their inheritance and is seeking to gain another advantage in a similar manner. Trying to dissuade him from such practices, Hesiod recounts in the first part of the poem two myths illustrating the necessity for honest, hard work in the wretched life of humankind. One continues the story of Pandora, who out of curiosity opens a jar, loosing multifarious evils on humanity; the other traces human decline since the Golden Age. Against the brutality and injustice of his contemporaries, Hesiod affirms his unshakable belief in the power of justice. For him, Justice is a deity and, indeed, Zeus's favourite daughter, and the happiness of individuals as well as of communities depends on their treatment of her.

The part of Hesiod's message that exalts justice and deprecates hubris is addressed to the leaders of his community, who seem inclined to abet Perses. Hesiod also speaks to Perses directly, urging him to abandon his schemes and thenceforth to gain his livelihood through strenuous and persistent work: "Before success the immortal gods have placed the sweat of our brows." Hard work is for Hesiod the only way to prosperity and distinction. The concept of life that Hesiod here develops is in conscious opposition to the more glorious ideals of the heroic epic of Homer.

In the second half of the poem, Hesiod describes with much practical detail the kind of work appropriate to each part of the calendar and explains how to set about it. The description of the rural year is enlivened by a vivid feeling for the rhythm of human life and the forces of nature, from the overpowering winter storm, which drives people back into their homes, to the parching heat of summer, during which humans must have respite from their labours.

The poem ends with a series of primitive taboos and superstitions, followed by a section explaining which parts of the month are auspicious for sowing, threshing, shearing, and the begetting of children. It is difficult to believe that either of these sections could have been composed by Hesiod.

Spurious Works

Such was the power of Hesiod's name that epics by other poets were soon attributed to him. These are often included in editions of his works. The *Precepts of Chiron*, the *Astronomy*, the *Ornithomanteia* ("Divination by Birds"), the *Melampodeia*, which described a contest between two seers, and the *Aigimios* are today little more than names.

ARCHILOCHUS

(fl. *c.* 650 BCE, Paros [Cyclades, Greece])

The poet and soldier Archilochus was the earliest Greek writer of iambic, elegiac, and personal lyric poetry whose works have survived to any considerable extent. Archilochus's father was Telesicles, a wealthy

Parian who founded a colony on the island of Thasos. Archilochus lived on both Paros and Thasos. Fragments of his poetry mention the solar eclipse of April 6, 648 BCE, and the wealth of the Lydian king Gyges (*c.* 680–645 BCE). The details of Archilochus's life, in the ancient biographical tradition, are derived for the most part from his poems — an unreliable source because the events he described may have been fictitious, or they may have involved imaginary personae or ritual situations.

Modern discoveries, however, have supported the picture given in the poetry. Two inscriptions dedicated to Archilochus were discovered in a sacred area on Paros; they are named, after the men who dedicated them, the Mnesiepes inscription (3rd century BCE) and the Sosthenes inscription (1st century BCE). Archilochus's self-presentation was taken seriously as early as the late 5th century BCE by the Athenian politician and intellectual Critias, who denounced him for presenting himself as impoverished, quarrelsome, foul-mouthed, lascivious, and lower-class. Some scholars feel that the Archilochus portrayed in his poems is too scurrilous to be real.

Archilochus probably served as a soldier. According to ancient tradition, he fought against Thracians on the mainland near Thasos and died when the Thasians were fighting against soldiers from the island of Naxos. In one famous poem, Archilochus tells, without embarrassment or regret, of throwing his shield away in battle. ("I saved my life. What do I care about my shield? The hell with it! I'll buy another just as good.") The motif of the abandoned shield appears again in the lyric poems of Alcaeus and Anacreon, in a parody by Aristophanes (*Peace*), and in a learned variation by the Latin poet Horace (*Carmina*).

Although the truth is difficult to discern with certainty from the poems and other evidence, Archilochus may have been disreputable. He was particularly famous in antiquity for his sharp satire and ferocious invective. It was said that a man named Lycambes betrothed his daughter Neobule to the poet and then later withdrew the plan. In a papyrus fragment published in 1974 (the "Cologne Epode")—the longest surviving piece of Archilochus's poetry—a man, who is apparently the poet himself, tells in alternately explicit and hinting language how he seduced the sister of Neobule after having crudely rejected Neobule herself. According to the ancient accounts, Lycambes and his daughters committed suicide, shamed by the poet's fierce mocking.

Archilochus was the first known Greek poet to employ the elegiac couplet and various iambic and trochaic metres, ranging from dimeter to tetrameter, as well as epodes, lyric metres, and *asinarteta* (a mixture of different metres). He was a master of the Greek language, moving from Homeric formulas to the language of daily life in a few lines. He was the first European author to make personal experiences and feelings the main subject of his poems: the controlled use of the personal voice in his verse marks a distinct departure from other surviving Greek verse, which is typically more formulaic and heroic. For his technical accomplishments Archilochus was much admired by later poets, such as Horace, but there was also severe criticism, especially of a moralistic character, by writers such as the poets Pindar and Critias (both 5th century BCE).

STESICHORUS

(b. 632/629 BCE, Mataurus, Bruttium, Magna Graecia [now in southern Italy]—d. 556/553 BCE, Catania [or Himera], Sicily)

Stesichorus, originally called Teisias, was a Greek poet known for his distinctive choral lyric verse on epic themes. Stesichorus, which in Greek means "instructor of choruses," was a byname derived from his professional activity, which he practiced especially in Himera, a town on the northern coast of Sicily.

Scholars at Alexandria in the 3rd or 2nd century BCE divided Stesichorus's work into 26 books, or papyrus rolls. Although many titles survive, there exist only a few fragments of the actual poetry. Late 20th-century publications of papyrus finds have furthered the study of his work. The titles suggest that he took the themes of his poems from the traditional epic heritage found in mainland Greece and Asia Minor as well as in Italy and Sicily. *Helen*, *Wooden Horse*, *Sack of Troy*, *Homecomings of the Heroes*, and *Oresteia* are based on stories about the Trojan War. *Cerberus*, *Geryoneis*, and *Cycnus* are about Heracles (Hercules). *Funeral Games for Pelias* is part of the legend of the Argonauts. Yet the poetry broke with the epic tradition, in which a single performer declaimed verse in dactylic hexameters, as Stesichorus's lyric verses in the Doric dialect were accompanied by a stringed instrument. The Roman educator Quintilian (1st century CE) wrote that Stesichorus supported the weight of the epic with his lyre. Some ancient sources placed Stesichorus in a line of solo kithara (lyre) performers.

Stesichorus was credited with the three-part articulation of choral lyric—strophic lines followed by antistrophic lines in the same metre, concluding with a summary line, called an epode, in a different metre—that became canonical. The apparent length of some of his poems (*Geryoneis* seems to have reached more than 1,300 verses, and the *Oresteia* is in two books) has caused some scholars to doubt that a chorus could have performed them. The ancient testimony, however, is unanimous in classifying his poetry as choral lyric; it is possible that the choruses performed appropriate movements while the solo performer (perhaps the poet) sang the words.

According to a story that was famous in the ancient world, Stesichorus was blinded by Helen after he blamed her in a poem for causing the Trojan War. He regained his sight by composing a double retraction, the *Palinode*. Scholars have doubted the poet's authorship of works such as *Calyce*, *Rhadine*, and *Daphne*, which seem to anticipate themes popular in the romantic poetry of the Hellenistic age (323–30 BCE).

Alcaeus

b. *c.* 620 BCE, Mytilene, Lesbos [Greece]—d. 580 BCE)

Alcaeus (Greek Alkaios) was a Greek lyric poet whose work was highly esteemed in the ancient world. He lived at the same time and in the same city as the poet Sappho. A collection of Alcaeus's surviving poems in 10 books (now lost) was made by scholars in Alexandria, Egypt, in the 2nd century BCE, and he was a favourite model of the Roman lyric poet Horace (1st century BCE), who borrowed the alcaic stanza. Only fragments and quotations from Alcaeus's work survived into the Byzantine Middle Ages and into the modern world, but papyrus texts discovered and published in the 20th century considerably expanded knowledge of his poetry, enabling scholars to evaluate his major themes and his quality as a poet.

Alcaeus's poems may be classed in four groups: hymns in honour of gods and heroes, love poetry, drinking songs, and political poems. Many of the fragments reflect the vigour of the poet's involvement in the social and political life of Mytilene. They express a closed world of aristocratic values and conservatism, in which realism and idealism coexist—although the idealism is limited by the norms and goals of the poet's political faction.

At the end of the 7th century BCE and the beginning of the 6th century, aristocratic families on Lesbos contended for power, among them the family of Alcaeus and his brothers, Antimenidas and Cicis. These families enrolled in *hetaireiai* ("factions"), societies of nobles united by an oath of loyalty and a community of ethical and political views. In the years 612–609 a conspiracy organized by Alcaeus's brothers and their ally Pittacus overthrew the tyrant Melanchrus. Alcaeus was probably too young to participate in the overthrow, but later he fought next to Pittacus in a war between Mytilene and Athens over the control of Sigeum, a promontory on the Troad near the Hellespont. He reportedly told his friend Melanippus how he had to abandon his shield to the enemy to save his own life.

A new tyrant, Myrsilus, came to power in Lesbos, and Alcaeus became his fierce opponent. After the failure of a conspiracy, Alcaeus went into exile in Pyrrha, a small town near Mytilene. During his exile Alcaeus wrote bitter polemics against Pittacus, who had joined another faction. The poet greeted Myrsilus's death with fierce joy: "Now we must get drunk and drink whether we want to or not, because Myrsilus is dead!" With this death, Alcaeus was able to return to his home.

To replace Myrsilus, the city appointed Pittacus as *aisymnētēs* ("organizer"); he held power for a decade (590–580 BCE). Pittacus enjoyed a reputation for benevolence and was later included among the Seven Sages (the 6th-century grouping of representative wise and clever men from all parts of Greece). For Alcaeus, however, Pittacus's rise to power meant a return to exile. (An ancient critic reported that he was exiled three times.) Alcaeus's poetry in this period dwells on his misfortunes, battles, and tireless rancour against Pittacus, whom he mocks for disloyalty, physical defects (including flat feet and a big stomach), rudeness, and low origins. There is little evidence regarding the poet's exile; he may have visited Egypt and perhaps Thrace and Boeotia. Pittacus may have recalled him from his second exile. His death is likewise a mystery, although he implied in his poetry that he was old, and some believe that he died in battle.

Alcaeus's most influential image is his allegory of the ship of state, found in a number of fragments. Another common topic is wine, the gift of Dionysus, "the mirror of a man," which in every season offers the poet a remedy against his woes. This theme supports the theory that much of his verse was composed for symposia, a context that would explain his allusive language, full of references that presuppose the shared experiences, values, and aspirations of political partisans (*hetairoi*) gathered together for drink and song. Horace reported that Alcaeus also wrote hymns and erotic verse for handsome young men.

Other fragments of Alcaeus's work convey the atmosphere of everyday life in 6th-century Mytilene. He wrote of ships and rivers, of a girls' beauty contest, of a flock of wigeon (a kind of dabbling duck) in flight, and of the flowers that herald the spring. He managed to convey the spirit and the values of the city-states of the Aegean, as, for example, when he declares that true greatness lies "not in well-fashioned houses, nor in walls, canals, and dockyards, but in men who use whatever Fortune sends them."

$\mathcal{S}$APPHO

(b. *c.* 610, Lesbos [now part of Greece]—d. *c.* 570 BCE)

Sappho (which was spelled Psappho in the Aeolic dialect spoken by the poet) was a Greek lyric poet greatly admired in all ages for the beauty of her writing style. She ranks with Archilochus and Alcaeus among Greek poets for her ability to impress readers with a lively sense of her personality. Her language contains elements from Aeolic vernacular speech and Aeolic poetic tradition, with traces of epic vocabulary familiar to readers of Homer. Her phrasing is concise, direct, and picturesque. She has the ability to stand aloof and judge critically her own ecstasies and grief, and her emotions lose nothing of their force by being (as the English poet William Wordsworth put it) recollected in tranquility.

Portrait of the Greek lyric poet Sappho, a proponent of educating young girls in her thiasos, *an exclusive school or community of young women.*
DEA/G. Nimatallah/De Agostini/Getty Images

Legends about Sappho abound, many having been repeated for centuries. She is said, for example, to have been married to Cercylas, a wealthy man from the island of Andros. But many scholars challenge this claim, finding evidence in the Greek words of the bawdry of later Comic poets. Most modern critics also consider it legend that Sappho leaped from the Leucadian rock to certain death in the sea because of her unrequited love of Phaon, a younger man and a sailor. She had at least two brothers, Larichus and Charaxus, and may have had a third. A fragment from Sappho that is dedicated to Charaxus has survived. One of her poems mentions a daughter named Cleis or Claïs. The tradition that she fled the island or was banished and went to Sicily may be true, but she lived most of her life in her hometown of Mytilene on Lesbos.

Her work contains only a few apparent allusions to the political disturbances of the time, which are so frequently reflected in the verse of her contemporary Alcaeus. Her themes are invariably personal—primarily concerned with her *thiasos*, the usual term (not found in Sappho's extant writings) for the female community, with a religious and educational background, that met under her leadership. Sappho herself attacks in her poems other *thiasoi* directed by other women.

The goal of the Sapphic *thiasos* is the education of young women, especially for marriage. Aphrodite is the group's tutelary divinity and inspiration. Sappho is the intimate and servant of the goddess and her intermediary with the girls. In the ode to Aphrodite, the poet invokes the goddess to appear, as she has in the past, and to be her ally in persuading a girl she desires to love her. Frequent images in Sappho's poetry include flowers, bright garlands, naturalistic outdoor scenes, altars smoking with incense, perfumed unguents to sprinkle on the body and bathe the hair—that is, all the elements of Aphrodite's rituals. In the *thiasos* the girls were educated and initiated into grace and elegance for seduction and love. Singing, dancing, and poetry played a central role in this educational process and other cultural occasions. As was true for other female communities, including the Spartan, and for the corresponding masculine institutions, the practice of homoeroticism within the *thiasos* played a role in the context of initiation and education. In Sappho's poetry love is passion, an inescapable power that moves at the will of the goddess; it is desire and sensual emotion; it is nostalgia and memory of affections that are now distant, but shared by the community of the *thiasos*. There is a personal poetic dimension, which is also collective because all the girls of the group recognize themselves in it. An important part of Sappho's poetic oeuvre is occupied by epithalamia, or nuptial songs.

It is not known how her poems were published and circulated in her own lifetime and for the following three or four centuries. In the era of Alexandrian scholarship (3rd and 2nd centuries BCE), what survived of her work was collected and published in a standard edition of nine books of lyrical verse, divided according to metre. This edition did not endure beyond the early Middle Ages. By the 8th or 9th century CE Sappho was represented only by quotations in other authors. Only the ode to Aphrodite, 28 lines long, is complete. The next longest fragment is 16 lines long. Since 1898 these fragments have been greatly increased by papyrus finds, though, in the opinion of some scholars, nothing equal in quality to the two longer poems.

Sappho's poetry continues to intrigue Classical scholars and poets alike. Among the noteworthy translations of the late 20th and early 21st centuries is Canadian poet Anne Carson's *If Not, Winter: Fragments of Sappho*, published in 2002.

Anacreon

(b. *c.* 582 BCE, Teos, Ionia [now Siğacık, Turkey]—d. *c.* 485 BCE)

The Greek lyric poet Anacreon was born in one of 12 cities that comprised the Ionian League, established to forestall Persian invasion. After Teos was conquered by the Persians in 546 BCE, Anacreon immigrated to the newly founded city of Abdera, on the coast of Thrace. He spent his working life largely at the courts of tyrants, who were important patrons of art and literature during that period. The first of Anacreon's patrons was Polycrates of Samos. After Polycrates was murdered by the Persians, Anacreon moved to Athens, writing under the patronage of Hipparchus. Even after Hipparchus's assassination in 514 BCE, the poet continued to enjoy popularity in Athens, as is shown by his appearances in works of art of the period. After Hipparchus's death Anacreon may have moved to Thessaly. He may have died at Teos, where his tomb was said to have been found.

Anacreon wrote both serious and light poetry. A serious fragment on politics, for example, names the opponents of Polycrates. The poems quoted by later sources, however, are in praise of love, wine, and revelry. Anacreon's treatment of these subjects is formal and elegant, since he disliked excess and vulgarity. His tone conveys ironic enjoyment, and his language and use of metre are smooth and simple but creative.

From his erotic verse there survive striking images of beloved young men: the peaceful character of Megistes, the eyes of Cleobulus, the blond locks of the Thracian Smerdies. Girls also appear, such as the girl from Lesbos and a shy and subdued Thracian girl. (Both are probably *hetairai* [highly cultivated courtesans], attending a symposium.) For

Anacreon love is light, fantastic, and bizarre—but never dramatic—as shown in his various images of Eros. The poet recommends the same approach, joyous and carefree rather than licentious and violent, for the dinner party. As ancient critics had already observed, Anacreon's poetry finds room for the same human types that would populate Greek dramatic performances, notably mime and New Comedy, such as the nouveau riche rascal Artemon and the bald and tiresomely pretentious Alexis.

Only fragments of Anacreon's verse have survived. The edition of Anacreon's poetry known to later generations was probably prepared in Alexandria by Aristarchus in the 2nd century BCE and divided into 9 or 10 books on the basis of metrical criteria. Still, Anacreon's poetic sentiments and style were widely imitated by Hellenistic and Byzantine Greek writers, though they tended to exaggerate the strain of drunken eroticism and frivolity present in his work. There thus arose the *Anacreontea*, a collection of about 60 short poems composed by post-Classical Greek writers at various dates and first published by French scholar-printer Henri II Estienne as the work of Anacreon in 1554. These had a great influence on Renaissance French poetry. The word *Anacreontics* was first used in England in 1656 by English poet and essayist Abraham Cowley to denote a verse metre supposedly used by the ancient Greek poet and consisting of seven or eight syllables with three or four main stresses. Anacreon himself, it should be noted, composed verse in a variety of Greek lyric metres. Robert Herrick, William Oldys, and William Shenstone wrote original Anacreontics in English, and Thomas Moore provided perhaps the finest translation of the *Anacreontea* in 1800, under the title *Odes of Anacreon*. The *Anacreontea* also influenced Italian and German literature. The *Anacreontea* and works by Anacreon, like those of most other significant ancient

Greek and Roman writers, are published in the extensive Loeb Classical Library.

SIMONIDES OF CEOS

(b. *c.* 556 BCE, Iulis, Ceos [now Kéa, Greece]—d. *c.* 468 BCE, Acragas [now Agrigento, Sicily, Italy])

The Greek poet Simonides was noted for his lyric poetry, elegiacs, and epigrams. He began writing poetry on Ceos, but he was soon called to the court of the Peisistratids (the tyrants of Athens), which in the 6th century BCE was a lively cultural and artistic centre. He later visited other powerful figures—such as Scopas, ruler of Crannon—in Thessaly, in northern Greece.

Simonides lived in Athens after the fall of the Peisistratid tyranny and the founding of the democracy. He befriended important people there, including the politician and naval strategist Themistocles, and he achieved numerous successes in dithyrambic competitions. (A later poet credited Simonides with 57 victories.) In the competition, Simonides was selected (above such celebrated poets as Aeschylus) to compose the elegiac verses commemorating those who fell in the Battle of Marathon. He celebrated the Greek victories of the Persian Wars, including a famous encomium for the Spartan dead at Thermopylae. Simonides maintained close ties with the Spartan general and regent Pausanias. He traveled to Sicily as a guest of the courts of Hieron I, tyrant of Syracuse, and Theron, tyrant of Acragas. Tradition there made him and his nephew Bacchylides, also a lyric poet, the rivals of Pindar. Simonides is said to have reconciled the two tyrants when they quarreled.

Of Simonides' extensive literary corpus, only fragments remain, most of them short. There are many epigrams written in elegiac couplets intended to be carved on monuments to celebrate a death, a victory, or other deeds worthy of memory. (However, scholars suspect that many of the epigrams attributed to Simonides were not composed by him.) Simonides' *threnoi*, songs of lamentation used for funerals, were particularly famous in antiquity—as the praise of the poets Catullus and Horace and the educator Quintilian demonstrates—because they showed genius in combining affecting poetry with praise of the deceased. Simonides played an important role in the development of the epinicion, a song in honour of an athletic victory. He is the author of the earliest epinicion for which the date (520 BCE) and the victor (Glaucus of Carystus, for boy's boxing) are certain. The fragments display an epinician tone that contrasts with Pindar's high seriousness, as Simonides praises the victor with ironic and humorous references. Simonides was known for his tendency toward concision and rejection of prolixity. He defined poetry as a speaking picture and painting as mute poetry.

There emerges from his longer fragments, such as the encomium of Scopas, an original and nonconformist personality that questions the innate and absolute values of the aristocratic ethic, which are the basis of Pindar's worldview. Simonides' worldview, in contrast, is in sympathy with the social setting determined by the rise of the new mercantile classes. His moral outlook is pragmatic, realistic, and relativistic; he is conscious of the imperfection and frailty of human accomplishments.

Simonides changed the conception and practice of poetic activity by insisting that a patron who commissioned a poem owed the poet fair remuneration. Simonides' professional policy gave rise to many anecdotes about his greed. The most famous in antiquity concerned a poem he was commissioned to write for Scopas of Thessaly. When Simonides delivered the poem, Scopas paid him only half the sum they had agreed on, telling him to get the rest from the Dioscuri, to whose praise the poet had devoted much of the poem. During the banquet at the palace to celebrate Scopas's victory, Simonides was summoned outside at the request of two young men; when he went outside, the young men were gone. When the palace then collapsed and he alone survived, he realized that the young men had been the Dioscuri. Having insisted on being paid and having been credited with the invention of a (now-lost) method of memorization, Simonides can be seen as a precursor of the 5th-century Sophists.

In 1992 new papyrus fragments of his elegies were published. Among them are parts of a long composition on the Battle of Plataea (479 BCE), in which the decisive role of the Spartans is emphasized. The fragments also include pederastic works and poems that were of the type meant for symposia (dinner parties).

AESOP

A esop, who is the supposed author of a collection of Greek fables, is almost certainly a legendary figure. Various attempts were made in ancient times to establish him as an actual personage. Herodotus in the 5th century BCE said that he had lived in the 6th century and that he was a slave, and Plutarch in the 1st century CE made him adviser to Croesus, the 6th-century-BCE king of Lydia. One tradition holds that he came from Thrace, while a later one styles him a Phrygian. An Egyptian biography of the 1st century CE places him on the island of Samos as a slave who gained his freedom from his master, thence going to Babylon as riddle solver to King Lycurgus, and,

Aesop, with a fox, from the central medallion of a kylix, *or wide, shallow drinking vessel, c. 470* BCE; *in the Gregorian Etruscan Museum, Vatican City.* Alinari/Art Resource, New York

finally, meeting his death at Delphi. The probability is that Aesop was no more than a name invented to provide an author for fables centring on beasts, so that "a story of Aesop" became synonymous with "fable." The importance of fables lay not so much in the story told as in the moral derived from it.

Fables teach a general principle of conduct by presenting a specific example of behaviour. Thus, to define the moral that "People who rush into things without using judgment run into strange and unexpected dangers," Aesop—the traditional "father" of the fable form—told the following story:

There was a dog who was fond of eating eggs. Mistaking a shell-fish for an egg one day, he opened his mouth wide and swallowed it down in one gulp. The weight of it in his stomach caused him intense pain. "Serve me right," he said, "for thinking that anything round must be an egg."

By a slight change of emphasis, the fabulist could have been able to draw a moral about the dangerous effects of gluttony.

Because the moral is embodied in the plot of the fable, an explicit statement of the moral need not be given, though it usually is. Many of these moral tag lines have taken on the status of proverb because they so clearly express commonly held social attitudes.

Aesopian fables emphasize the social interactions of human beings, and the morals they draw tend to embody advice on the best way to deal with the competitive realities of life. With some irony, fables view the world in terms of its power structures. One of the shortest Aesopian fables says: "A vixen sneered at a lioness because she never bore more than one cub. 'Only one,' she replied, 'but a lion.'" Foxes and wolves, which the poet Samuel Taylor Coleridge called "Everyman's metaphor" for cunning and cruelty, appear often as characters in fables chiefly because, in the human world, such predatory cunning and cruelty are able to get around restraints of justice and authority. The mere fact that fables unmask the "beast in me," as James Thurber, the 20th-century American humorist and fabulist, put it, suggests their satiric force. Subversive topical satire in tsarist and Soviet Russia was often called "Aesopism." All comic strips that project a message (such as the Charles Schulz creation *Peanuts* and Walt Kelly's *Pogo*) have affinities with Aesop's method.

The first-known collection of the fables ascribed to Aesop was produced by Demetrius Phalareus in the 4th century BCE, but it did not survive beyond the 9th century CE. A collection of fables that relied heavily on the Aesop corpus was that of Phaedrus, which was produced at Rome in the 1st century CE. Phaedrus's treatment of them greatly influenced the way in which they were used by later writers, notably by the 17th-century French poet and fabulist Jean de La Fontaine.

Aeschylus

(b. 525/524 BCE—d. 456/455 BCE, Gela, Sicily)

Aeschylus grew up in the turbulent period when the Athenian democracy, having thrown off its tyranny (the absolute rule of one man), had to prove itself against both self-seeking politicians at home and invaders from abroad. Aeschylus himself took part in his city's first struggles against the invading Persians. Later Greek chroniclers believed that Aeschylus was 35 years old in 490 BCE when he participated in the Battle of Marathon, in which the Athenians first repelled the Persians; if this is true it would place his birth in 525 BCE. Aeschylus's father's name was Euphorion, and the family probably lived at Eleusis (west of Athens).

Writing Career

Aeschylus was a notable participant in Athens' major dramatic competition, the Great Dionysia, which was a part of the festival of Dionysus. Every year at this festival, each of three dramatists would produce three tragedies, which either could be unconnected in plot sequence or could have a connecting theme. This trilogy was followed by a satyr play, which was a kind of lighthearted burlesque. Aeschylus is recorded as having participated in this competition, probably for the first time, in 499 BCE. He won his first victory in the theatre in the spring of 484 BCE. In the meantime, he had fought and possibly been wounded at Marathon, and Aeschylus singled out his participation in this battle years later for mention on the verse epitaph he wrote for himself. Aeschylus's brother was killed in this battle. In 480 the Persians again invaded Greece, and once again Aeschylus saw service,

A study of the Greek tragedians, including Aeschylus (holding the scroll), for the painting "The Apotheosis of Homer," by Jean-Auguste-Dominique Ingres. **The Bridgeman Art Library/Getty Images**

fighting at the Battles of Artemisium and Salamis. His responses to the Persian invasion found expression in his play *Persians*, the earliest of his works to survive. This play was produced in the competition of the spring of 472 BCE and won first prize.

Around this time Aeschylus is said to have visited Sicily to present *Persians* again at the tyrant Hieron I's court in Syracuse. Aeschylus's later career is a record of sustained dramatic success, though he is said to have suffered one memorable defeat, at the hands of the novice Sophocles, whose entry at the Dionysian festival of 468 BCE was victorious over the older poet's entry. Aeschylus recouped the loss with victory in the next year, 467, with his Oedipus trilogy (of which the third play, *Seven Against Thebes*, survives). After producing the masterpiece among his extant works, the *Oresteia* trilogy, in 458, Aeschylus went to Sicily again. The chronographers recorded Aeschylus's death at Gela (on Sicily's south coast) in 456/455, aged 69. A ludicrous story that he was killed when an eagle dropped a tortoise on his bald pate was presumably fabricated by a later comic writer. At Gela he was accorded a public funeral, with sacrifices and dramatic performances held at his grave, which subsequently became a place of pilgrimage for writers.

Aeschylus wrote approximately 90 plays, including satyr plays as well as tragedies; of these, about 80 titles are known. Only seven tragedies have survived entire. One account, perhaps based on the official lists, assigns Aeschylus 13 first prizes, or victories; this would mean that well over half of his plays won, since sets of four plays rather than separate ones were judged. Aeschylus's two sons also achieved prominence as tragedians. One of them, Euphorion, won first prize in his own right in 431 BCE over Sophocles and Euripides.

Dramatic and Literary Achievements

Aeschylus's influence on the development of tragedy was fundamental. Previous to him, Greek drama was limited to one actor (who became known as the protagonist, meaning first actor, once others were added) and a chorus engaged in a largely static recitation. (The chorus was a group of actors who responded to and commented on the main action of a play with song, dance, and recitation.) The actor could assume different roles by changing masks and costumes, but he was limited to engaging in dialogue only with the chorus. By adding a second actor (the deuteragonist, or second actor) with whom the first could converse, Aeschylus vastly increased the drama's possibilities for dialogue and dramatic tension and allowed more variety and freedom in plot construction. Although the dominance of the chorus in early tragedy is ultimately only hypothesis, it is probably true that, as Aristotle says in his *Poetics*, Aeschylus "reduced the chorus' role and made the plot the leading actor." Aeschylus was an innovator in other ways as well. He made good use of stage settings and stage machinery, and some of his works were noted for their spectacular scenic effects. He also designed costumes, trained his choruses in their songs and dances, and probably acted in most of his own plays, this being the usual practice among Greek dramatists.

But Aeschylus's formal innovations account for only part of his achievement. His plays are of lasting literary value in their majestic and compelling lyrical language, in the intricate architecture of their plots, and in the universal themes they explore so honestly. Aeschylus's language in both dialogue and choral lyric is marked by force, majesty, and emotional intensity. He makes bold use of compound epithets, metaphors, and figurative turns of speech, but this rich language is firmly harnessed to the dramatic action rather than used as mere decoration. It is characteristic of Aeschylus to sustain an image or group of images throughout a play; the ship of state in *Seven Against Thebes*, the birds of prey in *Suppliants*, the snare in *Agamemnon*. More generally, Aeschylus deploys throughout a play or trilogy of plays several leading motifs that are often associated with a particular word or group of words. In the *Oresteia*, for example, such themes as wrath, mastery, persuasion, and the contrasts of light and darkness, of dirge and triumphal song, run throughout the trilogy. This sort of dramatic orchestration as applied to careful plot construction enabled Aeschylus to give Greek drama a more truly artistic and intellectual form.

The Oresteia trilogy consists of three closely connected plays, all extant, that were presented in 458 BCE. In *Agamemnon* the great Greek king of that name returns triumphant from the siege of Troy, along with his concubine, the Trojan prophetess Cassandra, only to be humiliated and murdered by his fiercely vengeful wife, Clytemnestra. She is driven to this act partly by a desire to avenge the death of her daughter Iphigenia, whom Agamemnon has sacrificed for the sake of the war, partly by her adulterous love for Aegisthus, and partly as agent for the curse brought on Agamemnon's family by the crimes of his father, Atreus. At the play's end Clytemnestra and her lover have taken over the palace and now rule Argos. Many regard this play as one of the greatest Greek tragedies. From its extraordinarily sustained dramatic and poetic power one might single out the fascinating, deceitful richness of Clytemnestra's words and the huge choral songs, which raise in metaphorical and often enigmatic terms the complex of major themes—of theology, politics, and blood relationships—which are elaborated throughout the trilogy.

The second play in the Oresteia trilogy, *Libation Bearers* (Greek *Choephoroi*) is the second play in the trilogy and takes its title from the chorus of women servants who come to pour propitiatory offerings at the tomb of the murdered Agamemnon. At the start of this play Orestes, the son of Agamemnon and Clytemnestra, who was sent abroad as a child, returns as a man to take vengeance upon his mother and her lover for their murder of his father. He is reunited with his sister Electra, and together they invoke the aid of the dead Agamemnon in their plans. Orestes then slays Aegisthus, but Orestes' subsequent murder of Clytemnestra is committed reluctantly, at the god Apollo's bidding. Orestes' attempts at self-justification then falter and he flees, guilt-wracked, maddened, and pursued by the female incarnations of his mother's curse, the Erinyes (Furies), the goddesses of revenge. At this point the chain of vengeance seems interminable.

Eumenides, the title of the third play, means "The Kind Goddesses." The play opens at the shrine of Apollo at Delphi, where Orestes has taken sanctuary from the Furies. At the command of the Delphic oracle, Orestes journeys to Athens to stand trial for his matricide. There the goddess Athena organizes a trial with a jury of citizens. The Furies are his accusers, while Apollo defends him. The jury divides evenly in its vote, and Athena casts the tie-breaking vote for Orestes' acquittal. The Furies then turn their vengeful resentment against the city itself, but Athena persuades them, in return for a home and cult, to bless Athens instead and reside there as the "Kind Goddesses" of the play's title. The trilogy thus ends with the cycle of retributive bloodshed ended and supplanted by the rule of law and the justice of the state.

As the Oresteia trilogy reveals, Aeschylean tragedy deals with the plights, decisions, and fates of individuals with whom the destiny of the community or state is closely bound up; in turn, both individual and community stand in close relation to the gods. Personal, social, and religious issues are thus integrated, as they still were in the Greek civilization of the poet's time. Theodicy (i.e., the justifying of the gods' ways to mortals) was in some sense the concern of Aeschylus, though it might be truer to say that he aimed through dramatic conflict to throw light on the nature of divine justice. Aeschylus and his Greek contemporaries believed that the gods begrudged human greatness and sent infatuation on mortals at the height of their success, thus bringing them to disaster. The foolish act was frequently one of impiety or pride (*hubris*), for which a downfall could be seen as a just punishment. In this scheme of things, divine jealousy and eternal justice formed the common fabric of a moral order of which Zeus, supreme among the gods, was the guardian.

But the unjust are not always punished in their lifetime. It is upon their descendants that justice may fall. This tradition of belief in a just Zeus and in hereditary guilt was accepted by Aeschylus, and it is evinced in many of his plays. The simplest illustration of this is in *Persians*, in which Xerxes and his invading Persians are punished for their own offenses. But in a play such as *Agamemnon*, the issues of just punishment and moral responsibility, of human innocence and guilt, of individual freedom versus evil heredity and divine compulsion are more complex and less easily disentangled, thus presenting contradictions which still baffle the human intellect.

Finally, to Aeschylus, divine justice uses human motives to carry out its decrees. Chief among these motives is the desire for vengeance, which was basic to the ancient Greek scheme of values. In the one complete extant trilogy, the *Oresteia*, this notion of vengeance or retaliation is dominant. Retaliation is a motive of Agamemnon, Clytemnestra, Aegisthus, and Orestes. But significantly, the chain of retaliatory murder that pursues Agamemnon and his family ends not by a perfect balance of blood guilt, not by a further perpetuation of violence, but rather through reconciliation and the rule of law as established by Athena and the Athenian courts of justice.

Aeschylus is almost unequaled in writing tragedy that, for all its power of depicting evil and the fear and consequences of evil, ends, as in the *Oresteia*, in joy and reconciliation. Living at a time when the Greek people still truly felt themselves surrounded by the gods, Aeschylus nevertheless had a capacity for detached and general thought, which was typically Greek and which enabled him to treat the fundamental problem of evil with singular honesty and success.

PINDAR

(b. probably 518 BCE, Cynoscephalae, Boeotia, Greece—d. after 446, probably *c.* 438 BCE, Argos)

Pindar, known in Greek as Pindaros and in Latin as Pindarus, was perhaps the greatest lyric poet of ancient Greece. He was a master at writing epinicia, choral odes celebrating victories achieved in Hellenic athletic games.

Early Training

Pindar was of noble birth, possibly belonging to a Spartan family, the Aegeids, though the evidence for this is inconclusive. His parents, Daiphantus and Cleodice, survive only as names. His uncle Scopelinus, a skilled performer on the *aulos* (a single- or double-reed pipe played in pairs), doubtless helped with Pindar's early musical training. The family possessed a town house in Thebes (to be spared by express command of Alexander the Great in the general destruction of that city by the Macedonians in 335 BCE). Such a background would have given Pindar a ready entrée into aristocratic circles in other Greek cities. Pindar's poetry borrowed certain fundamental characteristics from the cultural traditions of his native Boeotia, a region that remained rather at the margins of political and economic trends of the Archaic (*c.* 650–480) and Classical (*c.* 450–323) periods. His poetry evinces a conservative attitude of absolute adherence to aristocratic values, a rigorous sense of piety, and a familiarity with the great mythological heritage that descended from the Mycenaean period (*c.* 16th–12th century BCE) and achieved a first systematic presentation, significantly, in the work of Pindar's Boeotian predecessor Hesiod at the end of the 8th century. Ancient authorities make Pindar the contemporary of the Boeotian poet Corinna (Korinna), who was supposed to have beaten him in poetic competitions.

The ancient biographical tradition reports that as a young man Pindar went to Athens to complete and refine his poetic education. It is unclear whether he studied there with Lasus of Hermione, who had introduced important innovations into the dithyramb (choral song in honour of Dionysus, the god of wine and ecstasy), or whether he learned from him at second hand. At any rate, in 497 or 496 Pindar, scarcely more than 20 years of age, won first place in the dithyrambic competition at the Great Dionysia, an event that had been introduced in 508.

Professional Career

Seventeen volumes of Pindar's poetry, comprising almost every genre of choral lyric, were known in antiquity. Only four books of epinicia have survived complete, doubtless because they were chosen by a teacher as a schoolbook in the 2nd century CE. They are supplemented by numerous fragments, and 20th-century finds of papyri contributed to a deeper understanding of Pindar's achievement, especially in paeans and dithyrambs.

All the evidence, however, suggests that the epinicia were Pindar's masterpieces. These are divided as Olympic, Pythian, Isthmian, or Nemean—the games in which the victories he celebrated were held; the epinicia number 44 odes in all. The earliest surviving epinicion (Pythian ode 10) dates from 498, and Pindar already had an assured mastery of his medium when he wrote it. No doubt Pindar visited the Panhellenic festivals, at Delphi (where the Pythian games were held) and Olympia in particular, to absorb the atmosphere of the games and celebrate his victories. He would also have seen in person the homes of the aristocrats and the courts of the tyrants whose triumphs he sang. But in general he preferred to remain loyal to his native land and reside in Thebes; characteristically, Pindar's standards and values, like his poetry, changed little if at all over the years.

Pindar's early poems have almost all been lost; it is probable, however, that what gave him a growing reputation beyond the borders of Boeotia were hymns in honour of the gods. Pindar was born at the time of the Pythian festival, and from his youth he had a close connection with the Pythian priesthood, which served the oracular shrine of Apollo at Delphi. Pindar and his descendants, indeed, enjoyed special privileges at Delphi, where his memory was cherished in later times and where an iron chair, in which it was said he had sat to sing, was exhibited. The first commissions for epinicia came mostly from aristocratic connections. Progress in winning recognition seems to have been steady, if slow.

A significant breakthrough came when Pindar established a link with the court of Theron of Acragas through the tyrant's brother Xenocrates, whose chariot won the Pythian contest (Pythian odes 6 and 12, composed for the victory of the *aulete* Midas in musical competitions; 490). But the Persian invasion of Greece came before the promise of this new connection could be fulfilled. Pindar faced a crisis of divided loyalties, torn between a sense of solidarity with the aristocracy of Boeotia, who followed a pro-Persian policy, and a growing appreciation of Spartan and Athenian heroic resistance. Pindar was first and foremost a Theban, and he stood by his friends, many of whom paid for their policy with their lives. But it was Simonides, not Pindar, who wrote the poems of rejoicing at Greece's victories and of mourning for its glorious dead.

It took Pindar some years to reestablish himself; fortunately, his friends in Aegina were staunch (Isthmian ode 8; 478). It is virtually certain that he visited Sicily in 476–474 and was made welcome at the courts of Theron of Acragas and Hieron I of Syracuse. They were to elicit much of his greatest poetry, and it was through these connections that Pindar's reputation spread throughout the Greek world and commissions flowed in from the mainland, the islands, and also from the remoter outposts of Hellenism. Promising new contacts were made with the royal houses of Macedon and Cyrene (Alexander of Macedon, fragment 120; Arcesilas of Cyrene, Pythian odes 4 and 5; 462 BCE).

Theron and Hieron respected and admired Pindar, but his aristocratic temper made him dangerously outspoken. Diplomatic tact and finesse were not among his qualities, and his adroit rivals, Simonides and Bacchylides, were more pliant and adaptable (Bacchylides, not Pindar, celebrated Hieron's Olympic victory in the chariot race in 468). Echoes of Pindar's bitter resentment sound in his poetry. So too Pindar's intervention on behalf of Damophilus, a noble exile from Cyrene (Pythian ode 4), seems to have been taken amiss, and he was not invited to commemorate Arcesilas's triumph at Olympia in 460. Nevertheless, these were the years of supreme achievement, and Pindar found a growing demand for his poetry and a growing appreciation of his skill. His debt to Athens was amply paid in a famous tribute (fragment 76) that the Athenians never tired of citing, one that earned the poet special honours in that city (and, according to ancient tradition, a fine at Thebes). It was probably in this period that Pindar married.

The subsequent decade of Athenian domination in central Greece coincided with a period when Delphi was controlled by Phocis in northern Greece. These were dark years for Pindar, and his poetic output dwindled. Pindar's last datable epinicion is from 446 BCE. According to the ancient biographical tradition, Pindar died in Argos at age 80, in the arms of a handsome boy, Theoxenus, whose name appears in a fragment of an encomium the poet dedicated to him.

BACCHYLIDES

(b. c. 510 BCE, Ceos [now Kéa, Greece])

The Greek lyric poet Bacchylides was a nephew of the poet Simonides and a younger contemporary of the Boeotian poet Pindar, with whom he competed in the composition of epinician poems (odes commissioned by victors at the major athletic festivals).

The 3rd-century-BCE scholars at the great library at Alexandria, Egypt, listed Bacchylides among the canonical nine lyric poets, and they produced an edition of his poems. The poems remained popular until at least the 4th century CE, when the emperor Julian was said by the Latin historian Ammianus Marcellinus to have enjoyed them. The works were lost (except as they were quoted by others) until the discovery of papyrus texts that reached the

British Museum in 1896 and were published in 1897. The papyri contained the texts of 21 poems in whole or in part; 14 are epinicia, and the remainder are dithyrambs (choral songs in honour of Dionysus). Fragments derived from quotations by ancient authors and later papyrus finds include passages from paeans (hymns in honour of Apollo and other gods) and encomiums (songs in honour of distinguished men).

Hieron I, ruler of Syracuse, commissioned several epinician odes to celebrate his victories in horse and chariot races in 476, 470, and 468 BCE. For the first two, Hieron obtained odes from both Bacchylides and Pindar; but for his most prestigious victory, the four-horse chariot race at Olympia in 468, Hieron commissioned an epinicion only from Bacchylides. The victory of Pitheas of Aegina in the pancratium at the Nemean Games was also celebrated by both Pindar (Nemean ode 5) and Bacchylides (ode 13). Ancient scholars took seriously Pindar's remarks about rival poets in the first Pythian ode, concluding that Pindar actively disliked Simonides and Bacchylides; later scholars, however, viewed such remarks as poetic convention more than personal truth.

Bacchylides, who described himself as "the Caen nightingale," wrote in a style that was simpler and less sublime than Pindar's. He excelled in narrative, pathos, and clarity of expression. A good example of all three is the encounter of Heracles with the ghost of Meleager in the underworld (ode 5), an episode treated also by Pindar (fragment 249a). Another memorable narrative is the story of the miraculous rescue of Croesus from the burning pyre (ode 3).

Like his uncle Simonides, Bacchylides wrote dithyrambs for the Dionysian festival at Athens—notably the unique semidramatic ode 18, which takes the form of a dialogue between Theseus's father, Aegeus, and an answering chorus of Athenians. Literary historians differ about

45

the relationship of ode 18 to the development of Attic drama. Older scholars, following statements in Aristotle's *Poetics*, saw in the dithyramb the foundations of Attic tragedy. Present-day scholars, however, believe that ode 18 was influenced by contemporary Attic drama and that ode 16, *Heracles* or *Deianeira,* was influenced by Sophocles' tragedy *Trachinian Women*. In another dithyramb (ode 17), Bacchylides gives a spirited account of a contest between Minos and Theseus: Theseus dives into the sea to recover a ring that Minos has thrown there as a challenge; Theseus emerges from the water with the ring, dry-haired and surrounded by enthusiastic Naiads. Bacchylides' poetic activity led him to Sicily, Aegina, Thessaly, Macedonia, the Peloponnesus, Athens, and Metapontum. His last dated poems (odes 6 and 7) were composed in 452 BCE.

SOPHOCLES

(b. *c.* 496 BCE, Colonus, near Athens [Greece]—d. 406, Athens)

S ophocles was one of the three great tragic playwrights of Classical Athens (the other two being Aeschylus and Euripides). Of his more than 120 dramas, the best known is *Oedipus the King*.

Life and Career

Sophocles was born in a village outside the walls of Athens, where his father, Sophillus, was a wealthy manufacturer of armour. Sophocles himself received a good education. Because of his beauty of physique, his athletic prowess, and his skill in music, he was chosen in 480, when he was 16, to lead the paean (choral chant to a god) celebrating

A sculpted bust of Sophocles, one of three great tragic playwrights (along with Aeschylus and Euripides) of ancient Greece. The Bridgeman Art Library/Getty Images

the decisive Greek sea victory over the Persians at the Battle of Salamis.

The relatively meagre information about Sophocles' civic life suggests that he was a popular favourite who participated actively in his community and exercised outstanding artistic talents. In 442 he served as one of the treasurers responsible for receiving and managing tribute money from Athens' subject-allies in the Delian League. In 440 he was elected one of the 10 *stratēgoi* (high executive officials who commanded the armed forces) as a junior colleague of the great Athenian statesman Pericles. Sophocles later served as *stratēgos* perhaps twice again. In 413, then aged about 83, Sophocles was a *proboulos*, one of 10 advisory commissioners who were granted special powers and were entrusted with organizing Athens' financial and domestic recovery after its terrible defeat at Syracuse in Sicily. Sophocles' last recorded act was to lead a chorus in public mourning for his deceased rival, Euripides, before the festival of 406. He died that same year.

These few facts are about all that is known of Sophocles' life. They imply steady and distinguished attachment to Athens, its government, religion, and social forms. Sophocles was wealthy from birth, highly educated, noted for his grace and charm, on easy terms with the leading families, a personal friend of prominent statesmen, and in many ways fortunate to have died before the final surrender of Athens to Sparta in 404. In one of his last plays, *Oedipus at Colonus*, he still affectionately praises both his own birthplace and the great city itself.

Sophocles was the younger contemporary of Aeschylus and the older contemporary of Euripides. He won his first victory at the Dionysian dramatic festival in 468, however, defeating the great Aeschylus in the process. This began a career of unparalleled success and longevity. In total, Sophocles wrote 123 dramas for the festivals. Since each author who was chosen to enter the competition usually presented four plays, this means he must have competed about 30 times. Sophocles won perhaps as many as 24 victories, compared to 13 for Aeschylus and four for Euripides, and indeed he may have never received lower than second place in the competitions he entered.

Dramatic and Literary Achievements

Only seven of Sophocles' tragedies survive in their entirety, along with 400 lines of a satyr play, numerous fragments of plays now lost, and 90 titles. All seven of the complete plays are works of Sophocles' maturity, but only two of them, *Philoctetes* and *Oedipus at Colonus*, have fairly certain dates. *Ajax* is generally regarded as the earliest of the extant plays. Some evidence suggests that *Antigone* was first performed in 442 or 441 BCE. *Philoctetes* was first performed in 409, when Sophocles was 90 years old, and *Oedipus at Colonus* was said to have been produced after Sophocles' death by his grandson.

The best known of Sophocles' plays is *Oedipus the King* (Greek *Oidipous Tyrannos*; Latin *Oedipus Rex*). It is a structural marvel that marks the summit of Classical Greek drama's formal achievements. The play's main character, Oedipus, is the wise, happy, and beloved ruler of Thebes. Though hot-tempered, impatient, and arrogant at times of crisis, he otherwise seems to enjoy every good fortune. But Oedipus mistakenly believes that he is the son of King Polybus of Corinth and his queen. He became the ruler of Thebes because he rescued the city from the Sphinx by answering its riddle correctly, and so was awarded the city's widowed queen, Jocasta. Before overcoming the Sphinx, Oedipus left Corinth forever because the Delphic oracle had prophesied to him that he would kill his father and marry his mother. While journeying to Thebes from

Corinth, Oedipus encountered at a crossroads an old man accompanied by five servants. Oedipus got into an argument with him and in a fit of arrogance and bad temper killed the old man and four of his servants

The play opens with the city of Thebes stricken by a plague and its citizens begging Oedipus to find a remedy. He consults the Delphic oracle, which declares that the plague will cease only when the murderer of Jocasta's first husband, King Laius, has been found and punished for his deed. Oedipus resolves to find Laius's killer, and much of the rest of the play centres upon the investigation he conducts in this regard. In a series of tense, gripping, and ominous scenes Oedipus's investigation turns into an obsessive reconstruction of his own hidden past as he begins to suspect that the old man he killed at the crossroads was none other than Laius. Finally, Oedipus learns that he himself was abandoned to die as a baby by Laius and Jocasta because they feared a prophecy that their infant son would kill his father; that he survived and was adopted by the ruler of Corinth, but in his maturity he has unwittingly fulfilled the Delphic oracle's prophecy of him; that he has indeed killed his true father, married his own mother, and begot children who are also his own siblings.

With this and others of his powerfully written plays, Sophocles was credited by ancient authorities with several major and minor dramatic innovations. Among the latter is his invention of some type of "scene paintings" or other pictorial prop to establish locale or atmosphere. He also may have increased the size of the chorus from 12 to 15 members. Sophocles' major innovation was his introduction of a third actor into the dramatic performance. It had previously been permissible for two actors to "double" (i.e., assume other roles during a play), but the addition of a third actor onstage enabled the dramatist both to increase the number of his characters and widen the variety of their interactions. The scope of the dramatic conflict was thereby extended, plots could be more fluid, and situations could be more complex.

As in *Oedipus the King*, the typical Sophoclean drama presents a few characters, impressive in their determination and power and possessing a few strongly drawn qualities or faults that combine with a particular set of circumstances to lead them inevitably to a tragic fate. Sophocles develops his characters' rush to tragedy with great economy, concentration, and dramatic effectiveness, creating a coherent, suspenseful situation whose sustained and inexorable onrush came to epitomize the tragic form to the Classical world. Sophocles emphasizes that most people lack wisdom, and he presents truth in collision with ignorance, delusion, and folly. Many scenes dramatize flaws or failure in thinking (deceptive reports and rumours, false optimism, hasty judgment, madness). The chief character does something involving grave error; this affects others, each of whom reacts in his own way, thereby causing the chief agent to take another step toward ruin—his own and that of others as well. Equally important, those who are to suffer from the tragic error usually are present at the time or belong to the same generation. It was this more complex type of tragedy that demanded a third actor. Sophocles thus abandoned the spacious Aeschylean framework of the connected trilogy and instead comprised the entire action in a single play. From his time onward, "trilogy" usually meant no more than three separate tragedies written by the same author and presented at the same festival.

Sophocles' language responds flexibly to the dramatic needs of the moment; it can be ponderously weighty or swift-moving, emotionally intense or easygoing, highly decorative or perfectly plain and simple. His mastery of form and diction was highly respected by his contemporaries. Sophocles has also been universally admired for the sympathy and vividness with which he delineates his characters; especially notable are his tragic women, such as Electra and Antigone. Few dramatists have been able to handle situation and plot with more power and certainty; the frequent references in the *Poetics* to Sophocles' *Oedipus the King* show that Aristotle regarded this play as a masterpiece of construction, and few later critics have dissented. Sophocles is also unsurpassed in his moments of high dramatic tension and in his revealing use of tragic irony.

The criticism has been made that Sophocles was a superb artist and nothing more; he grappled neither with religious problems as Aeschylus had nor with intellectual ones as Euripides had done. He accepted the gods of Greek religion in a spirit of unreflecting orthodoxy, and he contented himself with presenting human characters and human conflicts. But it should be stressed that to Sophocles "the gods" appear to have represented the natural forces of the universe to which human beings are unwittingly or unwillingly subject. To Sophocles, human beings live for the most part in dark ignorance because they are cut off from these permanent, unchanging forces and structures of reality. Yet it is pain, suffering, and the endurance of tragic crisis that can bring people into valid contact with the universal order of things. In the process, an individual can become more genuinely human.

HERODOTUS

(b. 484 BCE?, Halicarnassus, Asia Minor [now Bodrum, Turkey]?— d. 430–420 BCE)

The Greek historian Herodotus is believed to have been born at Halicarnassus, a Greek city in southwest Asia Minor that was then under Persian rule. The precise dates of his birth and death are alike uncertain. He is thought to have resided in Athens and to have met Sophocles and then to have left for Thurii, a new colony in southern Italy sponsored by Athens. The latest event alluded to in his *History*, an account of the Greco-Persian Wars, belongs to 430, but how soon after or where he died is not known. There is good reason to believe that he was in Athens, or at least in central Greece, during the early years of the Peloponnesian War, from 431, and that his work was published and known there before 425.

Herodotus was a wide traveler. His longer wandering covered a large part of the Persian Empire: he went to Egypt, at least as far south as Elephantine (Aswān), and he also visited Libya, Syria, Babylonia, Susa in Elam, Lydia, and Phrygia. He journeyed up the Hellespont to Byzantium, went to Thrace and Macedonia, and traveled northward to beyond the Danube and to Scythia eastward along the northern shores of the Black Sea as far as the Don River and some way inland. These travels would have taken many years.

Structure and Scope of the History

Herodotus's subject in his *History* is the wars between Greece and Persia (499–479 BCE) and their preliminaries. As it has survived, the *History* is divided into nine books (the division is not Herodotus's own): Books I–V describe the background to the Greco-Persian Wars; Books VI–IX contain the history of the wars, culminating in an account of the Persian king Xerxes' invasion of Greece (Book VII) and the great Greek victories at Salamis, Plataea, and Mycale in 480–479 BCE. There are two parts in the *History,* one being the systematic narrative of the war of 480–479 with its preliminaries from 499 onward (including the Ionic revolt and the Battle of Marathon in Book VI),

the other being the story of the growth and organization
of the Persian Empire and a description of its geography,
social structure, and history.

There has been much debate among modern scholars
whether Herodotus from the first had this arrangement in
mind or had begun with a scheme for only one part, either a
description of Persia or a history of the war, and if so, with
which. One likely opinion is that Herodotus began with a
plan for the history of the war and that later he decided on
a description of the Persian Empire itself. For a man like
Herodotus was bound to ask himself what the Persian-led
invasion force meant. Herodotus was deeply impressed not
only by the great size of the Persian Empire but also by the
varied and polyglot nature of its army, which was yet united
in a single command, in complete contrast to the Greek
forces with their political divisions and disputatious com-
manders, although the Greeks shared a common language,
religion, and way of thought and the same feeling about what
they were fighting for. This difference had to be explained
to his readers, and to this end he describes the empire.

A logical link between the two main sections is to be
found in the account in Book VII of the westward march
of Xerxes' immense army from Sardis to the Hellespont on
the way to the crossing by the bridge of boats into Greece
proper. First comes a story of Xerxes' arrogance and pet-
ulance, followed by another of his savage and autocratic
cruelty, and then comes a long, detailed description of the
separate military contingents of the army marching as if
on parade, followed by a detailed enumeration of all the
national and racial elements in the huge invasion force.

Herodotus describes the history and constituent parts
of the Persian Empire in Books I–IV. His method in the
account of the empire is to describe each division of it
not in a geographical order but as each was conquered by
Persia—by the successive Persian kings Cyrus, Cambyses,

and Darius. (The one exception to this arrangement is Lydia, which is treated at the very beginning of the history not because it was first conquered but because it was the first foreign country to attack and overcome the Greek cities of Asia Minor.)

The first section of Book I, the history and description of Lydia and its conquest by the Persians, is followed by the story of Cyrus himself, his defeat of the Medes and a description of Persia proper, his attack on the Massagetae (in the northeast, toward the Caspian), and his death. Book II contains the succession of Cambyses, Cyrus' son, his plan to attack Egypt, and an immensely long account of that unique land and its history. Book III describes the Persians' conquest of Egypt, the failure of their invasions to the south (Ethiopia) and west; the madness and death of Cambyses; the struggles over the succession in Persia, ending with the choice of Darius as the new king; the organization of the vast new empire by him, with some account of the most distant provinces as far east as Bactria and northwest India; and the internal revolts suppressed by Darius. Book IV begins with the description and history of the Scythian peoples, from the Danube to the Don, whom Darius proposed to attack by crossing the Bosporus, and of their land and of the Black Sea.

Then follows the story of the Persian invasion of Scythia, which carried with it the submission of more Greek cities, such as Byzantium; of the Persians' simultaneous attack from Egypt on Libya, which had been colonized by Greeks; and the description of that country and its colonization. Book V describes further Persian advances into Greece proper from the Hellespont and the submission of Thrace and Macedonia and many more Greek cities to Persian might, then the beginning of the revolt of the Greek cities of Ionia against Persia in 499, and so to the main subject of the whole work.

Method of Narration

This brief account of the first half of Herodotus's *History* not only conceals its infinite variety but is positively misleading insofar as it suggests a straightforward geographical, sociological, and historical description of a varied empire. The *History*'s structure is more complex than that, and so is Herodotus's method of narration. For example, Herodotus had no need to explain Greek geography, customs, or political systems to his Greek readers, but he did wish to describe the political situation at the relevant times of the many Greek cities later involved in the war. This he achieved by means of digressions skillfully worked into his main narrative. He thus describes the actions of Croesus, the king of Lydia, who conquered the Greeks of mainland Ionia but who was in turn subjugated by the Persians, and this account leads Herodotus into a digression on the past history of the Ionians and Dorians and the division between the two most powerful Greek cities, the Ionian Athens and the Doric Sparta. Athens' complex political development in the 6th century BCE is touched upon, as is the conservative character of the Spartans. All of this, and much besides, some of it only included because of Herodotus's personal interest, helps to explain the positions of these Greek states in 490, the year of the Battle of Marathon, and in 480, the year in which Xerxes invaded Greece.

One important and, indeed, remarkable feature of Herodotus's *History* is his love of and gift for narrating history in the storyteller's manner (which is not unlike Homer's). In this regard he inserts not only amusing short stories but also dialogue and even speeches by the leading historical figures into his narrative, thus beginning a practice that would persist throughout the course of historiography in the Classical world.

Outlook on Life

The story of Croesus in Book I gives Herodotus the occasion to foreshadow, as it were, in Croesus's talk with Solon the general meaning of the story of the Greco-Persian Wars, and so of his whole *History*—that great prosperity is "a slippery thing" and may lead to a fall, more particularly if it is accompanied by arrogance and folly as it was in Xerxes. The story of Xerxes' invasion of Greece is a clear illustration of the moral viewpoint here; a war that by all human reasoning should have been won was irretrievably lost. To Herodotus, the old moral "pride comes before a fall" was a matter of common observation and had been proved true by the greatest historical event of his time. Herodotus believes in divine retribution as a punishment of human impiety, arrogance, and cruelty, but his emphasis is always on the actions and character of men, rather than on the interventions of the gods, in his descriptions of historical events. This fundamentally rationalistic approach was an epochal innovation in Western historiography.

Qualities as a Historian

Herodotus was a great traveler with an eye for detail, a good geographer, with an indefatigable interest in the customs and past history of the region, and a man of the widest tolerance, with no bias toward the Greeks and against the barbarians. He was neither naive nor easily credulous. It is this which makes the first half of his work not only so readable but of such historical importance. In the second half he is largely, but by no means only, writing military history, and it is evident that he knew little of military matters. Yet he understood at least one essential of the strategy of Xerxes' invasion, the Persians' dependence on their fleet though they came by land, and therefore

Herodotus understood the decisive importance of the naval battle at Salamis. Similarly, in his political summaries he is commonly content with explaining events on the basis of trivial personal motives, yet here again he understood certain essentials: that the political meaning of the struggle between the great territorial empire of Persia and the small Greek states was not one of Greek independence only but the rule of law as the Greeks understood it; and that the political importance of the Battle of Marathon for the Greek world was that it foreshadowed the rise of Athens (confirmed by Salamis) to a position of equality and rivalry with Sparta and the end of the long-accepted primacy of the latter. He knew that war was not only a question of victory or defeat, glorious as the Greek victory was, but brought its own consequences in its train, including the internal quarrels and rivalry between the leading Greek city-states, quarreling that was to later culminate in the devastating internecine strife of the Peloponnesian War (431–404 BCE).

Herodotus had his predecessors in prose writing, especially Hecataeus of Miletus, a great traveler whom Herodotus mentions more than once. But these predecessors, for all their charm, wrote either chronicles of local events, of one city or another, covering a great length of time, or comprehensive accounts of travel over a large part of the known world, none of them creating a unity, an organic whole. In the sense that he created a work that is an organic whole, Herodotus was the first of Greek, and so of European, historians. Herodotus's work is not only an artistic masterpiece; for all his mistakes (and for all his fantasies and inaccuracies) he remains the leading source of original information not only for Greek history of the all-important period between 550 and 479 BCE but also for much of that of western Asia and of Egypt at that time.

EURIPIDES

(b. c. 484 BCE, Athens [Greece] — d. 406, Macedonia)

It is possible to reconstruct only the sketchiest biography of Euripides. His mother's name was Cleito, and his father's name was Mnesarchus or Mnesarchides. One tradition states that his mother was a greengrocer who sold herbs in the marketplace. Aristophanes joked about this in comedy after comedy; but there is better indirect evidence that Euripides came of a well-off family. Euripides first received the honour of being chosen to compete in the dramatic festival in 455, and he won his first victory in 441. He left Athens for good in 408, accepting an invitation from Archelaus, king of Macedonia. He died in Macedonia in 406.

Euripides' only known public activity was his service on a diplomatic mission to Syracuse in Sicily. He was passionately interested in ideas, however, and owned a large library. He is said to have associated with Protagoras, Anaxagoras, and other

Euripides, marble bust copied from a Greek original, c. 340–330 BCE; in the Museo Archeologico Nazionale, Naples. **Courtesy of the Soprintendenza alle Antichità della Campania, Naples**

Sophists and philosopher-scientists. His acquaintance with new ideas brought him restlessness rather than conviction, however, and his questioning attitude toward traditional Greek religion is reflected in some of his plays. Of Euripides' private life, little can be said. Later tradition invented for him a spectacularly disastrous married life. It is known that he had a wife called Melito and produced three sons. One of these was something of a poet and produced the *Bacchants* after his father's death. He may also have completed his father's unfinished play *Iphigenia at Aulis*.

The ancients knew of 92 plays composed by Euripides. Nineteen plays are extant, if one of disputed authorship is included. At only four festivals was Euripides awarded the first prize — the fourth posthumously, for the tetralogy that included *Bacchants* and *Iphigenia at Aulis*. As Sophocles won perhaps as many as 24 victories, it is clear that Euripides was comparatively unsuccessful. More to the point is that on more than 20 occasions Euripides was chosen, out of all contestants, to be one of the three laureates of the year. Furthermore, the regularity with which Aristophanes parodied him is proof enough that Euripides' work commanded attention. It is often said that disappointment at his plays' reception in Athens was one of the reasons for his leaving his native city in his old age; but there are other reasons why an old poet might have left Athens in the 23rd year of the Peloponnesian War.

Dramatic and Literary Achievements

Euripides' plays exhibit his iconoclastic, rationalizing attitude toward both religious belief and the ancient legends and myths that formed the traditional subject matter for Greek drama. These legends seem to have been for him a mere collection of stories without any particular authority.

He also apparently rejected the gods of Homeric theology, whom he frequently depicts as irrational, petulant, and singularly uninterested in meting out "divine justice." That the gods are so often presented on the stage by Euripides is partly due to their convenience as a source of information that could not otherwise be made available to the audience.

Given this attitude of sophisticated doubt on his part, Euripides invents protagonists who are quite different from the larger-than-life characters drawn with such conviction by Aeschylus and Sophocles. They are, for the most part, commonplace, down-to-earth men and women who have all the flaws and vulnerabilities ordinarily associated with human beings. Furthermore, Euripides makes his characters express the doubts, the problems and controversies, and in general the ideas and feelings of his own time. They sometimes even take time off from the dramatic action to debate each other on matters of current philosophical or social interest.

Euripides differed from Aeschylus and Sophocles in making his characters' tragic fates stem almost entirely from their own flawed natures and uncontrolled passions. Chance, disorder, and human irrationality and immorality frequently result not in an eventual reconciliation or moral resolution but in apparently meaningless suffering that is looked upon with indifference by the gods. The power of this type of drama lies in the frightening and ghastly situations it creates and in the melodramatic, even sensational, emotional effects of its characters' tragic crises.

Given this strong strain of psychological realism, Euripides shows moments of brilliant insight into his characters, especially in scenes of love and madness. His depictions of women deserve particular attention; it is easy to extract from his plays a long list of heroines who are fierce, treacherous, or adulterous, or all three at once.

Misogyny is altogether too simple an explanation here, although Euripides' reputation in his own day was that of a woman hater, and a play by Aristophanes, *Women at the Thesmophoria*, comically depicts the indignation of the Athenian women at their portrayal by Euripides.

The chief structural peculiarities of Euripides' plays are his use of prologues and of the providential appearance of a god (deus ex machina) at the play's end. Almost all of the plays start with a monologue that is in effect a bare chronicle explaining the situation and characters with which the action begins. Similarly, the god's epilogue at the end of the play serves to reveal the future fortunes of the characters. This latter device has been criticized as clumsy or artificial by modern authorities, but it was presumably more palatable to the audiences of Euripides' own time. Another striking feature of his plays is that over time Euripides found less and less use for the chorus; in his successive works it tends to grow detached from the dramatic action.

The word habitually used in antiquity to describe Euripides' ordinary style of dramatic speech is *lalia* ("chatter"), alluding probably both to its comparatively light weight and to the volubility of his characters of all classes. Notwithstanding this, Euripides' lyrics at times have considerable charm and sweetness. In the works written after 415 BCE his lyrics underwent a change, becoming more emotional and luxuriant. At its worst this style is hardly distinguishable from Aristophanes' parody of it in his comedy *Frogs*, but where frenzied emotion is appropriate, as in the tragedy *Bacchants*, Euripides' songs are unsurpassed in their power and beauty.

During the last decade of his career Euripides began to write "tragedies" that might actually be called romantic dramas, or tragicomedies with happy endings. These plays have a highly organized structure leading to a recognition scene in which the discovery of a character's true identity produces a complete change in the situation, and in general a happy one. Extant plays in this style include *Ion*, *Iphigenia Among the Taurians*, and *Helen*. Plays of the tragicomedy type seem to anticipate the New Comedy of the 4th century BCE.

The fame and popularity of Euripides eclipsed that of Aeschylus and Sophocles in the cosmopolitan Hellenistic period. The austere, lofty, essentially political and "religious" tragedy of Aeschylus and Sophocles had less appeal than that of Euripides, with its more accessible realism and its obviously emotional, even sensational, effects. Euripides thus became the most popular of the three for revivals of his plays in later antiquity; this is probably why at least 18 of his plays have survived compared to seven each for Aeschylus and Sophocles, and why the extant fragmentary quotations from his works are more numerous than those of Aeschylus and Sophocles put together.

Selected Plays

The dates of production of nine of Euripides' plays are known with some certainty from evidence that goes back to the official Athenian records. Those plays whose dates are prefixed by "*c.*" can be dated to within a few years by the internal evidence of Euripides' changing metrical techniques.

One of Euripides' most powerful and best known plays, *Medea* (431 BCE; Greek *Mēdeia*) is a remarkable study of the mistreatment of a woman and of her ruthless revenge. The Colchian princess Medea has been taken by the hero Jason to be his wife. They have lived happily for some years at Corinth and have two sons. But then Jason casts Medea off and decides to marry the Princess of Corinth. Medea is determined on revenge, and after a dreadful mental struggle between her passionate sense of injury and her love for her children, she decides to punish her husband by murdering both the Corinthian princess and their own sons, thereby leaving her husband to grow old with neither wife nor child. She steels herself to commit these deeds and then escapes in the chariot of her grandfather, the sun-god Helios, leaving Jason without even the satisfaction of punishing her for her crimes. Euripides succeeds in evoking sympathy for the figure of Medea, who becomes to some extent a representative of women's oppression in general.

The play *Bacchants* (*c.* 406 BCE; Greek *Bakchai*; Latin *Bacchae*) is regarded by many as Euripides' masterpiece. In it the god Dionysus arrives in Greece from Asia intending to introduce his orgiastic worship there. He is disguised as a charismatic young Asian holy man and is accompanied by his women votaries, who make up the play's chorus. He expects to be accepted first in Thebes, but the Thebans reject his divinity and refuse to worship him, and the city's young king, Pentheus, tries to arrest him. In the end Dionysus drives Pentheus insane and leads him to the mountains, where Pentheus's own mother, Agave, and the women of Thebes in a bacchic frenzy tear him to pieces. Agave returns to Thebes triumphant carrying Pentheus's head, and her father, Cadmus, has to lead her back to sanity and recognition. The play shows how the liberating and ecstatic side of the Dionysiac religion must be balanced against the dangerous irresponsibility that goes with the Dionysiac loss of reason and self-consciousness.

Euripides' *Cyclops* (Greek *Kyklōps*) is noteworthy as the only complete surviving satyr play. The play's cowardly, lazy satyrs with their disgraceful old father Silenus are slaves of the man-eating one-eyed Cyclops Polyphemus in Sicily. Odysseus arrives, driven to Sicily by adverse weather, and eventually succeeds (as in Homer's *Odyssey*) in blinding the Cyclops. He thus enables the Cyclops's victims to escape.

THUCYDIDES

(b. 460 BCE or earlier? — d. after 404 BCE?)

Thucydides was the greatest of ancient Greek historians and author of the *History of the Peloponnesian War*,
which recounts the struggle between Athens and Sparta
in the 5th century BCE. His work was the first recorded
political and moral analysis of a nation's war policies.

All that is certainly known (perhaps all that ancient
scholars knew) of Thucydides' life is what he reveals
about himself in the course of his narrative. He was an
Athenian, old enough when the war began to estimate its
importance and judge that it was likely to be a long one
and to write an account of it, observing and making notes
from its beginning. He was probably born, therefore,
not later than 460 — perhaps a few years earlier since
his detailed narrative begins, just before 431, with the
events which provoked the war. He was certainly older
than 30 when he was elected *stratēgos,* a military magistrate of great importance, in 424. Hence, he belongs to
the generation younger than that of the Greek historian
Herodotus.

Thucydides was in Athens when the great pestilence
of 430–429 raged. He caught the disease himself and saw
others suffer. Later, in 424, he was elected one of the 10
stratēgoi of the year and, because of his connections, was
given command of the fleet in the Thraceward region,
based at Thasos. He failed to prevent the capture of the
important city of Amphipolis by the Spartan general
Brasidas, who launched a sudden attack in the middle of
winter. Because of this blunder, Thucydides was recalled,
tried, and sentenced to exile. This, he says later, gave

him greater opportunity for undistracted study for his *History* and for travel and wider contacts, especially on the Peloponnesian side—Sparta and its allies.

He lived through the war, and his exile of 20 years ended only with the fall of Athens and the peace of 404. The time and manner of his death are uncertain, but that he died shortly after 404 is probable, and that he died by violence in the troubled times following the peace may well be true, for the *History* stops abruptly, long before its appointed end. His tomb and a monument to his memory were still to be seen in Athens in the 2nd century CE.

Scope and Plan of the History

The *History*, which is divided into eight books, probably not by Thucydides' design, stops in the middle of the events of the autumn of 411 BCE, more than six and a half years before the end of the war. This much at least is known: that three historians, Cratippus (a younger contemporary), Xenophon (who lived a generation later), and Theopompus (who lived in the last third of the 4th century), all began their histories of Greece where Thucydides left off. Xenophon, one might say, began the next paragraph nearly as abruptly as Thucydides ended his.

So it is certain that Thucydides' work was well known soon after publication and that no more was ever published other than the eight books that have survived; it may reasonably be inferred from the silence of the available sources that no separate section of the work was published in his lifetime. It may also be inferred that parts of the *History,* and the last book in particular, are defective, in the sense that he would have written at greater length had he known more and that he was trying still to learn more—e.g., of internal Athenian politics in the years of "uneasy truce." His existing narrative is in parts barely understandable without some imaginative guesswork.

It may be assumed, then, that there are three fairly definable stages in his work: first, the "notes" he made of events as they occurred; secondly, the arrangement and rewriting of these notes into a consecutive narrative, as a "chronicle," but by no means in the final form that Thucydides intended; thirdly, the final, elaborated narrative—of the preliminaries of the war (Book I), of the "Ten Years' War," and of the Athenian expedition to conquer Sicily. Thucydides supplemented his note stage throughout the project; even the most elaborated parts of the *History* may have been added right up to the time of his death—certainly many additions were made after the war was over.

All this is significant because Thucydides was writing what few others have attempted—a strictly contemporary history of events that he lived through and that succeeded each other almost throughout his adult life. He endeavoured to do more than merely record events, in some of which he took an active part and in all of which he was a direct or indirect spectator; he attempted to write the final history for later generations, and, as far as a man can and as no other man has, he succeeded.

It is obvious that he did not rush his work; the last of the complete narrative (stage three, above) took him to the autumn of 413, eight and a half years before the end of the war, the last of stage two, to six and a half years before. During these last years he was observing, inquiring, writing his notes, adding to or modifying what he had already written; at no time before the end, during all the 27 years of the war, did he know what that end would be nor, therefore, what would be the length and the final shape of his own *History*. It is evident that he did not long survive the war since he did not leave any connected account, even at stage two, of the last six years. But in what he lived to complete, he wrote a definitive history.

Character Studies

Besides the political causes of the war, Thucydides was interested in and emphasized the conflict between two types of character: the ever-active, innovating, revolutionary, disturbing Athenians and the slower-moving, more cautious Peloponnesians, especially the Spartans, "not excited by success nor despairing in misfortune," but quietly self-confident.

Thucydides was not really concerned with individuals but rather with the actions, sufferings, and the characters of states ("the Athenians," "the Syracusans," etc.). But he did understand the significance of personalities. Besides depicting by their words and deeds the characters of some who influenced events—such as Cleon, the harsh demagogue of Athens; Hermocrates, the would-be moderate leader in Syracuse; the brave Nicostratus; and the incompetent Alcidas—he goes out of his way to give a clear picture of the characters and influence of four men: Themistocles (in a digression, the Athenian hero of the Second Persian War), Pericles, Brasidas, and Alcibiades. All four of them were of the active, revolutionary type. Pericles of Athens was indeed unique for Thucydides in that he combined caution and moderation in action and great stability of character with a daring imagination and intellect; he was a leader of the new age. During the war each of them—Pericles and Alcibiades in Athens, Brasidas in Sparta—was in conflict with a conservative, quietist opposition within his own country.

The conflict between the revolutionary and the conservative also extended between the generally daring Athenian state and the generally cautious Peloponnesians.

It is a great loss that Thucydides did not live to write the story of the last years of the war, when Lysander, the other great revolutionary Spartan, played a larger part than any other single man in the defeat of Athens. This defeat was, in one aspect, the defeat of intellectual brilliance and daring by "stolidity" and stability of character (this last the quality most lacking in Alcibiades, the most brilliant Athenian of the second half of the war); but it was largely brought about by Brasidas and Lysander, the two Spartans who rivaled the Athenians in daring and intellect.

Study of the War's Technical Aspects

Thucydides was also interested in the technical aspect of the war. The most important problems in the war, besides protecting food supplies during land fighting, centred around the difficulties and possibilities of war between an all-powerful land force (Sparta and its allies) and an all-powerful naval force (Athens). Thucydides also studied the details of siege warfare; the difficulties of the heavily armed combat in mountain country and of fighting against the fierce but unruly barbarians of the north; an army trying to force a landing from ships against troops on shore; the one great night battle, at Syracuse; the skill and the daring maneuvers of the Athenian sailors and the way these maneuvers were overcome by the Syracusans; the unexpected recovery of the Athenian fleet after the Sicilian disaster—in all these aspects of the war he took a keen professional interest.

In Thucydides' introductory pages on the early history of Greece he lays much stress on the development of sea trading and naval power and on the accumulation of capital resources: they help to explain the great war between a land power and a sea power.

Style and Historical Aims

Thucydides was himself an intellectual of the Athenian kind; markedly individualistic, his style shows a man brought up in the company of Sophocles and Euripides, the playwrights, and the philosophers Anaxagoras, Socrates, and the contemporary Sophists. His writing is condensed and direct, almost austere in places, and is meant to be read rather than delivered orally. He explains in a scientific and impartial manner the intricacies and complexities of the events he observed. Only in his speeches does he sometimes fall short of the lucidity of the narrative prose.

In a prefatory note near the beginning of the *History*, Thucydides speaks a little of the nature of his task and of his aims. It was difficult, he says, to arrive at the truth of the speeches made—whether he heard them himself or received a report from others—and of the actions of the war. For the latter, even if he himself observed a particular battle, he made as thorough an enquiry as he could—for he realized that eyewitnesses, either from faulty memory or from bias, were not always reliable.

He wrote the speeches out of his own words, appropriate to the occasion, keeping as closely as possible to the general sense of what had actually been said. He could never have omitted them, for it is through the speeches that he explains the motives and ambitions of the leading men and states; and this, the study of the human mind in time of war, is one of his principal aims. (The omission of speeches from the last book is a great loss and is caused, no doubt, by the difficulty he had in getting information about Athens at this period.) He avoided, he says, all "storytelling" (this is a criticism of Herodotus), and his work might be the less attractive in consequence;

but I have written not for immediate applause but for posterity, and I shall be content if the future student of these events, or of other similar events which are likely in human nature to occur in after ages, finds my narrative of them useful.

This is all that he expressly tells of his aim and methods. Moreover, in the course of his narrative (except for the pestilence of 430 and his command in 424) he never gives his authority for a statement. He does not say which of the speeches he actually heard, which of the other campaigns he took part in, what places he visited, or what persons he consulted. Thucydides insisted in doing all the work himself; and he provides, for the parts he completed, only the finished structure, not the plans or the consultations.

Authority of His Work

He kept to a strict chronological scheme, and, where it can be accurately tested by the eclipses that he mentions, it fits closely. There are also a fair number of contemporary documents recorded on stone, most of which confirm his account both in general and in detail. There is the silent testimony of the three historians who began where he left off, not attempting, in spite of much independence of opinion, to revise what he had already done, not even the last book, which he clearly did not complete. Another historian, Philistus, a Syracusan who was a boy during the Athenian siege of his city, had little to alter or to add to Thucydides' account in his own *History of Sicily*. Above all, there are the contemporary political comedies of Aristophanes—a man about 15 years younger than Thucydides with as different a temper and writing purpose as could be—which remarkably reinforce the reliability of the historian's dark picture of Athens at war. The modern historian of this war is in much the same position as the ancient: he cannot do much more than translate, abridge, or enlarge upon Thucydides.

For Thucydides kept rigidly to his theme: the history of a war—that is, a story of battles and sieges, of alliances hastily made and soon broken, and, most important, of the behaviour of peoples as the war dragged on and on, of the inevitable "corrosion of the human spirit." He vividly narrates exciting episodes and carefully describes tactics on land and sea. He gives a picture, direct in speeches, indirect in the narrative, of the ambitious imperialism of Athens—controlled ambition in Pericles, reckless in Alcibiades, debased in Cleon—ever confident that nothing was impossible for them, resilient after the worst disaster. He shows also the opposing picture of the slow steadiness of Sparta, sometimes so successful, at other times so accommodating to the enemy.

His record of Pericles' speech on those killed in the first year of the war is the most glowing account of Athens and Athenian democracy that any leading citizen could hope to hear. It is followed (in, of course, due chronological order) by a minutely accurate account of the symptoms of the pestilence ("so that it may be recognized by medical men if it recurs") and a moving description of the demoralizing despair that overtook men after so much suffering and such heavy losses—probably more than a quarter of the population, most of it crowded within the walls of the city, died.

Equally moving is the account of the last battles in the great harbour of Syracuse and of the Athenian retreat. In one of his best-known passages he analyzes by a most careful choice of words, almost creating the language as he writes, the moral and political effects of civil strife within a state in time of war. By a different method, in speeches, he portrays the hard fate of the town of Plataea due to the long-embittered envy and cruelty of Thebes and the faithlessness of Sparta, and the harsh brutality of Cleon when he proposed to execute all the men of the Aegean island city of Mytilene. Occasionally, he is forced into personal comment, as on the pathetic fate of the virtuous and much-liked Athenian Nicias.

He had strong feelings, both as a man and as a citizen of Athens. He was filled with a passion for the truth as he saw it, which not only kept him free from vulgar partiality against the enemy but served him as a historian in the accurate narrative of events—accurate in their detail and order and also in their relative importance.

ARISTOPHANES

(b. *c.* 450 BCE—d. *c.* 388 BCE)

Aristophanes was the greatest representative of ancient Greek comedy and the one whose works have been preserved in greatest quantity. He is the only extant representative of the Old Comedy, that is, of the phase of comic dramaturgy in which chorus, mime, and burlesque still played a considerable part and which was characterized by bold fantasy, merciless invective and outrageous satire, unabashedly licentious humour, and a marked freedom of political criticism. But Aristophanes belongs to the end of this phase, and, indeed, his last extant play, which has no choric element at all, may well be regarded as the only extant specimen of the short-lived Middle Comedy, which, before the end of the 4th century BCE, was to be superseded in turn by the milder and more realistic social satire of the New Comedy.

Life and Career

Little is known about the life of Aristophanes, and most of the known facts are derived from references in his own plays. Born *c.* 450 BCE, he was an Athenian citizen belonging to the *deme*, or clan, named Pandionis, but his actual birthplace is uncertain. (The fact that he or his father, Philippus, owned property on the island of Aegina may have been the cause of an accusation by his fellow citizens that he was not of Athenian birth.) He began his dramatic career in 427 BCE with a play, the *Daitaleis* (*The Banqueters*), which appears, from surviving fragments, to have been a satire on his contemporaries' educational and moral theories. He is thought to have written about 40 plays in all. A large part of his work is concerned with the social, literary, and philosophical life of Athens itself and with themes provoked by the great Peloponnesian War (431–404 BCE). This war was essentially a conflict between imperialist Athens and conservative Sparta and so was long the dominant issue in Athenian politics. Aristophanes was naturally an opponent of the more or less bellicose statesmen who controlled the government of Athens throughout the better part of his maturity. Aristophanes lived to see the revival of Athens after its defeat by Sparta. He died in about 388 BCE.

Dramatic and Literary Achievements

Aristophanes' reputation has stood the test of time. His plays continue to be produced on the 21st-century stage in numerous translations, which manage with varying degrees of success to convey the flavour of Aristophanes' puns, witticisms, and topical allusions. Aristophanes' greatness lies in the wittiness of his dialogue; in his generally good-humoured though occasionally malevolent satire; in the brilliance of his parody, especially when he mocks the controversial tragedian Euripides; in the ingenuity and inventiveness, not to say the laughable absurdity, of his comic scenes born of imaginative fantasy; in the peculiar charm of his choric songs, whose freshness can still be conveyed in languages other than Greek; and, at least for audiences of a permissive age, in the licentious frankness of many scenes and allusions in his comedies. A few of his more popular plays are described in the following paragraphs.

Aristophanes' comedy *Wasps* (422 BCE; Greek *Sphēkes*) satirized the litigiousness of the Athenians in the person of the mean and waspish old man Philocleon ("Love-Cleon"), who has a passion for serving on juries. In the play, Philocleon's son, Bdelycleon ("Loathe-Cleon"), arranges for his father to hold a "court" at home; but, since the first "case" to be heard is that of the house dog accused of the theft of a cheese, Philocleon is finally cured of his passion for the law courts and instead becomes a boastful and uproarious drunkard. The play's

Bust of the Greek comic playwright Aristophanes. His plays continue to be staged by theatrical troupes in the 21st century. **Hulton Archive/ Getty Images**

main political target is the exploitation by Cleon of the Athenian system of large subsidized juries.

The play *Peace* (421 BCE; Greek *Eirēnē*) was staged seven months or so after both Cleon and Brasidas, the two main champions of the war policy on the Athenian and Spartan sides respectively, had been killed in battle and, indeed, only a few weeks before the ratification of the Peace of Nicias (March? 421 BCE), which suspended hostilities between Athens and Sparta for six uneasy years. In *Peace*, the war-weary farmer Trygaeus ("Vintager") flies to heaven on a monstrous dung beetle to find the lost goddess Peace, only to discover that the God of War has buried Peace in a pit. With the help of a chorus of farmers Trygaeus rescues her, and the play ends with a joyful celebration of marriage and fertility.

Some scholars see *Birds* (414 BCE; Greek *Ornithes*) as a political satire on the imperialistic dreams that had led the Athenians to undertake their ill-fated expedition of 415 BCE to conquer Syracuse in Sicily. Peisthetaerus ("Trusty") is so disgusted with his city's bureaucracy that he persuades the birds to join him in building a new city that will be suspended in between heaven and earth; it is named Nephelokokkygia and is the original Cloudcuckooland. The city is built, and Peisthetaerus and his bird comrades must then fend off the undesirable humans who want to join them in their new Utopia. He and the birds finally even starve the Olympian gods into cooperating with them.

Written not long after the catastrophic defeat of the Athenian expedition to Sicily (413 BCE) and not long before the revolt of the Four Hundred in Athens, whereby an oligarchic regime ready to make peace with Sparta was set up (411 BCE), the popular *Lysistrata* (411 BCE; Greek *Lysistratē*) depicts the seizure of the Acropolis and of the treasury of Athens by the city's women. At Lysistrata's instigation, these women have, together with all the women of Greece, declared a moritorium on sex until the men make peace and end the war. The women defy their menfolk until the peace is arranged, after which both the Athenian and Spartan wives are reunited with their husbands. The play is a strange mixture of humour, indecency, gravity, and farce.

In *Women at the Thesmophoria* (411 BCE; Greek *Thesmophoriazousai*) Euripides has discovered that the women of Athens, angered by his constant attacks upon them in his tragedies, mean to discuss during their coming festival (the Thesmophoria) the question of contriving his death. Euripides tries to persuade the effeminate Agathon, a tragic poet, to plead his cause. Agathon refuses, and Euripides persuades his brother-in-law Mnesilochus to undertake the assignment. Mnesilochus is disguised with great thoroughness as a woman and sent on his mission, but his true sex is discovered and he is at once seized by the women. There follow three scenes in which he tries unsuccessfully to escape; all three involve brilliant parodies of Euripides' tragedies, and all three attempts fail. Finally, Euripides himself arrives and succeeds in rescuing his advocate by promising never again to revile women.

In the literary comedy *Frogs* (405 BCE; Greek *Batrachoi*) Dionysus, the god of drama, is concerned about the poor quality of present-day tragedy in Athens now that his recent favourite, Euripides, is dead. Dionysus disguises himself as the hero Heracles and goes down to Hades to bring Euripides back to the land of the living. As the result, however, of a competition arranged between Euripides and his great predecessor, Aeschylus, Dionysus is won over to the latter's cause and returns to earth with Aeschylus, instead, as the one more likely to help Athens in its troubles.

XENOPHON

(b. *c.* 430 BCE, Attica, Greece—d. shortly before 350, Attica)

The Greek historian and philosopher Xenophon wrote a number of surviving works that are valuable for their depiction of late Classical Greece. His *Anabasis* ("Upcountry March") in particular was highly regarded in antiquity and had a strong influence on Latin literature.

Life

Xenophon's life history before 401 is scantily recorded. At that time, prompted by a Boeotian friend, he left postwar Athens, joined the Greek mercenary army of the Achaemenian prince Cyrus the Younger, and became involved in Cyrus's rebellion against his brother, the Persian king Artaxerxes II. After Cyrus's defeat at Cunaxa (about 50 miles [80 km] from Babylon in what is now Iraq), the Greeks (later known as the Ten Thousand) returned to Byzantium via Mesopotamia, Armenia, and northern Anatolia. Xenophon was one of the men selected to replace five generals seized and executed by the Persians. The persistence and skill of the Greek soldiers were used by proponents of Panhellenism as proof that the Persians were vulnerable. Initially viewed with hostility by Sparta (the current Greek hegemonic power), the mercenaries found employment in the winter of 400–399 with the Thracian prince Seuthes but then entered Spartan service for a war to liberate Anatolian Greeks from Persian rule. Unpersuaded by Seuthes's offers of land and marriage to his daughter and evidently disinclined (despite protestations to the contrary) to return home, Xenophon remained with his comrades. Although the *Anabasis* narrative stops at this point and further details are lacking, he clearly became closely involved with senior Spartans, notably (after 396) King Agesilaus II. When a Greek coalition, including Athens, rebelled against Spartan hegemony in mainland Greece, Xenophon fought (at Coronea in 394) for Sparta.

Whether his service to Sparta caused or reflected his formal exile from Athens remains a matter of some dispute, but exiled he certainly was. The Spartans gave him somewhere to live at Scillus (across the Alpheus River from Olympia), a small city in the Triphylian state created after Sparta's defeat of Elis in 400. During his years there, Xenophon served as Sparta's representative at Olympia, and he sent his sons to Sparta for their education. Some historians believe that he also made a trip to Sicily during this period. He certainly used his mercenary booty to buy land and erect a small-scale copy of Artemis's famous temple at Ephesus. (In *Anabasis*, Book V, there is a well-known description of this sacred estate and of the annual quasi-civic festival celebrated there.)

Too prominent to be unscathed by Sparta's loss of authority after the Battle of Leuctra (371), Xenophon was expelled from Scillus and is said to have settled in Corinth—though here, as elsewhere, the biographical tradition is of debatable authority, since the episode does not appear in Xenophon's own writings. The claim that his exile was formally repealed is another case in point, but his *Hipparchicus* (*Cavalry Commander*) and *Vectigalia* (*Ways and Means*) suggest that Xenophon had a sympathetic interest in Athens' fortunes, and rapprochement is reflected in his sons' service in the Athenian cavalry at the second Battle of Mantinea (362). The death of Xenophon's son Gryllus there unleashed such a profusion of eulogies that Aristotle later gave the subtitle *Gryllus* to a dialogue that criticized Isocrates' views of rhetoric. At the time of his own death, Xenophon's standing—as author of a considerable oeuvre and hero of an adventure nearly five decades old but ideo-logically vivid in a Greek world defined by its relationship to Persia—had never been higher.

Works

Xenophon produced a large body of work, all of which survives to the present day. (Indeed, the manuscript tradition includes *Constitution of the Athenians*, which is not by Xenophon.) The great majority of his works were probably written during the last 15 to 20 years of his life, but their chronology has not been decisively established. His output was formally varied—the main categories were long histori-cal or ostensibly historical narratives, Socratic texts, and short technical, biographical, or political treatises—but these had common features, as enumerated below.

First, Xenophon's work is characterized by novelty. His output includes the earliest or earliest surviving examples of the short nonmedical treatise and of autobiographical narrative (*Anabasis*). Other works, although not without precedent in genre, are unusual in various ways; this is true of the idiosyncratic contemporary history of *Hellenica* ("Greek History") and the fictive history of *Cyropaedia* ("Education of Cyrus"); the second-order, philosophically nontechnical response to (or exploitation of) Socratic literature found in *Memorabilia*, *Symposium* ("Drinking Party"), *Oeconomicus* ("Household Management"), and *Apology*; and the novel form of encomiastic biography exemplified by *Agesilaus*.

Second, the subject matter reflects Xenophon's per-sonal experiences. *Anabasis* and *Cyropaedia* flowed from the adventure of 401–400; the Socratic writings stemmed from youthful association with a charismatic teacher; *Hellenica* arose from a personal take on the politico-military history of his times; treatises on military com-mand, horsemanship, household management, and hunting derived from prolonged personal experience of each; *Ways and Means* was inspired by concern about Athens' finances and political fortunes; and *Hiero* may have originated in a visit to Sicily.

Third, Xenophon's agenda was essentially didactic (usually with direct or indirect reference to military or leadership skills), and it was often advanced through the use of history as a source of material. As a narrative historian Xenophon has a reputation for inaccuracy and incompleteness, but he clearly assumed that people and events from the past were tools for promoting political and ethical improvement. His ethical system contained little that jars in modern terms; but in today's cynical world, the apparent ingenuousness of its expression strikes some as by turns bland and irritating. The system's interconnection with the gods may challenge readers who either disavow the divine or are not reconciled to a pagan theological environment, simply because—in ethical contexts, though not in specific ritual ones (as illustrated in *Anabasis*, Book VII)—divine power in Xenophon is frequently anonymous and often singular or because he could apparently take a pragmatic attitude (e.g., posing a question to the Delphic oracle that was framed to produce the "right" answer). His contemporaries perhaps saw things differently: for them the gods were unproblematic (not that everyone thought the same way about them, but Xenophon's terms of reference were readily understood), and his insistence on a moral component to practical and (broadly) political skills may have been distinctive.

Fourth, charges of ingenuousness have been partly fueled by Xenophon's style. Judged in antiquity to be plain, sweet, persuasive, graceful, poetic, and a model of Attic purity, it now strikes some as jejune. A more charitable, and fairer, description would be that his style is understated—the range of stylistic figures is modest, and the finest effects are produced by his simplicity of expression. Rereading a famous passage in which the Ten Thousand first glimpse the sea, one is struck by the disproportion between its remembered impact and its brevity and indirect approach. Xenophon does not describe seeing the sea; instead he describes, first, his gradual realization that a commotion up ahead is caused by the shouts of those who have seen the sea and, second, the scenes of celebration as men embrace with tears and laughter, build a huge cairn of stones, and shower gifts upon their local guide.

Of his works with historical themes, *Hellenica* is a seven-book account of 411–362 in two distinct (perhaps chronologically widely separated) sections: the first (Book I and Book II through chapter 3, line 10) "completes" Thucydides (in largely un-Thucydidean fashion) by covering the last years of the Peloponnesian War (i.e., 411–404); the second (the remainder) recounts the long-term results of Spartan victory, ending with Greece in an unabated state of uncertainty and confusion after the indecisive second Battle of Mantinea (362). It is an idiosyncratic account, notable for omissions, an unexpected focus, a critical attitude to all parties, and a hostility to hegemonic aspirations—an intensely personal reaction to the period rather than an orderly history.

Anabasis, which probably initially circulated pseudonymously (under the name Themistogenes of Syracuse), tells the story of the Ten Thousand in a distinctive version, one in which Xenophon himself plays a central role in Books III–VII. The work provides a narrative that is varied and genuinely arresting in its own right, but it also invites the reader to think about the tactical, strategic, and leadership skills of those involved. On a political and ethnocultural front, it expresses a general view of Greek superiority to "barbarians," but, although it evokes Panhellenism (the thesis that Persia was vulnerable to concerted attack—and should therefore be attacked), it does not provide unambiguous support for that view.

In *Cyropaedia* Xenophon investigated leadership by presenting the life story of Cyrus II, founder of the Persian Empire. Because the story differs flagrantly from other sources and the narrative's pace and texture are unlike those of ordinary Greek historiography, many analysts have classed the work as fiction. Story line is certainly subordinate to didactic agenda, but Xenophon may have drawn opportunistically on current versions of the Cyrus story rather than pure imagination. The result is fictive history, more analogous to Socratic literature than to the Greek novel (to which it is sometimes pictured as antecedent). In the *Cyropaedia*, techniques of military and political leadership are exposed both through example and through direct instruction; but Cyrus's achievement (i.e., absolute autocracy) is not an unambiguous (or readily transferable) good, and the final chapter recalls that, Cyrus notwithstanding, Persia had declined. (As is often the case in the stories of Classical Greece, barbarian achievements worthy of respect lie in the past.)

Xenophon was long characterized as a second-rate practitioner of other people's literary trades, but more-sympathetic study suggests that the artfully simple style masks a writer of some sophistication. In the early 21st century, Xenophon was starting to be taken seriously as a distinctive voice on the history, society, and intellectual attitudes of the later Classical era.

ANONYMOUS: *THE* Mahabarata

Written circa 400 BCE, the *Mahabarata* (Sanskrit *Mahābhārata*, "Great Epic of the Bharata

Dynasty") is one of the two Sanskrit great epic poems of ancient India (the other being the *Ramayana*). The *Mahabharata* is an important source of information on the development of Hinduism between 400 BCE and 200 CE and is regarded by Hindus as both a text about *dharma* (Hindu moral law) and a history (*itihasa*, literally "that's what happened"). Appearing in its present form about 400 CE, the *Mahabharata* consists of a mass of mythological and didactic material arranged around a central heroic narrative that tells of the struggle for sovereignty between two groups of cousins, the Kauravas (sons of Dhritarashtra, the descendant of Kuru) and the Pandavas (sons of Pandu). The poem is made up of almost 100,000 couplets—about seven times the length of the *Iliad* and the *Odyssey* combined—divided into 18 *parvans*, or sections, plus a supplement titled *Harivamsha* ("Genealogy of the God Hari"; i.e., of Vishnu). Although it is unlikely that any single person wrote the poem, its authorship is traditionally ascribed to the sage Vyasa, who appears in the work as the grandfather of the Kauravas and the Pandavas. The traditional date for the war that is the central event of the *Mahabharata* is 1302 BCE, but most historians assign it a later date.

The story begins when the blindness of Dhritarashtra, the elder of two princes, causes him to be passed over in favour of his brother Pandu as king on their father's death. A curse prevents Pandu from fathering children, however, and his wife Kunti asks the gods to father children in Pandu's name. As a result, Dharma fathers Yudhishtira, the Wind fathers Bhima, Indra fathers Arjuna, and the Ashvins (twins) father Nakula and Sahadeva (also twins; born to Pandu's second wife, Madri). The enmity and jealousy that develops between the cousins forces the Pandavas to leave the kingdom when their father dies. During their exile the five jointly marry Draupadi (who is born out of a sacrificial fire and whom Arjuna wins by shooting an arrow through a row of targets) and meet their cousin Krishna, who remains their friend and companion thereafter. Although the Pandavas return to the kingdom, they are again exiled to the forest, this time for 12 years, when Yudhishthira loses everything in a game of dice with Duryodhana, the eldest of the Kauravas.

The feud culminates in a series of great battles on the field of Kurukshetra (north of Delhi, in Haryana state). All the Kauravas are annihilated, and, on the victorious side, only the five Pandava brothers and Krishna survive. Krishna dies when a hunter, who mistakes him for a deer, shoots him in his one vulnerable spot—his foot—and the five brothers, along with Draupadi and a dog who joins them (the god Dharma, Yudhisththira's father, in disguise), set out for Indra's heaven. One by one they fall on the way, and Yudhisthira alone reaches the gate of heaven. After further tests of his faithfulness and constancy, he is finally reunited with his brothers and Draupadi, as well as with his enemies, the Kauravas, to enjoy perpetual bliss.

The central plot constitutes little more than one fifth of the total work. The remainder of the poem addresses a wide range of myths and legends, including the romance of Damayanti and her husband Nala (who gambles away his kingdom just as Yudhishthira gambles away his) and the legend of Savitri, whose devotion to her dead husband persuades Yama, the god of death, to restore him to life. The poem also contains descriptions of places of pilgrimages.

Along with its basic plot and accounts of numerous myths, the *Mahabharata* reveals the evolution of Hinduism and its relations with other religions during its composition. The period during which the epic took shape was one of transition from Vedic sacrifice to sectarian Hinduism, as well as a time of interaction—sometimes

Gate at Angkor Thom, Cambodia, c. *1200.* R. Manley/Shostal Associates

friendly, sometimes hostile—with Buddhism and Jainism. Different sections of the poem express varying beliefs, often in creative tension. Some sections, such as the *Narayaniya* (a part of Book 13), the *Bhagavadgita* (Book 6), the *Anugita* (Book 14), and the *Harivamsha*, are important sources of early Vaishnava theology, in which Krishna is an avatar of the god Vishnu. Above all, the *Mahabharata* is an exposition of *dharma* (codes of conduct), including the proper conduct of a king, of a warrior, of an individual living in times of calamity, and of a person seeking to attain freedom from rebirth. The poem repeatedly demonstrates that the conflicting codes of *dharma* are so "subtle" that, in some situations, the hero cannot help but violate them in some respect, no matter what choice he makes.

The *Mahabharata* story has been retold in written and oral Sanskrit and vernacular versions throughout South and Southeast Asia. Its various incidents have been portrayed in stone, notably in sculptured reliefs at Angkor Wat and Angkor Thom in Cambodia, and in Indian miniature paintings.

QU YUAN

(b. 340, Quyi [now Zigui, Hubei province], China—
d. 278 BCE, Hunan)

Qu Yuan (in an earlier transliteration system spelled Ch'ü Yüan) was one of the greatest poets of ancient China and the earliest known by name. He was born a member of the ruling house of Chu, a large state in the central valley of the Yangtze River. While still in his 20s he was appointed a trusted, favoured counselor of his kinsman Huaiwang, the ruler of Chu. Qu Yuan advocated the unpopular policy of resistance to Qin, the most powerful of the Warring States, causing his rival courtiers to intrigue successfully against him. Estranged from the throne through the malice of his rivals, Qu Yuan was banished to the south of the Yangtze River by Huaiwang's successor, Qingxiangwang.

In despair over his banishment, Qu Yuan wandered about southern Chu, writing poetry and observing the shamanistic folk rites and legends that greatly influenced his works. He eventually drowned himself in despair in the Miluo River, a tributary of the Yangtze. The famous Dragon Boat Festival, held on the fifth day of the fifth

An elaborate relief showing Qu Yuan (right), who is considered to be one of China's greatest poets and a national hero. **Christian Kober/ AWL Images/Getty Images**

month of the Chinese lunar year, originated as a search for the poet's body.

The works of Qu Yuan have survived in an early anthology, the *Chuci* ("Elegies of Chu"; Eng. trans. *Elegies of the South*, 2011), much of which must be attributed to later poets writing about the legendary life of Qu Yuan. The anthology begins with the long melancholic poem *Lisao* ("On Encountering Sorrow"), Qu Yuan's most famous work, which initiated a tradition of romanticism in Chinese literature. His highly original and imaginative verse had an enormous influence over early Chinese poetry.

CALLIMACHUS

(b. *c.* 305 BCE, Cyrene, North Africa [now Shaḥḥāt, Libya]—d. *c.* 240)

The Greek poet and scholar Callimachus was the most representative poet of the erudite and sophisticated Alexandrian school. He migrated to Alexandria, where King Ptolemy II Philadelphus of Egypt gave him employment in the Library of Alexandria, the most important such archive in the Hellenistic world. Of Callimachus's voluminous writings—he is said to have produced more than 800 books—only six hymns, about 60 epigrams, and fragments survive, many of them discovered in the 20th century. His most famous poetical work, illustrative of his antiquarian interests, was the *Aitia* (*Causes*), probably produced between 270 and 245 BCE. This work is a narrative elegy in four books, containing a medley of recondite tales from Greek mythology and history by which the author seeks to explain the legendary origin of obscure customs, festivals, and names. The structure of the poem, with its short episodes loosely connected by a common theme, became the model for the *Fasti* and *Metamorphoses* of the Roman poet Ovid. Of his elegies for special occasions, the best known is the *Lock of Berenice* (itself included in the *Aitia* as the last episode of the collection), a polished piece of court poetry later freely adapted into Latin by Catullus.

Callimachus's other works include the *Iambi*, 13 short poems on occasional themes, and the *Hecale* a small-scale epic, or epyllion, which set a new poetic fashion for concise, miniaturistic detail. Callimachus insisted on the exercise of consummate literary craftsmanship and virtuosity within poems of relatively short length. He raised the hexameter to new heights of order and euphony, and his poetry may well be considered the peak of refinement of Greek verse of the period. In the *Hymns,* Callimachus adapted the traditional religious form of the Homeric Hymns (a collection of 34 ancient Greek poems of unknown authorship) to an original and purely literary use. The *Epigrams* of Callimachus treat a variety of personal themes with consummate artistry. Of his prolific prose works, certainly the most famous was the *Pinakes* ("Tables of Those Who Have Distinguished Themselves in Every Form of Culture and of What They Wrote") in 120 books. This work consisted of an elaborate critical and biographical catalog of the authors of the works held in the Library of Alexandria. Discoveries in the 19th and 20th centuries of ancient Egyptian papyruses confirm the fame and popularity of Callimachus. No other Greek poet except Homer is so often quoted by the grammarians of late antiquity. He was taken as a model by many Roman poets, notably Catullus and Propertius, and by the most sophisticated Greek poets, from Euphorion, Nicander, and Parthenius to Nonnus and his followers in the 5th century CE.

VALMIKI

(fl. probably not before 300 BCE, India)

The poet and sage Valmiki was hailed by later classical poets as the first true poet (*kavi*). Indeed, much of his work in the *Ramayana* (Sanskrit *Rāmāyaṇa*, "Romance of Rama"), one of the two great Sanskrit epics, possesses a poetic freshness and literary intention that is largely absent from its near-contemporary the *Mahabharata.* Valmiki's great tools are metaphor and simile. He delights in description of pastoral scenes, in lamentations and

Rama and Sita (seated) *with Hanuman* (kneeling) *and Lakshmana, 18th century, India*. Photos.com/Thinkstock

grand martial spectacles, and in the idyll of the hermitage, which depicts a serene sage leading a life of quiet meditation and living on simple forest fare in a tranquil woodland close to a sacred river. And the entire work is suffused with a confident, unwavering morality, for which the heroes of the *Mahabharata* are still searching.

In its present form, the *Ramayana* consists of some 24,000 couplets divided into seven books. It describes the royal birth of Rama in the kingdom of Ayodhya (Oudh), his tutelage under the sage Vishvamitra, and his success in bending Shiva's mighty bow at the bridegroom tournament of Sita, the daughter of King Janaka, thus winning her for his wife. After Rama is banished from his position as heir by an intrigue, he retreats to the forest with his wife and his favourite half brother, Lakshmana, to spend

14 years in exile. There Ravana, the demon-king of Lanka, carries off Sita to his capital, while her two protectors are busy pursuing a golden deer sent to the forest to mislead them. Sita resolutely rejects Ravana's attentions, and Rama and his brother set about

Ravana, the many-headed demon-king, detail from a painting of the Ramayana, c. 1720; in the Cleveland Museum of Art. **Courtesy of the Cleveland Museum of Art, Ohio, gift of George P. Bickford**

to rescue her. After numerous adventures they enter into alliance with Sugriva, king of the monkeys; and with the assistance of the monkey-general Hanuman and Ravana's own brother, Vibhishana, they attack Lanka. Rama slays Ravana and rescues Sita, who in a later version undergoes an ordeal by fire in order to clear herself of the suspicions of infidelity. When they return to Ayodhya, however, Rama learns that the people still question the queen's chastity, and he banishes her to the forest. There she meets the sage Valmiki (the reputed author of the *Ramayana*) and at his hermitage gives birth to Rama's two sons. The family is reunited when the sons become of age, but Sita, after again protesting her innocence, asks to be received by the earth, which swallows her up.

The poem enjoys immense popularity in India, where its recitation is considered an act of great merit. Many of its translations into the vernacular languages are themselves works of great literary merit, including the 12th-century *Iramavartaram* ("Rama's Incarnation") by the Tamil poet Kampan; the Bengali version of Krittibas Ojha (1450); and the Hindi version, *Ramcharitmanas* (1574–1576/77), of Tulsidas. Throughout North India the events of the poem are enacted in an annual pageant, the Ram Lila, and in South India the two epics, the *Ramayana* and the *Mahabharata*, even today make up the story repertoire of the *kathakali* dance-drama of Malabar. The *Ramayana* was popular even during the Mughal period (16th century), and it was a favourite subject of Rajasthani and Pahari painters of the 17th and 18th centuries.

The story also spread in various forms throughout Southeast Asia (especially Cambodia, Indonesia, and Thailand); and its heroes, together with the Pandava brothers of the *Mahabharata*, were the heroes of traditional Javanese-Balinese theatre, dance, and shadow plays. Incidents from the *Ramayana* are carved in bas-relief on many Indonesian monuments—for example, at Panataran in eastern Java.

PLAUTUS

(b. *c.* 254 BCE, Sarsina, Umbria? [Italy]—d. 184 BCE)

Little is known for certain about the life and personality of Plautus, who ranks with Terence as one of the two great Roman comic dramatists. His work, moreover, presents scholars with a variety of textual problems, since the manuscripts by which his plays survive are corrupt and sometimes incomplete. Nevertheless, his literary and dramatic skills make his plays enjoyable in their own right, while the achievement of his comic genius has had lasting significance in the history of Western literature and drama.

Life

According to the grammarian Festus (2nd or 3rd century CE), Plautus was born in northeastern central Italy. His customarily assigned birth and death dates are largely based on statements made by later Latin writers, notably Cicero in the 1st century BCE. Even the three names usually given to him—Titus Maccius Plautus—are of questionable historical authenticity. Internal evidence in some of the plays does, it is true, suggest that these were the names of their author, but it is possible that they are stage names, even theatrical jokes or allusions. ("Maccus," for example, was the traditional name of the clown in the so-called Atellan farces, long-established popular burlesque, native to the Neapolitan region of southern Italy. "Plautus," according to Festus, derives from *planis pedibus, planipes* [flat-footed] being a pantomime dancer.) There are further difficulties: the poet Lucius Accius (170–*c.*

86 BCE), who made a study of his fellow Umbrian, seems to have distinguished between one Plautus and one Titus Maccius. Tradition has it that Plautus was associated with the theatre from a young age. An early story says that he lost the profits made from his early success as a playwright in an unsuccessful business venture, and that for a while afterward he was obliged to earn a living by working in a grain mill.

Approach to Drama

The Roman predecessors of Plautus in both tragedy and comedy borrowed most of their plots and all of their dramatic techniques from Greece. Even when handling themes taken from Roman life or legend, they presented these in Greek forms, setting, and dress. Plautus, like them, took the bulk of his plots, if not all of them, from plays written by Greek authors of the late 4th and early 3rd centuries BCE (who represented the "New Comedy," as it was called), notably by Menander and Philemon. Plautus did not, however, borrow slavishly. Although the life represented in his plays is superficially Greek, the flavour is Roman, and Plautus incorporated into his adaptations Roman concepts, terms, and usages. He referred to towns in Italy; to the gates, streets, and markets of Rome; to Roman laws and the business of the Roman law courts; to Roman magistrates and their duties; and to such Roman institutions as the Senate.

Even more important was Plautus's approach to the language in which he wrote. His action was lively and slapstick, and he was able to marry the action to the word. In his hands, Latin became racy and colloquial, verse varied and choral.

Whether these new characteristics derived from now lost Greek originals—more vigorous than those of Menander—or whether they stemmed from the established forms and tastes of burlesque traditions native to Italy, cannot be determined with any certainty. The latter is the more likely. The result, at any rate, is that Plautus's plays read like originals rather than adaptations, such is his witty command of the Latin tongue—a gift admired by Cicero himself. It has often been said that Plautus's Latin is crude and vulgar, but it is in fact a literary idiom based upon the language of the Romans in his day.

The plots of Plautus's plays are sometimes well organized and interestingly developed, but more often they simply provide a frame for scenes of pure farce, relying heavily on intrigue, mistaken identity, and similar devices. Plautus is a truly popular dramatist, whose comic effect springs from exaggeration, burlesque and often coarse humour, rapid action, and a deliberately upside-down portrayal of life, in which slaves give orders to their masters, parents are hoodwinked to the advantage of sons who need money for girls, and the procurer or braggart soldier is outwitted and fails to secure the seduction or possession of the desired girls. Plautus, however, did also recognize the virtue of honesty (as in *Bacchides*), of loyalty (as in *Captivi*), and of nobility of character (as in the heroine of *Amphitruo*).

Although Plautus's original texts did not survive, some version of 21 of them did. Even by the time that Roman scholars such as Varro, a contemporary of Cicero, became interested in the playwright, only acting editions of his plays remained. These had been adapted, modified, cut, expanded, and generally brought up-to-date for production purposes. Critics and scholars have ever since attempted to establish a "Plautine" text, but 20th- and 21st-century editors have admitted the impossibility of successfully accomplishing such a task. The plays had an active stage life at least until the time of Cicero and were occasionally performed afterward.

During the Middle Ages, Plautus was little read—if at all—in contrast to the popular Terence. By the mid-14th century, however, the humanist scholar and poet Petrarch knew eight of the comedies. As the remainder came to light, Plautus began to influence European domestic comedy after the Renaissance poet Ariosto had made the first imitations of Plautine comedy in the Italian vernacular. His influence was perhaps to be seen at its most sophisticated in the comedies of Molière, and it can be traced up to the 20th century in such adaptations as Jean Giraudoux's *Amphitryon 38* (1929), Cole Porter's musical *Out of This World* (1950), and the musical and motion picture *A Funny Thing Happened on the Way to the Forum* (1963). Plautus's stock character types have similarly had a long line of successors: the braggart soldier of *Miles Gloriosus*, for example, became the Capitano of the Italian commedia dell'arte, is recognizable in Nicholas Udall's *Ralph Roister Doister* (16th century), in Shakespeare's Pistol, and even in his Falstaff, in Edmond Rostand's *Cyrano de Bergerac* (1897), and in Bernard Shaw's Sergius in *Arms and the Man* (1894), while a trace of the character perhaps remains in Bertolt Brecht's Eilif in *Mother Courage and Her Children* (1941). Thus, Plautus, in adapting Greek New Comedy to Roman conditions and taste, also significantly affected the course of the European theatre.

QUINTUS ENNIUS

(b. 239 BCE, Rudiae, southern Italy—d. 169 BCE)

Because of the place of his birth, Quintus Ennius was at home in three languages and had, as he put it, "three hearts": Oscan, his native tongue; Greek, in which he was educated; and Latin, the language of the army with which he served in the Second Punic War. The elder Cato took him to Rome (204), where he earned a meagre living as a teacher and by adapting Greek plays, but he was on familiar terms with many of the leading men in Rome, among them the elder Scipio. His patron was Marcus Fulvius Nobilior, whom he accompanied on his campaign in Aetolia and whose son Quintus obtained Roman citizenship for Ennius (184 BCE). Nothing else of significance is known about his life.

Ennius is best known for his *Annales*, a narrative poem telling the story of Rome from the wanderings of Aeneas to the poet's own day. Only 600 lines of this work survive. In them, the poet introduced himself as a reincarnated Homer, addressed the Greek Muses, and composed in dactylic hexameter the metre of Homer. Ennius varied his accounts of military campaigns with autobiography, literary and grammatic erudition, and philosophical speculation. *Annales* was the national epic until it was eclipsed by Virgil's *Aeneid*.

Ennius excelled in tragedy. Titles survive of 20 tragedies adapted from the Greek, mostly Euripides (e.g., *Iphigenia at Aulis, Medea, Telephus,* and *Thyestes*). About 420 lines remain, indicating remarkable freedom from the originals, great skill in adapting the native Latin metres to the Greek framework, heightening the rhetorical element and the pathetic appeal (a feature of Euripides that he greatly admired) through skillful use of alliteration and assonance. His plays on Roman themes were *Sabinae* ("Sabine Women") and, if they really were plays, *Ambracia* (on the capture of that city in Aetolia by Fulvius) and *Scipio*.

In the *Saturae* (*Satires*) Ennius developed the only literary genre that Rome could call its own. Four books in a variety of metres on diverse subjects, they were mostly concerned with practical wisdom, often driving home a lesson with the help of a fable. More philosophical was a work on the theological and physical theories of

Epicharmus, the Sicilian poet and philosopher. *Euhemerus*, based on the ideas of Euhemerus of Messene, argued that the Olympian gods were originally great men honoured after death in human memory. Some epigrams, on himself and Scipio Africanus, are the first Latin elegiac couplets.

Ennius, who is credited also with the introduction of the double spelling of long consonants and the invention of Latin shorthand, was a man of wide interests and was conversant with the intellectual and literary movements of the Hellenistic world. He created and did not fall far short of perfecting a mode of poetic expression that reached its greatest beauty in Virgil and was to remain preeminent in Latin literature.

Cicero and others admired the work of Ennius throughout the republican period. Critical remarks appeared in Horace, becoming more severe in Seneca and Martial. The Neronian epic poet Lucan studied Ennius, and he was still read in the 2nd century CE; by the 5th century CE, copies of Ennius were rare.

POLYBIUS

(b. *c.* 200 BCE, Megalopolis, Arcadia, Greece — d. *c.* 118)

The Greek historian Polybius was the son of Lycortas, a distinguished Achaean statesman, and he received the upbringing considered appropriate for a son of rich landowners. His youthful biography of Philopoemen reflected his admiration for that great Achaean leader, and an interest in military matters found expression in his lost book, *Tactics*. He enjoyed riding and hunting, but his knowledge of literature was rather specialized (apart from the historians) and his acquaintance with philosophy superficial.

Statue of the Greek historian Polybius, whose 40-book treatise on the history of Rome exists largely in the form of excerpts noted by Greek historians of the 10th century. alessandro0770/Shutterstock.com

Before 170/169, when he was hipparch (cavalry commander) in the Achaean Confederation, almost nothing is known of his career. But he then became involved in critical events. Encumbered by their war with Perseus of Macedonia, the Romans were watching for disloyalty in the Greek states. Although Polybius declared for open support of Rome and was sent as an envoy to the consul Quintus Marcius Philippus, Achaean help was rejected. After Perseus's defeat at Pydna in 168, Polybius was one of 1,000 eminent Achaeans who were deported to Rome and detained in Italy without trial.

Residence in Rome

In Rome, Polybius had the good fortune to attract the friendship of the great Roman general Scipio Aemilianus; he became Scipio's mentor and through his family's influence was allowed to remain in Rome. It is probable that Polybius accompanied Scipio to Spain in 151, went with him to Africa (where he saw the Numidian king Masinissa), and crossed the Alps in Hannibal's footsteps on his way back to Italy. Shortly afterward, when his political detention had ended, Polybius joined Scipio at Carthage and was present at its siege and destruction in 146. It is likely that he then undertook a voyage of exploration in the Atlantic, which is related in Pliny the Elder's *Natural History*.

Meanwhile, hostilities had broken out between Achaea and Rome, and Polybius was in Corinth shortly after its destruction, in 146. He devoted himself to securing as favourable a settlement as possible for his countrymen and to reestablishing order; and, as the geographer Pausanias states, Achaean gratitude found expression in the erection of statues in his honour at Tegea, Pallantium, Mantineia, Lycosura—where the inscription declared that "Greece would never have come to grief, had she obeyed

Polybius in all things, and having come to grief, she found succour through him alone"—and Megalopolis, where it was recorded that "he had roamed over all the earth and sea, had been the ally of the Romans, and had quenched their wrath against Greece."

Of Polybius's life after 146 little is known. At some date he visited Alexandria and Sardis. He is known to have discussed political problems with Scipio and Panaetius of Rhodes. He wrote a history of the Numantine War, evidently after 133 BCE, and also a treatise on the habitability of the equatorial region; but when he composed the latter is unknown.

Polybius's History of Rome

The Histories on which his reputation rests consisted of 40 books, the last being indexes. Books I–V are extant. For the rest there are various excerpts, including those contained in the collection of passages from Greek historians assembled in the 10th century and rediscovered and published by various editors from the 16th to the 19th century.

Polybius's original purpose was to narrate the history of the 53 years (220–168 BCE)—from Hannibal's Spanish campaign to the Battle of Pydna—during which Rome had made itself master of the world. Books I–II form an introduction covering Roman history from the crossing into Sicily against the Carthaginians in 264 and including events in various other parts of the world (especially Achaea) between 264 and 220. In Book III, Polybius sketches a modified plan, proposing to add an account of how the Romans exercised their supremacy and to extend coverage to the destruction of Carthage, in 146.

The events of 168–146 were related in Books XXX–XXXIX. Polybius probably conceived his revision after 146, having by this date completed his narrative down to the end of the Second Punic War. At least Books I–VI seem to have been published by about 150; there is no information as to when the rest of the work, including the revised plan in Book III, appeared.

Conception of History

"All historians," according to Polybius,

> *have insisted that the soundest education and training for political activity is the study of history, and that the surest and indeed the only way to learn how to bear bravely the vicissitudes of fortune is to recall the disasters of others.*

Practical experience and fortitude in facing calamity are the rewards of studying history and are stressed repeatedly throughout the work. History is essentially didactic. Pleasure is not to be wholly excluded, but the scale comes down sharply on the side of profit. To be really profitable, history must deal with political and military matters; and this is *pragmatiké historia*, in contrast to other sorts of history (IX, 1–2) — genealogies and mythical stories, appealing to the casual reader, and accounts of colonies, foundations of cities, and ties of kindred, which attract the person with antiquarian interests. Its nature is austere, though it may include contemporary developments in art and science. He stands in contrast to the sensationalism of many of his predecessors, who confuse history with tragedy.

In Book II, in which he attacks the Greek historian Phylarchus for practices that might be called unprofessional today, Polybius states:

> *A historian should not try to astonish his readers by sensationalism, nor, like the tragic poets, seek after men's probable utterances and enumerate all the possible*

consequences of the events under consideration, but sim-
ply record what really happened and was said, however
commonplace. For the object of history is the very oppo-
site of that of tragedy. The tragic writer seeks by the
most plausible language to thrill and charm the audience
temporarily; the historian by real facts and real speeches
seeks to instruct and convince serious students for all
time. There it is the probable that counts, even though it
be false, the object being to beguile the spectator; here it is
the truth, the object being to benefit the student.

This attack on Phylarchus is not isolated. Similar faults
are castigated in other historians judged guilty of sensationalism. Nor are these their only weaknesses. Many
historians are prone to exaggeration—and that for a special reason. As writers of monographs whose subjects are
simple and monotonous, they are driven "to magnify small
matters, to touch up and elaborate brief statements and
to transform incidents of no importance into momentous
events and actions." In contrast to such practices, Polybius
stresses the universal character of his own theme, which is
to narrate "how and thanks to what kind of constitution
the Romans in under 53 years have subjected nearly the
whole inhabited world to their sole government—a thing
unique in history."

Polybius believed that he had a particular reason for
adopting a comprehensive view of history, apart from his
own predilection for such a view. He wrote:

Hitherto the affairs of the world had been as it were dis-
persed...; since this date [220 BCE] history has formed an
organic whole, and the affairs of Italy and Africa have
been interlinked with those of Greece and Asia, all tend-
ing towards one end (I, 3, 3–4).

Indeed, only universal history is capable of adequately treating Rome's rise to world power—the historian's synoptic view matches the organic character of history itself:

> *What gives my work its peculiar quality, and is nowadays most remarkable, is this. Tyche [Fortune] having guided almost all the world's affairs in one direction and having inclined them to one and the same goal, so the historian must bring under one conspectus for his readers the operations by which she has accomplished her general purpose. For it was chiefly this consideration, coupled with the fact that none of my contemporaries has attempted a general history, which incited and encouraged me to undertake my task (I, 4, 1–2).*

The role here allotted to Fortune is somewhat unusual. For clearly the value of history as a source of practical lessons is diminished if cause and effect are at the mercy of an incalculable and capricious power. Usually, although Polybius uses Fortune to cover a variety of phenomena, ranging from pure chance to something very like a purposeful providence, much of the apparent inconsistency springs from his use of purely verbal elaboration or the careless adoption of current Hellenistic terminology, which habitually made Fortune a goddess. Here, however, Fortune seems to be a real directive power, which raised Rome to world dominion—because Rome deserved it. Normally, Polybius lays great emphasis on causality, and his distinction between the causes of an event (*aitiai*) and its immediate origins (*archai*) is useful up to a point, though it is more mechanical than that of the great Greek historian Thucydides and allows nothing for the dialectical character of real historical situations.

An important place in Polybius's work is occupied by his study of the Roman constitution and army and the early history of the city in Book VI. His analysis of the mixed constitution, which had enabled Rome to avoid the cycle of change and deterioration to which simple constitutional forms were liable, is full of problems, but it has exercised widespread influence, from Cicero's *De republica* down to Machiavelli and Montesquieu.

Sources of Information

Polybius defines the historian's task as the study and collation of documents, acquaintance with relevant geographical features, and, finally, political experience; of these the last two are the most essential. And he practiced what he preached, for he possessed good political and military experience and had traveled widely throughout the Mediterranean and beyond. Nor did he neglect written sources; indeed, for his introductory books, covering the period from 264 to 220, they were essential. For the main part of his history, from 220 onward, he consulted many writers, Greek and Roman, but, following precedent, he rarely names them.

He had access to private sources; for example, Publius Cornelius Scipio's letter to Philip V of Macedonia describing the capture in Spain, in 209 BCE, of New Carthage, and a letter of Scipio Nasica to some Hellenistic king about the campaigns of the Third Macedonian War. He almost certainly consulted the Achaean record office and must have drawn on Roman records for such material as the treaty between Carthage and Philip V. It has not been proved that he had access to the Rhodian records. His detailed figures for Hannibal's troop formations in Italy came from an inscription left by Hannibal, which he found in the Temple of Juno on the Lacinian promontory.

Polybius regarded oral sources as his most important, and the questioning of witnesses as the most vital part of a historian's task; indeed, this is one reason why he chose to begin his main history at the year 220. Anything else would be "hearsay at one remove," a safe foundation for neither judgments nor statements.

TERENCE

(b. *c.* 195 BCE, Carthage, North Africa [now in Tunisia]—d. 159? BCE, in Greece or at sea)

Terence, like Plautus, was a great Roman comic dramatist. He was the author of six verse comedies that were long regarded as models of pure Latin. His plays form the basis of the modern comedy of manners (witty, cerebral comedy that satirizes contemporary behaviour and manners).

Life

Publius Terentius Afer was taken to Rome as a slave by Terentius Lucanus, an otherwise unknown Roman senator. The senator was impressed by Terence's ability and gave him a liberal education and, subsequently, his freedom.

Reliable information about the life and dramatic career of Terence is defective. There are four sources of biographical information on him: a short, gossipy life by the Roman biographer Suetonius, written nearly three centuries later; a garbled version of a commentary on the plays by the 4th-century grammarian Aelius Donatus; production notices prefixed to the play texts recording details of first (and occasionally also of later) performances; and Terence's own prologues to the plays, which, despite polemic and distortion, reveal something of his literary career. Most of the available information about Terence relates to his career as a dramatist. During his short life he produced six plays, to which the production notices assign the following dates: *Andria* (*The Andrian Girl*), 166 BCE; *Hecyra* (*The Mother-in-Law*), 165 BCE; *Heauton timoroumenos* (*The Self-Tormentor*), 163 BCE; *Eunuchus* (*The Eunuch*), 161 BCE; *Phormio*, 161 BCE; *Adelphi* (or *Adelphoe; The Brothers*), 160 BCE; *Hecyra,* second production, 160 BCE; *Hecyra*, third production, 160 BCE. These dates, however, pose several problems. The *Eunuchus*, for example, was so successful that it achieved a repeat performance and record earnings for Terence, but the prologue that Terence wrote, presumably a year later, for the *Hecyra*'s third production gives the impression that he had not yet achieved any major success. Yet alternative date schemes are even less satisfactory.

From the beginning of his career, Terence was lucky to have the services of Lucius Ambivius Turpio, a leading actor who had promoted the career of Caecilius, the major comic playwright of the preceding generation. Now in old age, the actor did the same for Terence. Yet not all of Terence's productions enjoyed success. The *Hecyra* failed twice: its first production broke up in an uproar when rumours were circulated among its audience of alternative entertainment by a tightrope walker and some boxers; and the audience deserted its second production for a gladiatorial performance nearby.

Terence faced the hostility of jealous rivals, particularly one older playwright, Luscius Lanuvinus, who launched a series of accusations against the newcomer. The main source of contention was Terence's dramatic method. It was the custom for these Roman dramatists to draw their material from earlier Greek comedies about rich young men and the difficulties that attended their amours. The adaptations varied greatly in fidelity, ranging from the creative freedom of Plautus to the literal rendering of Luscius. Although Terence was apparently fairly faithful to his Greek models, Luscius alleged that Terence was guilty of "contamination"—i.e., that he had incorporated material from secondary Greek sources into his plots, to their detriment. Terence sometimes did add extraneous material. In the *Andria,* which, like the *Eunuchus, Heauton timoroumenos,* and *Adelphi*, was adapted from a Greek play of the same title by Menander, he added material from another Menandrean play, the *Perinthia* (*The Perinthian Girl*). In the *Eunuchus* he added to Menander's *Eunouchos* two characters, a soldier and his "parasite"—a hanger-on whose flattery of and services to his patron were rewarded with free dinners—both of them from another play by Menander, the *Kolax* (*The Parasite*). In the *Adelphi,* he added an exciting scene from a play by Diphilus, a contemporary of Menander. Such conservative writers as Luscius objected to the freedom with which Terence used his models.

A further allegation was that Terence's plays were not his own work but were composed with the help of unnamed nobles. This malicious and implausible charge is left unanswered by Terence. Romans of a later period assumed that Terence must have collaborated with the Scipionic circle, a coterie of admirers of Greek literature, named after its guiding spirit, the military commander and politician Scipio Africanus the Younger.

Terence died young. When he was 35, he visited Greece and never returned from the journey. He died either in Greece from illness or at sea by shipwreck on the return voyage. Of his family life, nothing is known, except that he left a daughter and a small but valuable estate just outside Rome on the Appian Way.

Approach Toward Comedy

Modern scholars have been preoccupied with the question of the extent to which Terence was an original writer, as opposed to a mere translator of his Greek models. Positions on both sides have been vigorously maintained, but for the most part critical opinion seems to accept that Terence was faithful to the plots, ethos, and characterization of his Greek originals: thus, his humanity, his individualized characters, and his sensitive approach to relationships and personal problems all may be traced to Menander, and his obsessive attention to detail in the plots of *Hecyra* and *Phormio* derives from the Greek models of those plays by Apollodorus of Carystus of the 3rd century BCE. Nevertheless, in some important particulars he reveals himself as something more than a translator. First, he shows both originality and skill in the incorporation of material from secondary models, as well as occasionally perhaps in material of his own invention; he incorporates this material unobtrusively. Second, his Greek models probably had expository prologues, informing their audiences of vital facts, but Terence cut them out, leaving his audiences in the same ignorance as his characters. This omission increases the element of suspense, though the plot may become too difficult for an audience to follow, as in the *Hecyra*.

Striving for a refined but conventional realism, Terence eliminated or reduced such unrealistic devices as the actor's direct address to the audience. He preserved the atmosphere of his models with a nice appreciation of how much Greekness would be tolerated in Rome, omitting the unintelligible and clarifying the difficult. His language is a purer version of contemporary colloquial Latin, at times shaded subtly to emphasize a character's individual speech patterns. Because they are more realistic, his characters lack some of the vitality and panache of Plautus's adaptations (Phormio here is a notable exception); but they are often developed in depth and with subtle psychology. Individual scenes retain their power today, especially those presenting brilliant narratives, civilized emotion, or clever theatrical strokes.

The influence of Terence on Roman education and on the later European theatre was very great. His language was accepted as a norm of pure Latin, and his work was studied and discussed throughout antiquity.

Recommended English translations include *Terence* (2001), edited by John Barsby; *Terence, the Comedies* (1992), originally published as *The Complete Comedies of Terence* (1974), translated by Palmer Bovie, Constance Carrier, and Douglass Parker and edited by Palmer Bovie; and *The Comedies*, new ed. (2008), translated and with notes by Peter Brown.

SIMA XIANGRU

(b. 179 BCE, Chengdu [now in Sichuan province], China—d. 117 BCE, Maoling [now Xingping, Shaanxi province])

Chinese poet Sima Xiangru (in an earlier transliteration system spelled Ssu-ma Hsiang-ju) was renowned for his *fu*, a Chinese literary form combining elements of poetry and prose. Self-trained in literature and fencing, Sima was appointed bodyguard to the Han emperor Jingdi, but soon he took a new position at the court of Prince Xiao of Liang. There he began to compose his famous *fu Zixufu,* in which three imaginary characters (one of whom is named Zixu) from rival states describe the hunts and hunting preserves of their rulers.

After the death of Prince Xiao, Sima returned to Chengdu, where he eloped with Zhuo Wenjun, the recently widowed daughter of a wealthy man. The poet had entrusted his *Zixufu* to a friend, who had shown it to the emperor Wudi. Immediately charmed by the poem, the emperor asked Sima to write a *fu* on the imperial hunt. He extended his original work into a highly imaginative and successful *fu*, adding a third part entitled *Shanglinfu* ("Supreme Park"), which rhapsodically describes Wudi's hunting preserves. The poet was rewarded with a court post. Endowed with his wife's share of the immense family fortune, he lived in comfort while he continued to write his poetry, including *Darenfu* ("The Mighty One"), a panegyric to Wudi. Only 29 of Sima's *fu* and 4 prose selections survive.

SIMA QIAN

(b. *c.* 145 BCE, Longmen, Xiayang [now Hancheng, Shaanxi province], China—d. *c.* 87 BCE)

Sima Qian (in an earlier transliteration system spelled Ssu-ma Ch'ien) was an astronomer, calendar expert, and the first great Chinese historian. He is most noted for his authorship of the *Shiji* ("Historical Records"), which is considered to be the most important history of China down to the end of the 2nd century. He was the son of Sima Tan, the grand historian (sometimes translated as "astronomer royal") at the Han court during the period 140–110 BCE. The office of grand historian combined responsibility for astronomical observations and for the regulation of the calendar with the duties of keeping a daily record of state events and court ceremonies.

After traveling extensively in his youth, Sima Qian entered court service. In 111 he accompanied a military expedition into the southwest of China, and in 110 he was a member of the Wudi emperor's entourage when the latter visited Mount Tai to conduct the sacrifices symbolizing the dynasty's authority. In the same year, his father died, and after the mandatory period of mourning he was appointed in 108 to succeed him in the post of grand historian.

In 105 he was among those responsible for a complete reform of the Chinese calendar, a reform prompted by the Wudi emperor's inauguration of what was to be a "new beginning" to the Han dynasty. At about the same time, Sima Qian began to undertake the unfulfilled ambition of his father to write a definitive history of the Chinese past, an ambition strengthened by his belief that under Wudi the Han had reached a peak of achievement that deserved to be recorded for posterity. Before his history was completed, however, Sima Qian deeply offended the emperor by coming to the defense of a disgraced general. Sima Qian was arraigned for "defaming the emperor," a capital crime. Either because the emperor felt him too valuable a man to lose or because Sima Qian himself requested a reprieve so that he could complete his history, he was castrated instead of executed.

Wudi later relented, and Sima Qian again rose in the imperial favour, becoming palace secretary (*zhongshuling*). But he remained bitterly

Sima Qian, detail, ink and colour on silk; in the National Palace Museum, Taipei. **Courtesy of the Collection of the National Palace Museum, Taipei, Taiwan, Republic of China**

conscious of the shame he had suffered and lived a retiring life, devoting himself to the completion of his great masterpiece.

The *Shiji* is his great claim to fame. There had, of course, been many histories before Sima Qian's time. The keeping of court chronicles was already an established practice under the earlier dynasties. One such work, the *Chunqiu* ("Spring and Autumn [Annals]") of the petty state of Lu, was said to have been the work of Confucius. It had achieved status as a canonical book largely because of its ethical judgments on the events that it recounts.

Sima Qian denied that his work was in any way comparable to this great Classic. He termed himself not a "maker," like Confucius, but merely a "transmitter" of past events. His great successor as historian of the Han, Ban Gu (32?–92 CE), took him to task for his haphazard use of ideas from the various schools of philosophy and for his devotion to Daoism. But the ethical standards of Han Confucianism that Ban Gu and his contemporaries could take for granted had not in Sima Qian's lifetime achieved the authority they had by the 1st century CE. Like most of his contemporaries, Sima Qian was an eclectic, employed at a court at which magic and the supernatural were still deemed potent forces and where the state religious cult and accepted moral and political standards were still in a fluid state. Sima Qian's moral judgments are, thus, not in accordance with any consistent theories.

His main achievement was that he reduced to an orderly narrative the complex events of the past, recorded in often contradictory sources deriving from the many independent states, each of which employed its own chronology. He organized these facts not, as in previous histories, simply as a chronologically ordered record but according to a new five-part plan. The "Basic Annals" gave a dated chronological outline centred on events at the court considered to have been the paramount power at the time. The following section consisted of chronological tables in which he attempted to clarify the confusion of the history of the various independent feudal kingdoms and to enable his reader to see at a glance what was happening in each of the states at any given time. The detailed accounts of each state were given in chapters entitled "The Hereditary Houses." A number of monographs dealt with various crucial aspects of government. These sections show Sima Qian to have favoured the practical reformist statesmen who, in his own time, were formulating new policies for the increasingly centralized state, rather than the proponents of Confucian moral theories. The work ends with a collection of "Biographies" that deal with a variety of famous individuals, who are selected as exemplars of various types of conduct, and also with the affairs of the various foreign peoples, relations with whom were beginning to become increasingly important during the reign of Wudi.

The *Shiji* provided a model for the later dynastic histories but differs from them in many ways. Its time span is far longer: such attempts to encompass the whole of human history were rare among later Chinese historians. Its source material, too, was far more varied. It incorporated not only the court annals of the Qin and the Han dynasties but also various earlier histories, parts of court chronicles of various feudal states, and material from the canonical books and the philosophical writings of all the schools, even historical romances. Neither is his subject matter exclusively court-centred and "political," as were the later histories; it includes a far wider range of society, including businessmen and merchants, condottieri and bandits, actors and court favourites, good officials and bad.

Sima Qian did not attempt to compose "objective" history but rather belonged unmistakably to the didactic Chinese tradition of history. He makes moral judgments on his characters. He also attempts to characterize them in types, recording an individual's exemplary deeds in one chapter and his misdeeds elsewhere. But the lessons he derives from history are varied and often mutually incompatible. He is much more notable for the critical attention he devotes to his sources. His acute critical comments are appended at the end of each chapter.

Sima Qian is important not only as a historian but also as a master of racy, flexible Chinese prose. He exerted a potent influence on later writers, particularly upon the early writers of narrative prose and fiction. Since Sima Qian's time, his history has been acknowledged as the great historical masterpiece in Chinese, a standard against which all later histories would be measured and a model for large-scale historical composition, not only in China but in all East Asian countries influenced by the Chinese literary tradition.

Marcus Terentius Varro

(b. 116 BCE, probably Reate [now Rieti, Italy]—d. 27 BCE)

Rome's greatest scholar and a satirist of stature, Marcus Terentius Varro is best known for his *Saturae Menippeae* ("Menippean Satires"). He was a man of immense learning and a prolific author. Inspired by a deep patriotism, he intended his work, by its moral and educational quality, to further Roman greatness. Seeking to link Rome's future with its glorious past, his works exerted great influence before and after the founding of the Roman Empire (27 BCE).

Varro studied with a prominent Latin scholar and with the philosopher Antiochus of Ascalon at Athens. Though not attracted to a political career, he played some part in the public life of the Roman Republic and rose to the office of praetor. He served with Pompey the Great in Spain (76), became his pro-quaestor there, and also served under him in the war against the pirates (67).

In 59 Varro wrote a political pamphlet entitled *Trikaranos* ("The Three-Headed") on the coalition of Pompey, Julius Caesar, and Crassus. He sided with Pompey in Spain (49) but was pardoned (47) and appointed librarian by Caesar, to whom he dedicated the second part of his *Antiquitates rerum humanarum et divinarum* ("Antiquities of Human and Divine Things"). Under the second triumvirate Varro was outlawed by Mark Antony, and his books were burned, but his property was later restored by Augustus. He spent the rest of his life in study and writing.

Varro wrote about 74 works in more than 600 books on a wide range of subjects: jurisprudence, astronomy, geography, education, and literary history, as well as satires, poems, orations, and letters. The only complete work to survive is the *Res rustica* ("Farm Topics"), a three-section work of practical instruction in general agriculture and animal husbandry, written to foster a love of rural life.

Dedicated to Cicero, Varro's *De lingua Latina* ("On the Latin Language") is of interest not only as a linguistic work but also as a source of valuable incidental information on a variety of subjects. Of the original 25 books there remain, apart from brief fragments, only Books V to X, and even these contain considerable gaps.

Of Varro's 150 books of the *Saturae Menippeae*, some 90 titles and nearly 600 fragments remain. The satires are humorous medleys in mixed prose and verse in the manner of the 3rd-century-BCE Cynic philosopher Menippus of Gadara. The subjects range from eating and drinking to literature and philosophy. In these satires, Varro shows himself a man of the old stamp, making fun of the follies and absurdities of modern times. He preaches a simple life of old-fashioned Roman virtue and piety, opposes luxury and philosophic dogmatism, and shows considerable skill in handling several metres and poetic manners.

CICERO

(b. 106 BCE, Arpinum, Latium [now Arpino, Italy]—d. Dec. 7, 43 BCE, Formiae, Latium [now Formia])

The Roman statesman, lawyer, scholar, and writer known as Cicero (or sometimes, notably in Great Britain, Tully) tried in vain to uphold republican principles in the final civil wars that destroyed the Roman Republic. His writings include books of rhetoric, orations, philosophical and political treatises, and letters. He is remembered in modern times as the greatest Roman orator and innovator of what became known as Ciceronian rhetoric.

Early Life and Career

Cicero was the son of a wealthy family of Arpinium. Admirably educated in Rome and in Greece, he did military service in 89 under Pompeius Strabo (the father of the statesman and general Pompey) and made his first appearance in the courts defending Publius Quinctius in 81. His brilliant defense, in 80 or early 79, of Sextus Roscius against a fabricated charge of parricide established his reputation at the bar, and he started his public career as quaestor (an office of financial administration) in western Sicily in 75.

As praetor, a judicial officer of great power at this time, in 66 he made his first important political speech, when, against Quintus Lutatius Catulus and leading Optimates (the conservative element in the Roman Senate), he

Statue of Roman statesman, orator, and writer Cicero. His elegant and persuasive rhetorical style, known as Ciceronian rhetoric, is still emulated by speakers to this day. Renata Sedmakova/Shutterstock.com

spoke in favour of conferring on Pompey command of the campaign against Mithradates VI, king of Pontus (in northeastern Anatolia). His relationship with Pompey, whose hatred of Marcus Licinius Crassus he shared, was to be the focal point of his career in politics. His election as consul for 63 was achieved through Optimates who feared the revolutionary ideas of his rival, Catiline.

In the first of his consular speeches, he opposed the agrarian bill of Servilius Rullus, in the interest of the absent Pompey; but his chief concern was to discover and make public the seditious intentions of Catiline, who, defeated in 64, appeared again at the consular elections in 63 (over which Cicero presided, wearing armour beneath his toga). Catiline lost and planned to carry out armed uprisings in Italy and arson in Rome. Cicero had difficulty in persuading the Senate of the danger, but the "last decree" *(Senatus consultum ultimum)*, something like a proclamation of martial law, was passed on October 22. On November 8, after escaping an attempt on his life, Cicero delivered the first speech against Catiline in the Senate, and Catiline left Rome that night. Evidence incriminating the conspirators was secured and, after a senatorial debate in which Cato the Younger spoke for execution and Julius Caesar against, they were executed on Cicero's responsibility. Cicero, announcing their death to the crowd with the single word *vixerunt* ("they are dead"), received a tremendous ovation from all classes, which inspired his subsequent appeal in politics to *concordia ordinum*, "concord between the classes." He was hailed by Catulus as "father of his country." This was the climax of his career.

Alliance with the First Triumvirate

At the end of 60, Cicero declined Caesar's invitation to join the political alliance of Caesar, Crassus, and Pompey, the so-called First Triumvirate, which he considered unconstitutional, and also Caesar's offer in 59 of a place on his staff in Gaul. When Publius Clodius, whom Cicero had antagonized by speaking and giving evidence against him when he was tried for profanity early in 61, became tribune in 58, Cicero was in danger, and in March, disappointed by Pompey's refusal to help him, fled Rome. On the following day Clodius carried a bill forbidding the execution of a Roman citizen without trial. Clodius then carried through a second law, of doubtful legality, declaring Cicero an exile. Cicero went first to Thessalonica, in Macedonia, and then to Illyricum. In 57, thanks to the activity of Pompey and particularly the tribune Titus Annius Milo, he was recalled on August 4. Cicero landed at Brundisium (Brindisi) on that day and was acclaimed all along his route to Rome, where he arrived a month later.

In winter 57–56 Cicero attempted unsuccessfully to estrange Pompey from Caesar. Pompey disregarded Cicero's advice and renewed his compact with Caesar and Crassus at Luca in April 56. Cicero then agreed, under pressure from Pompey, to align himself with the three in politics, and he committed himself in writing to this effect (the "palinode"). The speech *De provinciis consularibus* (*On the Consular Provinces*) marked his new alliance. He was obliged to accept a number of distasteful defenses, and he abandoned public life. In the next few years he completed the *De oratore* (55; *On the Orator*) and *De republica* (52; *On the Republic*) and began the *De legibus* (52; *On Laws*). In 52 he was delighted when Milo killed Clodius but failed disastrously in his defense of Milo (later written for publication, the *Pro Milone*, or *For Milo*).

In 51 he was persuaded to leave Rome to govern the province of Cilicia, in southern Anatolia, for a year. The province had been expecting a Parthian invasion, but it never materialized, although Cicero did suppress some brigands on Mt. Amanus. The Senate granted a *supplicatio* (a period of public thanksgiving), although Cicero had hoped for a triumph, a processional return through the city, on his return to Rome. All admitted that he governed Cilicia with integrity.

By the time Cicero returned to Rome, Pompey and Caesar were struggling for complete power. He was on the outskirts of Rome when Caesar crossed the Rubicon and invaded Italy in January 49. Cicero met Pompey outside Rome on January 17 and accepted a commission to supervise recruiting in Campania. He did not leave Italy with Pompey on March 17, however. His indecision was not discreditable, though his criticism of Pompey's strategy was inexpert. In an interview with Caesar on March 28, Cicero showed great courage in stating his own terms—his intention of proposing in the Senate that Caesar should not pursue the war against Pompey any further—though they were terms that Caesar could not possibly accept. He disapproved of Caesar's dictatorship; yet he realized that in the succession of battles (which continued until 45) he would have been one of the first victims of Caesar's enemies, had they triumphed. This was his second period of intensive literary production, works of this period including the *Brutus, Paradoxa Stoicorum* (*Paradoxes of the Stoics*), and *Orator* (*The Orator*) in 46; *De finibus* (*On the Supreme Good*) in 45; and *Tusculanae disputationes* (*Tusculan Disputations*), *De natura deorum* (*On the Nature of the Gods*), and *De officiis* (*On Duties*), finished after Caesar's murder, in 44.

Last Months

Cicero was not involved in the conspiracy to kill Caesar on March 15, 44, and was not present in the Senate when he was murdered. On March 17 he spoke in the Senate in favour of a general amnesty, but then he returned to his philosophical writing and contemplated visiting his son, who was studying in Athens. But instead he returned to Rome at the end of August, and his 14 Philippic orations (so called in imitation of Demosthenes' speeches against Philip II of Macedonia), the first delivered on Sept. 2, 44, the last on April 21, 43, mark his vigorous reentry into politics. His policy was to make every possible use of Caesar's adopted son Octavian (the future emperor Augustus), whose mature intelligence he seriously underestimated, and to drive the Senate, against its own powerful inclination toward compromise, to declare war on Mark Antony, who had controlled events immediately following Caesar's death and who now was pursuing one of the assassins in Cisalpine Gaul. No letters survive to show how Octavian deceived Cicero in the interval between the defeat of Antony in Cisalpine Gaul on April 14 and Octavian's march on Rome to secure the consulship in August. It was in May that Octavian learned of Cicero's unfortunate remark that "the young man should be given praise, distinctions—and then be disposed of." The Second Triumvirate of Octavian, Antony, and Marcus Aemilius Lepidus was formed at the end of October, and Cicero was soon being sought for execution. He was captured and killed near Caieta on December 7. His head and hands were displayed on the *rostra*, the speakers' platform at the Forum, in Rome.

In politics Cicero constantly denigrated his opponents and exaggerated the virtues of his friends. As a "new man," a man without noble ancestry, he was never accepted by the dominant circle of Optimates, and he attributed his own political misfortunes after 63 partly to the jealousy, partly to the spineless unconcern, of the complacent Optimates. The close political association with Pompey for which he longed was never achieved. He was more ready than some men to compromise ideals in order to preserve the republic, but, though he came to admit in the *De republica* that republican government required the presence of a powerful individual—an idealized Pompey perhaps—to ensure its stability, he showed little appreciation of the intrinsic weaknesses of Roman republican administration.

Letters and Poetry

From Cicero's correspondence between 67 and July 43 BCE more than 900 letters survive, and, of the 835 written by Cicero himself, 416 were addressed to his friend, financial adviser, and publisher, the knight Titus Pomponius Atticus, and 419 to one or other of some 94 different friends, acquaintances, and relatives. The number obviously constitutes only a small portion of the letters that Cicero wrote and received. Many letters that were current in antiquity have not survived; for instance, the account of the suppression of Catiline's conspiracy, mentioned in the *Pro Sulla* and *Pro Plancio*, which Cicero sent to Pompey at the end of 63; Pompey hardly as much as acknowledged it, and Cicero was mocked about it in public later. Many letters were evidently suppressed for political reasons after Cicero's death.

There are four collections of the letters: to Atticus (*Ad Atticum*) in 16 books; to his friends (*Ad familiares*) in 16 books; to Brutus (*Ad Brutum*); and, in 3 books, to his brother (*Ad Quintum fratrem*). The letters constitute a primary historical source such as exists for no other part of the ancient world. They often enable events to be dated with a precision that would not otherwise be possible, and they have been used, though with no very great success, to discredit the accuracy of Caesar's commentaries on the civil war. On the other hand, his reporting of events, naturally enough, is not objective, and he was capable of misremembering or misrepresenting past events so as to enhance his own credit.

Cicero is a minor but by no means negligible figure in the history of Latin poetry. His best-known poems (which survive only in fragments) were the epics *De consulatu suo* (*On His Consulship*) and *De temporibus suis* (*On His Life and Times*), which were criticized in antiquity for their self-praise. Cicero's verse is technically important; he refined the hexameter, using words of two or three syllables at the end of a line, so that the natural word accent would coincide with the beat of the metre, and applying rhetorical devices to poetry; he is one of those who made possible the achievement of Virgil.

Oratory

Cicero made his reputation as an orator in politics and in the law courts, where he preferred appearing for the defense and generally spoke last because of his emotive powers. Unfortunately, not all his cases were as morally sound as the attack on the governor of Sicily, Gaius Verres, which was perhaps his most famous case. In his day Roman orators were divided between "Asians," with a rich, florid, grandiose style, of which Quintus Hortensius was the chief exponent, and the direct simplicity of the "Atticists," such as Caesar and Brutus. Cicero refused to attach himself to any school. He was trained by Molon of Rhodes, whose own tendencies were eclectic, and he believed that an orator should command and blend a variety of styles. He made a close study of the rhythms that were likely to appeal to an audience, especially in the closing cadences of a sentence or phrase. His fullness revolutionized the writing of Latin; he is the real creator of the "periodic" style, in which phrase is balanced against phrase, with subordinate clauses woven into a complex but seldom obscure whole. Cicero's rhetoric was a complex art form, and the ears of the audience were keenly attuned to these effects. Of the speeches, 58 have survived, some in an incomplete form; it is estimated that about 48 have been lost.

Cicero in *Brutus* implicitly gives his own description of his strengths as an orator—a thorough knowledge of literature, a grounding in philosophy, legal expertise, a storehouse of history, the capacity to tie up an opponent and reduce the jury to laughter, the ability to lay down general principles applicable to the particular case, entertaining digressions, the power of rousing the emotions of anger or pity, the faculty of directing his intellect to the point immediately essential. This is not an unjust picture. It is the *humanitas* of the speeches that turns them from an ephemeral tour de force into a lasting possession. His humour is at its best in his bantering of the Stoics in *Pro Murena* in order to discredit Cato, who was among the prosecutors, and at its most biting when he is attacking Clodia in *Pro Caelio.* His capacity for arousing anger may be seen in the opening sentences of the first speech against Catiline and, for arousing pity, in the last page of *Pro Milone*. His technique in winning a case against the evidence is exemplified by *Pro Cluentio,* a speech in an inordinately complex murder trial; Cicero later boasted of "throwing dust in the jurymen's eyes."

TIRUVALLUVAR

(fl. *c.* 1st century BCE or 6th century CE, India)

The Tamil poet-saint Tiruvalluvar (Thiruvalluvar, Valluvar) is the author of the *Tirukkural* ("Sacred Couplets"), considered a masterpiece of human thought. The *Tirukkural* is compared in India and abroad to the Bible, John Milton's *Paradise Lost*, and the works of Plato.

Little is known about the life of Tiruvalluvar except that he is believed to have lived in Mylapore (now part of Chennai [formerly Madras], Tamil Nadu, India) with his wife, Vasuki. He was probably a Jain ascetic of humble origins who worked as a weaver. Both Buddhists and Shaivites, however, claim him as their own, and he is especially revered by those of low caste.

Tiruvalluvar's couplets in the *Tirukkural* are highly aphoristic: "Adversity is nothing sinful, but / laziness is a disgrace"; "Wine cheers only when it is quaffed, but love / intoxicates at mere sight." Despite Tiruvalluvar's reasonable tone, many of his ideas were revolutionary. He dismissed the caste system: "One is not great because of one's birth in a noble family; one is not low because of one's low birth." The poet maintained that goodness is its own reward and should not be regarded as a mere means to a comfortable afterlife.

The *Tirukkural* is the most celebrated of the *Patiren-kirkkanakku* ("Eighteen Ethical Works") in Tamil literature, and it has had an immense influence on Tamil culture and life.

An all-inclusive ethical guide, the *Tirukkural* has as its foremost moral imperatives the avoidance of killing and the avoidance of falsehood. It also commends to the reader a feeling of compassion for all individuals, regardless of caste or creed. Its 133 sections of 10 couplets each are divided into three books: *aram* (virtue), *porul* (government and society), and *kamam* (love). The first section opens with praise of God, rain, renunciation, and a life of virtue. It then presents a world-affirming vision, the wisdom of human sympathy that expands from one's family and friends to one's clan, village, and country. The *porul* section projects a vision of an ideal state and relates good citizenship to virtuous private life. The *kamam* section addresses both "secret love" and married love; the section on married love is written as a dialogue between husband and wife.

*L*UCRETIUS

(fl. 1st century BCE)

The Latin poet and philosopher Titus Lucretius Carus is known for his single, long poem, *De rerum natura* (*On the Nature of Things*). The poem is the fullest extant statement of the physical theory of the Greek philosopher Epicurus. It also alludes to his ethical and logical doctrines.

Life

Apart from Lucretius's poem almost nothing is known about him. The little evidence available is quite inconclusive. Jerome, a leading Latin Church Father, in his chronicle for the year 94 BCE (or possibly 96 or 93 BCE), stated that Lucretius was born in that year and that years afterward a love potion drove him insane. Having written some books in lucid intervals, which Cicero afterward emended, he killed himself in his 44th year (51 or 50 BCE). In his *Life of Virgil*, Aelius Donatus, a grammarian and teacher of rhetoric, noted that Virgil put on the *toga virilis* (the toga of an adult) in his 17th year, on his birthday (i.e., 54 or 53 BCE), and that Lucretius died that same day. But Donatus contradicted himself by stating that the consuls that year were the same as in the year of Virgil's birth (i.e., Crassus and Pompey, in 55 BCE). This last date seems partly confirmed by a sentence in Cicero's reply to his brother in 54 BCE, which suggests that Lucretius was already dead and also that Cicero may have been involved in the publication of his poem: "The poems of Lucretius are as you write in your letter—they have many highlights of genius, yet also much artistry." Excepting the single mention in Cicero, the only contemporary who named Lucretius was a Roman historian, Cornelius Nepos (in his *Atticus*), in the phrase "after the death of Lucretius and Catullus." The only contemporary whom Lucretius named was one Memmius, to whom he dedicated his poem, probably Gaius Memmius (son-in-law of Sulla, praetor of 58 BCE, and patron of Catullus and Gaius Helvius Cinna), for whose friendship Lucretius "hopes."

De rerum Natura

The title of Lucretius's work translates that of the chief work of Epicurus, *Peri physeōs* (*On Nature*), as also of the didactic epic of Empedocles, a pluralist philosopher of nature, of whom Lucretius spoke with admiration only less than that with which he praised his master Epicurus.

Lucretius distributed his argument into six books, beginning each with a highly polished introduction. Books I and II establish the main principles of the atomic universe, refute the rival theories of the pre-Socratic cosmic philosophers Heracleitus, Empedocles, and Anaxagoras, and covertly attack the Stoics, a school of moralists rivaling that of Epicurus. Book III demonstrates the atomic structure and mortality of the soul and ends with a triumphant sermon on the theme "Death is nothing to us." Book IV describes the mechanics of sense perception, thought, and certain bodily functions and condemns sexual passion. Book V describes the creation and working of this world and the celestial bodies and the evolution of life and human society. Book VI explains remarkable phenomena of the earth and sky—in particular, thunder and lightning. The poem ends with a description of the plague at Athens, a sombre picture of death contrasting with that of spring and birth in the invocation to Venus, with which it opens.

Literary Qualities of the Poem

Setting aside its philosophical argument, the poem is notable for its linguistic style and spirit. The problem of Lucretius was to render the bald and abstract Greek prose of Epicurus into Latin hexameters at a time when Latin had no philosophical vocabulary. He succeeded by applying common words to a technical use. Thus, he used *concilium* ("assembly of people") for a "system of atoms" and *primordia* ("first weavings") for the "atoms" that make up the texture of things. When necessary, he invented words. In poetic diction and style he was in debt to the older Latin poets, especially to Quintus Ennius, the father of Roman poetry. He freely used alliteration and assonance, solemn and often metrically convenient archaic forms, and old constructions. He formed expressive compound adjectives of a sort rejected by Augustan taste—e.g., "the light-sleeping hearts of dogs," "forest-breaking winds." He imitated or echoed Homer; the dramatists Aeschylus and Euripides; Callimachus, a poet and critic; the historian Thucydides; and the physician Hippocrates. His hexameters stand halfway between those of Ennius, who introduced the metre into Latin, and Virgil, who perfected it. There is also some incoherence of rhythm, as well as harsh elisions and examples of unusual prosody.

The influence of Lucretius on Virgil was pervasive, especially in Virgil's *Georgics*; and it is in clear allusion to Lucretius that Virgil wrote, "Happy is the man who can read the causes of things."

Lucretius spoke in austere compassion for the ignorant, unhappy human race. His moral fervour expressed itself in gratitude to Epicurus and in hatred of the seers who inculcated religious fears by threats of eternal punishment after death, of the Etruscan soothsayers with their lore of thunder and lightning, of the false philosophers—Stoics with their belief in divine providence or Platonists and Pythagoreans who taught the transmigration of immortal souls. The first appearance of *religio* ("religion" or "piety") in the poem is as a monster that thrusts its fearful head from the regions of the sky. Epicurus, not intimidated by these spectres, had ranged beyond the "flaming ramparts of the world" through the infinite universe, broken into the citadel of nature, and brought back in triumph the knowledge of what can and what cannot be, of that "deep-set boundary stone" that divides the separate properties of things, the real from the not real. And "so religion is crushed beneath our feet and his [Epicurus's] victory lifts us to the skies."

SALLUST

(b. *c.* 86 BCE, Amiternum, Samnium [now San Vittorino, near L'Aquila, Italy]—d. 35/34 BCE)

The Roman historian Gaius Sallustius Crispus was one of the great Latin literary stylists. He is known for his narrative writings dealing with political personalities, corruption, and party rivalry.

Life

Sallust's family was Sabine and probably belonged to the local aristocracy, but he was the only member known to have served in the Roman Senate. Thus, he embarked on a political career as a *novus homo* ("new man"); that is, he was not born into the ruling class, which was an accident that influenced both the content and tone of his historical judgments. Nothing is known of his early career, but he probably gained some military experience, perhaps in the east in the years from 70 to 60 BCE. His first political office, which he held in 52, was that of a tribune of the plebs. The office, originally designed to represent the lower classes, by Sallust's time had developed into one of the most powerful magistracies. The evidence that Sallust held a quaestorship, an administrative office in finance, sometimes dated about 55, is unreliable.

Because of electoral disturbances in 53, there were no regular government officials other than the tribunes, and the next year opened in violence that led to the murder of Clodius Pulcher, a notorious demagogue and candidate for the praetorship (a magistracy ranking below that of consul), by a gang led by Titus Annius Milo. The latter was a candidate for consul. In the trial that followed, Cicero defended Milo, while Sallust and his fellow tribunes harangued the people in speeches attacking Cicero. While these events were not of lasting significance, Sallust's experience of the political strife of that year provided a major theme for his writings.

In 50 Sallust was expelled from the Senate. The anonymous "Invective Against Sallust" alleges immorality as the cause, but the real reason may have been politics. In 49

Sallust sought refuge with Julius Caesar, and, when the civil war between Caesar and Pompey broke out in that year, he was placed in command of one of Caesar's legions. His only recorded action was unsuccessful. Two years later, designated praetor, he was sent to quell a mutiny among Caesar's troops, again without success. In 46 he took part in Caesar's African campaign (with modest success), and, when Africa Nova was formed from Numidian territory (modern Algeria), Sallust became its first governor. He remained in office until 45 or early 44.

Upon returning to Rome, Sallust was accused of extortion and of plundering his province, but through Caesar's intervention he was never brought to trial according to the "Invective Against Sallust," as reported by Dio Cassius. The evidence draws moralizing contrasts between Sallust's behaviour and his censorious writings and suggests a source for the ill-gotten wealth that created the splendid Sallustian Gardens (Horti Sallustiani). The tradition about his morals seems to have originated in scurrilous gossip and by a confusion between the historian and his adopted son, Augustus's minister Sallustius Crispus, a man of great wealth and luxurious tastes.

Sallust's political career ended soon after his return to Rome. His retirement may have been voluntary, as he himself maintains, or forced upon him by the withdrawal of Julius Caesar's favour or even by Caesar's assassination in 44.

Works

Sallust may have begun to write even before the Triumvirate was formed late in 43. He was born in a time of civil war. As he grew to maturity, foreign war and political strife were commonplace; thus, it is not surprising that his writings are preoccupied with violence. His first monograph,

Bellum Catilinae (43–42 BCE; *Catiline's War*), deals with corruption in Roman politics by tracing the conspiracy of Catiline, a ruthlessly ambitious patrician who had attempted to seize power in 63 BCE after the suspicions of his fellow nobles and the growing mistrust of the people prevented him from attaining it legally. Catiline was supported by certain members of the upper classes who were prompted either by ambition or by the hope of solving their financial problems by Catiline's accession to power. But he also had the backing of Italy's dissatisfied veterans, impoverished peasants, and overburdened debtors.

In Sallust's view, Catiline's crime and the danger he presented were unprecedented. Indeed, alarmed contemporaries may have exaggerated the significance of the incident; yet, had the government not acted as firmly as it did (effectively declaring martial law), a catastrophe could have occurred. Sallust describes the course of the conspiracy and the measures taken by the Senate and Cicero, who was then consul. He brings his narrative to a climax in a senatorial debate concerning the fate of the conspirators, which took place on Dec. 5, 63. In Sallust's eyes, not Cicero but Caesar and Cato represented civic virtue and were the significant speakers in the debate; he regarded the deaths of Caesar and Cato as marking the end of an epoch in the history of the republic. A digression in this work indicates that he considered party strife as the principal factor in the republic's disintegration.

In Sallust's second monograph, *Bellum Jugurthinum* (41–40 BCE; *The Jugurthine War*), he explored in greater detail the origins of party struggles that arose in Rome when war broke out against Jugurtha, the king of Numidia, who rebelled against Rome at the close of the 2nd century BCE. This war provided the opportunity for the rise to the consulship of Gaius Marius, who, like Sallust and Cicero, was a "new man." His accession to power represented a successful attack on the traditionally exclusive Roman political elite, but it caused the kind of political conflict that, in Sallust's view, resulted in war and ruin. Sallust considered Rome's initial mismanagement of the war the fault of the "powerful few" who sacrificed the common interest to their own avarice and exclusiveness. Political turmoil in Rome during the late republic had social and economic causes (not overlooked by Sallust), but essentially it took the form of a power struggle between the aristocratic group in control of the Senate and those senators who enlisted popular support to challenge the oligarchy. This is the underlying framework of Sallust's schematic analysis of the events of that time—the clash between the nobility, or Senate, and the people, or plebeians.

The *Histories*, of which only fragments remain, describes the history of Rome from 78 to at least 67 BCE on a year-to-year basis. Here Sallust deals with a wider range of subject matter, but party conflict and attacks on the politically powerful remain a central concern. Hints of hostility to the Triumvirate on Sallust's part may be detected in both *Bellum Jugurthinum* and the *Histories*. Two "Letters to Caesar" and an "Invective Against Cicero," Sallustian in style, have often been credited, although probably incorrectly, to Sallust; the former title was attributed to him by the 1st-century-CE Roman educator Quintilian.

Sallust's influence pervades later Roman historiography, whether men reacted against him, as Livy did, or exploited and refined his manner and views, as Tacitus did. Sallust himself was influenced by Thucydides more than by any other Greek writer. Sallust's narratives were enlivened with speeches, character sketches, and digressions, and, by skillfully blending archaism and innovation, he created a style of classic status. And to the delight of moralists he revealed that Roman politics were not all that official rhetoric depicted them to be. His monographs excel in suggesting larger themes in the treatment of particular episodes.

Sallust is somewhat limited as a historian; his work shows many instances of anachronisms, inaccuracies, and prejudice. Whatever his weaknesses, his own experiences in politics imbued his analysis and his idiom with an energy and passion that compel the attention of readers. Sallust's moralizing and brilliant style made him popular in the Middle Ages, and he was an important influence on the English Classical republicans of the 17th century (who, during a period of revolution and turmoil, advocated for a government modeled on the Roman Republic) and the U.S. Founding Fathers in the 18th century.

CATULLUS

(b. 84 BCE, Verona, Cisalpine Gaul [now in Italy]—d. *c.* 54 BCE, Rome)

The Roman poet Gaius Valerius Catullus is considered to have written the finest lyric poetry of ancient Rome. No ancient biography of Catullus survives. A few facts can be pieced together from external sources, in the works of his contemporaries or of later writers, supplemented by inferences drawn from his poems, some of which are certain, some only possible. The unembroidered, certain facts are scanty.

Life

Catullus was alive 55–54 BCE on the evidence of four of his poems and died young according to the poet Ovid—at age 30 as stated by St. Jerome (writing about the end of the 4th century), who nevertheless dated his life erroneously 87–57 BCE. Catullus was thus a contemporary of the statesmen Cicero, Pompey, and Caesar, who are variously addressed by him in his poems. He preceded the poets of the immediately succeeding age of the emperor Augustus, among whom Horace, Sextus Propertius, Tibullus, and Ovid name him as a poet whose work is familiar to them. On his own evidence and that of Jerome, he was born at Verona in what is now northern Italy and was therefore a native of Cisalpine Gaul (Gaul This Side of the Alps). He owned property at Sirmio, the modern Sirmione, on Lake Garda, though he preferred to live in Rome and owned a villa near the Roman suburb of Tibur, in an unfashionable neighbourhood.

According to an anecdote in the Roman biographer Suetonius's *Life of Julius Caesar*, Catullus's father was Caesar's friend and host, but the son nevertheless lampooned not only the future dictator but also his son-in-law Pompey and his agent and military engineer Mamurra with a scurrility that Caesar admitted was personally damaging and would leave its mark on history; the receipt of an apology was followed by an invitation to dinner "the same day," and Caesar's relations with the father continued uninterrupted. (Suetonius cites the episode as an example of Caesar's clemency.)

Catullus's poetry reports one event, externally datable to *c.* 57–56 BCE, a journey to Bithynia in Asia Minor in the retinue of Gaius Memmius, the Roman governor of the province, from which he returned to Sirmio. It also records two emotional crises, the death of a brother whose grave he visited in the Troad, also in Asia Minor, and an intense and unhappy love affair, portrayed variously in 25 poems, with a woman who was married and whom he names Lesbia, a pseudonym (Ovid states) for Clodia, according to the 2nd-century writer Apuleius. His poems also record, directly or indirectly, a homosexual affair with a youth named Juventius.

Such are the stated facts. The conjectural possibilities to be gleaned mostly from the internal evidence of Catullus's poetry extend a little further. It is accepted that Catullus was born *c.* 84 BCE and that he died *c.* 54 BCE. His father's hospitality to Caesar may have been exercised in Cisalpine Gaul when Caesar was governor of the province, but equally well at Rome—Suetonius does not indicate time or place. Catullus's Roman villa may have been heavily mortgaged (depending on the choice of manuscript reading of one poem). A yacht retired from active service and celebrated in an iambic poem may have been his own, built in Bithynia, in northwestern Asia Minor, and therefore available to convey him on his way home to Sirmio after his tour of duty. His fellow poet Cinna may have accompanied him to Bithynia. For the governor Memmius, himself a litterateur (to whom the Roman philosophic poet Lucretius dedicated his poem on the nature of things, *De rerum natura*), such company might be congenial, and it is possible to speculate that Cinna was on board the yacht. The brother's grave could have been visited en route to or from Bithynia.

The poet's Clodia may have been a patrician, one of the three Clodia sisters of Cicero's foe Publius Clodius Pulcher, all three the subject of scandalous rumour, according to Plutarch. If so, she was most probably the one who married the aristocrat Metellus Celer (consul 60 BCE, died 59 BCE), who in 62 BCE was governor of Cisalpine Gaul. It may have been at that time that the youthful poet first met her and possibly fell under her spell. She is accorded a vivid if unflattering portrait in Cicero's *Pro Caelio,* in which the orator had occasion to blacken her character in order to defend his client against Clodia's charge that as her lover after her husband's death he had tried to poison her. The client was Marcus Caelius Rufus, conceivably the Rufus reproached by Catullus in poem LXXVII as a trusted friend who had destroyed his happiness (but if so, the Caelius of poem C is a different person). This identification of Clodia, suggested by an Italian scholar of the 16th century, has found support in some uncertain inferences from the Lesbia poems: the poet's mistress besides being married perhaps moved in society, enjoyed fashionable amusements, was cultivated and witty, and was licentious enough to justify Cicero's attack. On the other hand, the poet twice appears to have included the protection of his own rank among the gifts he had laid at her feet.

The Poetry

A consideration of the text of Catullus's poems and of its arrangement is of unusual interest. Its survival has been as precarious as his biography is brief. Not being part of the school syllabus, from roughly the end of the 2nd century to the end of the 12th century, it passed out of circulation. Knowledge of it depends on a single manuscript discovered *c.* 1300, copied twice, and then lost. Of the two copies, one in turn was copied twice, and then it was lost. From the three survivors—in the Bodleian Library at Oxford, the Bibliothèque Nationale in Paris, and the Vatican Library in Rome—scholars have been able to reconstruct the lost "archetype." Incorrect transcription in the preceding centuries (some 14 instances are beyond repair), however, has invited frequent and often uncertain emendation.

Depending on whether one poem is divided or not, 113 or 114 poems survive. In the printed total of 116, numbers XVIII to XX were inserted by early editors without proof that they were written by Catullus. In 14 instances gaps are visible (eight of these of one or more lines), and in possibly six poems fragments of lost poems have been left attached to existing ones. Ancient citations indicate the existence of at least five more poems. The surviving body of work is therefore mutilated and incomplete and (in contrast to the *Odes* of Horace) cannot in its present published form represent the intentions of either author or executors, despite the elegant dedication to the historian Cornelius Nepos that heads it. With these qualifications, it permits the reconstruction of a poetic personality and art unique in Latin letters.

The collection is headed by 57 "short poems," ranging in length between 5 and 25 lines (number X, an exception, has 34) in assorted metres, of which, however, 51 are either hendecasyllabic—that is, having a verse line of 11 syllables (40 such)—or iambic—basically of alternate short and long syllables (11). These rhythms, though tightly structured, can be characterized as occasional or conversational. There follow eight "longer poems," ranging from 48 lines to 408 (number LXV, of 24 lines, is prefatory to number LXVI) in four different metres. The collection is completed by 48 "epigrams" written in the elegiac distich, or pair of verse lines, and extending between 2 and 12 lines, a limit exceeded only by two poems, one of 26 lines and the other of 16.

This mechanical arrangement, by indirectly recognizing the poet's metrical virtuosity and proposing three kinds of composition, justly calls attention to a versatility disproportionate to the slim size of the extant work. The occasional-verse metres and the elegiac distich had been introduced into Latin before his day. Traditionally both forms, as practiced by Greek writers after the 4th century BCE and their Roman imitators, had served for inscriptions and dedications and as verse of light occasions, satirical comment, and elegant sentiment. Catullus and his contemporaries continued this tradition; but in some 37 instances the poet uniquely converts these verse forms to serve as vehicles of feelings and observations expressed with such beauty and wit, on the one hand, or such passion, on the other, as to rank him, in modern terms, among the masters of the European lyric—the peer of Sappho and Percy Bysshe Shelley, of Robert Burns and Heinrich Heine—but exhibiting a degree of complexity and contradiction that the centuries-later Romantic temperament would scarcely have understood. The conversational rhythms in particular, as he managed them for lyric purposes, achieved an immediacy that no other classic poet can rival.

In his longer poems Catullus produced studies that deeply influenced the writers and poets of the Augustan Age: two charming marriage hymns; one frenzied cult hymn of emasculation; one romantic narrative in hexameters (lines of six feet) on the marriage of Peleus with the sea goddess Thetis; and four elegiac pieces, consisting of an epistle introducing a translation of an elegant conceit by the Alexandrian poet Callimachus, followed by a pasquinade, or scurrilous conversation, between the poet and a door (of poor quality, perhaps a youthful effort), and lastly a soliloquy (unless indeed this be two poems) addressed to a friend and cast in the form of an encomium, or poem of praise. The Augustan poet Virgil is content to imitate Catullus without naming him, even going so far, in the *Aeneid*, as to borrow whole lines from him in three instances. Horace both imitated Catullus and criticized him. Tibullus, Propertius, Ovid, and later Martial both imitate and affectionately commemorate him.

For the general reader, the 25 Lesbia poems are likely to remain the most memorable, recording as they do a love that could register ecstasy and despair and all the divided emotions that intervene. Two of them with unusual metre recall Sappho, the poet of Lesbos, as also does his use of the pseudonym Lesbia. As read today, these two seem to evoke the first moment of adoring love (number LI, a poem that actually paraphrases its Sapphic model) and the last bitterness of disillusionment (number XI). On the other hand, the poems of invective, which spare neither Julius Caesar nor otherwise unknown personalities, male and female, may not have received the critical attention some of them deserve. Between these two poles of private feeling lie a handful of transcendent and unforgettable compositions: the lament at his brother's grave; the salute to Sirmio his beloved retreat; the exchange of vows between Acme and Septimius; his elegy for his friend Calvus's wife; and even that vivid mime of a moment's conversation in a leisured day, in which the insouciance of a few young persons of fashion, the poet included, going about their affairs in the last days of the Roman Republic, is caught and preserved for posterity.

VIRGIL

(b. Oct. 15, 70 BCE, Andes, near Mantua [Italy]—
d. Sept. 21, 19 BCE, Brundisium)

The Roman poet Publius Vergilius Maro, better known as Virgil (Vergil), was regarded by the Romans as their greatest poet. His fame rests chiefly upon the *Aeneid* (from *c.* 30 BCE; unfinished at his death), which tells the story of Rome's legendary founder and proclaims the Roman mission to civilize the world under divine guidance. Virgil's reputation as a poet endures not only for the music and diction of his verse and for his skill in constructing an intricate work on the grand scale but also because he embodied in his poetry aspects of experience and behaviour of permanent significance.

Virgil was born of peasant stock, and his love of the Italian countryside and of the people who cultivated it

Portrait of Virgil, regarded by many to be one of ancient Rome's greatest poets. The Bridgeman Art Library/Getty Images

colours all his poetry. He was educated at Cremona, at Milan, and finally at Rome, acquiring a thorough knowledge of Greek and Roman authors, especially of the poets, and receiving a detailed training in rhetoric and philosophy.

Political Background

During Virgil's youth, as the Roman Republic neared its end, the political and military situation in Italy was confused and often calamitous. The civil war between Marius and Sulla had been succeeded by conflict between Pompey and Julius Caesar for supreme power. When Virgil was 20, Caesar with his armies swooped south from Gaul, crossed the Rubicon, and began the series of civil wars that were not to end until Augustus's victory at Actium in 31 BCE. Hatred and fear of civil war is powerfully expressed by both Virgil and his contemporary Horace. The key to a proper understanding of the Augustan Age and its poets lies, indeed, in a proper understanding of the turmoil that had preceded the Augustan peace.

Virgil's life was devoted entirely to his poetry and to studies connected with it; his health was never robust, and he played no part in military or political life. It is said that he spoke once in the lawcourts without distinction and that his shy and retiring nature caused him to give up any ideas he might have had of taking part in the world of affairs. He never married, and the first half of his life was that of a scholar and near recluse. But, as his poetry won him fame, he gradually won the friendship of many important men in the Roman world. Gradually, also, he became a Roman as well as a provincial. (The area in which he had spent his youth, the area around the Po River known as the province of Cisalpine Gaul, was not finally incorporated into Italy until 42 BCE. Thus Virgil came, as it were, to Rome from the outside. The enthusiasm of a provincial for Rome is seen in the first eclogue, one of his earliest poems, in which the shepherd Tityrus tells of his recent visit to the capital and his amazement at its splendours.)

Literary Career

Virgil's earliest certain work is the *Eclogues*, a collection of 10 pastoral poems composed between 42 and 37 BCE. Some of them are escapist, literary excursions to the idyllic pastoral world of Arcadia based on the Greek poet Theocritus (fl. *c*. 280 BCE) but more unreal and stylized. They convey in liquid song the idealized situations of an imaginary world in which shepherds sing in the sunshine of their simple joys and mute their sorrows (whether for unhappy love or untimely death) in a formalized pathos. But some bring the pastoral mode into touch with the real world, either directly or by means of allegory, and thus gave a new direction to the genre. The fifth eclogue, on the death of Daphnis, king of the shepherds, clearly has some relationship with the recent death of Julius Caesar; the 10th brings Gallus, a fellow poet who also held high office as a statesman, into the pastoral world; the first and ninth are lamentations over the expulsion of shepherds from their farms. (It was widely believed in antiquity that these poems expressed allegorically Virgil's own loss of his family farm when the veteran soldiers of Antony and Octavian—later the emperor Augustus—were resettled after the Battle of Philippi in 42 BCE. It was thought that he subsequently recovered his property through the intervention of his powerful friends. However that may be, it is certain that the poems are based on Virgil's own experience, whether in connection with his own farm or with those of his friends; and they express, with a poignant pathos that has come to be regarded as specially Virgilian, the sorrow of the dispossessed.)

But one eclogue in particular stands out as having relevance to the contemporary situation, and this is the fourth (sometimes called the Messianic, because it was later regarded as prophetic of Christianity). It is an elevated poem, prophesying in sonorous and mystic terms the birth of a child who will bring back the Golden Age, banish sin, and restore peace. It was clearly written at a time when the clouds of civil war seemed to be lifting; it can be dated firmly to 41–40 BCE, and it seems most likely that Virgil refers to an expected child of the triumvir Antony and his wife Octavia, sister of Octavian.

One of the most disastrous effects of the civil wars— and one of which Virgil, as a countryman, would be most intensely aware—was the depopulation of rural Italy. The farmers had been obliged to go to the war, and their farms fell into neglect and ruin as a result. The *Georgics*, composed between 37 and 30 BCE (the final period of the civil wars), is a superb plea for the restoration of the traditional agricultural life of Italy. In form it is didactic, but, as Seneca later said, it was written "not to instruct farmers but to delight readers." The practical instruction (about plowing, growing trees, tending cattle, and keeping bees) is presented with vivid insight into nature, and it is interspersed with highly wrought poetical digressions on such topics as the beauty of the Italian countryside (Book II. line 136 ff.) and the joy of the farmer when all is gathered in (II.458 ff.).

The *Georgics* is dedicated (at the beginning of each book) to Maecenas, one of the chief of Augustus's ministers, who was also the leading patron of the arts. By this time Virgil was a member of what might be called the court circle, and his desire to see his beloved Italy restored to its former glories coincided with the national requirement of resettling the land and diminishing the pressure on the cities. It would be wrong to think of Virgil as writing political propaganda; but equally it would be wrong to regard his poetry as unconnected with the major currents of political and social needs of the time. Virgil was personally committed to the same ideals as the government.

In the year 31 BCE, when Virgil was 38, Augustus (still known as Octavian) won the final battle of the civil wars at Actium against the forces of Antony and Cleopatra and from that time dates the Augustan Age. Virgil, like many of his contemporaries, felt a great sense of relief that the senseless civil strife was at last over and was deeply grateful to the man who had made it possible. Augustus was anxious to preserve the traditions of the republic and its constitutional forms, but he was in fact sole ruler of the Roman world. He used his power to establish a period of peace and stability and endeavoured to reawaken in the Romans a sense of national pride and a new enthusiasm for their ancestral religion and their traditional moral values, those of bravery, parsimony, duty, responsibility, and family devotion.

Virgil, too, as a countryman at heart, felt a deep attachment to the simple virtues and religious traditions of the Italian people. All his life he had been preparing himself to write an epic poem (regarded then as the highest form of poetic achievement), and he now set out to embody his ideal Rome in the *Aeneid*, the story of the foundation of the first settlement in Italy, from which Rome was to spring, by an exiled Trojan prince after the destruction of Troy by the Greeks in the 12th century BCE.

The theme he chose gave him two great advantages: one was that its date and subject were very close to those of Homer's *Iliad* and *Odyssey*, so that he could remodel episodes and characters from his great Greek predecessor; and the other was that it could be brought into relationship with his contemporary Augustan world by presenting Aeneas as the prototype of the Roman way of life (the last of the Trojans and the first of the Romans). Moreover, by the use of prophecies and visions and devices such as the description of the pictures on Aeneas's shield or of the origins of contemporary customs and institutions, it could foreshadow the real events of Roman history. The poem, then, operates on a double time scale; it is heroic and yet Augustan.

The enthusiasm that Virgil felt for the reborn Rome promised by Augustus's regime is often reflected in the poem. The sonorous and awe-inspiring prophecy by Jupiter (I.257 ff.), giving a picture of Rome's divinely inspired destiny, has a moving patriotic impact: "To these I set no bounds in space or time—I have given them rule without end" (278–279); and again, under Augustus, "Then shall the harsh generations be softened, and wars shall be laid aside" (291). The speech ends with a memorable image depicting the personified figure of Frenzy in chains, gnashing its bloodstained teeth in vain. At the end of the sixth book, Aeneas visits the underworld, and there pass before his eyes the figures of heroes from Roman history, waiting to be born. The ghost of his father (Anchises) describes them to him and ends by defining the Roman mission as one concerned with government and civilization (compared with the Greek achievement in art and literature and theoretical science). "Rule the people with your sway, spare the conquered, and war down the proud": this is the vision of Rome's destiny that the emperor Augustus and the poet Virgil had before them—that Rome was divinely appointed first to conquer the world in war and then to spread civilization and the rule of law among the peoples.

The vision of Rome that the *Aeneid* expresses is a noble one, but the real greatness of the poem is due to Virgil's awareness of the private, as well as the public, aspects of human life. The *Aeneid* is no panegyric; it sets the achievements and aspirations of the giant organization of Roman governmental rule in tension with the frustrated hopes and sufferings of individuals. The most memorable figure in the poem—and, it has been said, the only character to be created by a Roman poet that has passed into world literature—is Dido, Queen of Carthage, opponent of the Roman way of life. In a mere panegyric of Rome, she could have been presented in such a way that Aeneas's rejection of her would have been a victory to applaud; but, in fact, in the fourth book she wins so much sympathy that the reader wonders whether Rome should be bought at this price.

The *Aeneid* occupied Virgil for 11 years and, at his death, had not yet received its final revision. In 19 BCE, planning to spend a further three years on his poem, he set out for Greece—doubtless to obtain local colour for the revision of those parts of the *Aeneid* set in Greek waters. On the voyage he caught a fever and returned to Italy but died soon after arrival at Brundisium. Whether the *Aeneid* would have undergone major changes cannot be guessed; the story goes that Virgil's dying wish was for his poem to be burned, but that this request was countermanded by the order of Augustus. As it stands, the poem is a major monument both to the national achievements and ideals of the Augustan Age of Rome and to the sensitive and lonely voice of the poet who knew the "tears in things" as well as the glory.

Virgil's Legacy

Virgil's poetry immediately became famous in Rome and was admired by the Romans for two main reasons—first, because he was regarded as their own national poet, spokesman of their ideals and achievements; second, because he seemed to have reached the ultimate of perfection in his art (his structure, diction, metre). For the latter reason, his poems were used as school textbooks, and the 1st-century Roman critic and teacher Quintilian recommended that the educational curriculum should be based on Virgil's works. A few years after his death, Virgil was being imitated and echoed by the younger poet Ovid, and this process continued throughout the Silver Age. The study of Virgil in the schools has lasted as long as Latin has been studied.

Virgil's influence on English literature has been enormous. He was Edmund Spenser's constant inspiration for the fanciful beauty of *The Faerie Queene*. The *Aeneid* was the model for John Milton's *Paradise Lost* not only in epic structure and machinery but also in style and diction. In the English Augustan age, John Dryden and countless others held that Virgil's poetry had reached the ultimate perfection of form and ethical content. There was some reaction against him in the Romantic period, but the Victorians, such as Matthew Arnold and Alfred, Lord Tennyson, rediscovered in full measure that sensitivity and pathos that the Romantics had complained that Virgil lacked.

HORACE

(b. December 65 BCE, Venusia [now Venosa, Italy] —
d. Nov. 27, 8 BCE, Rome)

Quintus Horatius Flaccus was the outstanding Latin lyric poet and satirist under the emperor Augustus. He was probably of the Sabellian hillman stock of Italy's central highlands. His father had once been a slave but gained freedom before Horace's birth and became an auctioneer's assistant. He also owned a small property and

could afford to take his son to Rome and ensure personally his getting the best available education in the school
of a famous fellow Sabellian named Orbilius (a believer,
according to Horace, in corporal punishment). In about
46 BCE Horace went to Athens, attending lectures at the
Academy. After Julius Caesar's murder in March 44 BCE,
the eastern empire, including Athens, came temporarily
into the possession of his assassins Brutus and Cassius,
who could scarcely avoid clashing with Caesar's partisans,
Mark Antony and Octavian (later Augustus), the young
great-nephew whom Caesar, in his will, had appointed as
his personal heir. Horace joined Brutus's army and was
made *tribunus militum*, an exceptional honour for a freedman's son.

In November 42, at the two Battles of Philippi against
Antony and Octavian, Horace and his fellow tribunes (in
the unusual absence of a more senior officer) commanded
one of Brutus's and Cassius's legions. After their total
defeat, he fled back to Italy—controlled by Octavian—
but his father's farm at Venusia had been confiscated to
provide land for veterans. Horace, however, proceeded to
Rome, obtaining, either before or after a general amnesty
of 39 BCE, the minor but quite important post of one of
the 36 clerks of the treasury (*scribae quaestorii*). Early in 38
BCE he was introduced to Gaius Maecenas, a man of letters
from Etruria in central Italy who was one of Octavian's
principal political advisers. He now enrolled Horace in the
circle of writers with whom he was friendly. Before long,
through Maecenas, Horace also came to Octavian's notice.

During these years, Horace was working on Book I of
the *Satires,* 10 poems written in hexameter verse and published in 35 BCE. The *Satires* reflect Horace's adhesion to
Octavian's attempts to deal with the contemporary chal-
lenges of restoring traditional morality, defending small
landowners from large estates (*latifundia*), combating debt

and usury, and encouraging *novi homines* ("new men") to take their place next to the traditional republican aristocracy. The *Satires* often exalt the new man, who is the creator of his own fortune and does not owe it to noble lineage. Horace develops his vision with principles taken from Hellenistic philosophy: *metriotes* (the just mean) and *autarkeia* (the wise man's self-sufficiency). The ideal of the just mean allows Horace, who is philosophically an Epicurean, to reconcile traditional morality with hedonism. Self-sufficiency is the basis for his aspiration for a quiet life, far from political passions and unrestrained ambition.

In the 30s BCE his 17 *Epodes* were also under way. Mockery here is almost fierce, the metre being that traditionally used for personal attacks and ridicule, though Horace attacks social abuses, not individuals. The tone reflects his anxious mood after Philippi. Horace used his commitment to the ideals of Alexandrian poetry to draw near to the experiences of Catullus and other *poetae novi* (New Poets) of the late republic. Their political verse, however, remained in the fields of invective and scandal, while Horace, in *Epodes* 7, 9, and 16, shows himself sensitive to the tone of political life at the time, the uncertainty of the future before the final encounter between Octavian and Mark Antony, and the weariness of the people of Italy in the face of continuing violence. In doing so, he drew near to the ideals of the Archaic Greek lyric, in which the poet was also the bard of the community, and the poet's verse could be expected to have a political effect. In his erotic *Epodes*, Horace began assimilating themes of the Archaic lyric into the Hellenistic atmosphere, a process that would find more mature realization in the *Odes*.

In the mid-30s he received from Maecenas, as a gift or on lease, a comfortable house and farm in the Sabine hills (identified with considerable probability as one near

Licenza, 22 miles [35 kilometres] northeast of Rome), which gave him great pleasure throughout his life. After Octavian had defeated Antony and Cleopatra at Actium, off northwestern Greece (31 BCE), Horace published his *Epodes* and a second book of eight *Satires* in 30–29 BCE.

In the first *Satires* Horace had limited himself to attacking relatively unimportant figures (e.g., businessmen, courtesans, and social bores). The second *Satires* is even less aggressive, insisting that satire is a defensive weapon to protect the poet from the attacks of the malicious. The autobiographical aspect becomes less important; instead, the interlocutor becomes the depository of a truth that is often quite different from that of other speakers. The poet delegates to others the job of critic.

While the victor of Actium, styled Augustus in 27 BCE, settled down, Horace turned, in the most active period of his poetical life, to the *Odes*, of which he published three books, comprising 88 short poems, in 23 BCE. Horace, in the *Odes*, represented himself as heir to earlier Greek lyric poets but displayed a sensitive, economical mastery of words all his own. He sings of love, wine, nature (almost romantically), of friends, of moderation; in short, his favourite topics.

The *Odes* describe the poet's personal experiences and familiarize the reader with his everyday world; they depict the customs of a sophisticated and refined Roman society that is as fully civilized as the great Hellenistic Greek cities. The unique charm of Horace's lyric poetry arises from his combination of the metre and style of the distant past—the world of the Archaic Greek lyric poets—with descriptions of his personal experience and the important moments of Roman life. He creates an intermediate space between the real world and the world of his imagination, populated with fauns, nymphs, and other divinities.

The last ode of the first three books suggests that Horace did not propose to write any more such poems.

The tepid reception of the *Odes* following their publication in 23 BCE and his consciousness of growing age may have encouraged Horace to write his *Epistles*. Book I may have been published in 20 BCE, and Book II probably appeared in 14 BCE. These two books are very different in theme and content. Although similar to the *Satires* in style and content, the *Epistles* lack the earlier poems' aggressiveness and their awareness of the great city of Rome. They are literary letters, addressed to distant correspondents, and they are more reflective and didactic than the earlier work.

The third book, now called *Ars poetica*, is conceived as a letter to members of the Piso family. It is not really a systematic history of literary criticism or an exposition of theoretical principles. It is rather a series of insights into writing poetry, choosing genres, and combining genius with craftsmanship. For Horace, writing well means uniting natural predisposition with long study and a solid knowledge of literary genres.

The "Epistle to Florus" of Book II may have been written in 19 BCE, the *Ars poetica* in about 19 or 18 BCE, and the last epistle of Book I in 17–15 BCE. This last named is dedicated to Augustus, from whom there survives a letter to Horace in which the emperor complains of not having received such a dedication hitherto.

By this time Horace was virtually in the position of poet laureate, and in 17 BCE he composed the *Secular Hymn* (*Carmen saeculare*) for ancient ceremonies called the Secular Games, which Augustus had revived to provide a solemn, religious sanction for the regime and, in particular, for his moral reforms of the previous year. The hymn was written in a lyric metre, Horace having resumed his compositions in this form; he next completed a fourth book of 15 *Odes,* mainly of a more serious (and political) character than their predecessors. The latest of these poems belongs to 13 BCE. In 8 BCE Maecenas, who had been less in

Augustus's counsels during recent years, died. One of his last requests to the emperor was: "Remember Horace as you would remember me." A month or two later, however, Horace himself died, after naming Augustus as his heir. He was buried on the Esquiline Hill near Maecenas's grave.

The portrait of Horace that emerges from a study of his work is that of an individual who is kindly, tolerant, and mild but capable of strength; consistently humane, realistic, astringent, and detached, he is a gentle but persistent mocker of himself quite as much as of others. His self-portrait is also a confession of an attitude that descends from melancholy to depression. Some critics believe that he may have been clinically depressed.

His attitude to love, on the whole, is flippant; without telling the reader a single thing about his own amorous life, he likes to picture himself in ridiculous situations within the framework of the appropriate literary tradition—and relating, it should be added, to women of Greek names and easy virtue, not Roman matrons or virgins. To his male friends, however—the men to whom his *Odes* are addressed—he is affectionate and loyal, and such friends were perhaps the principal mainstay of his life. The gods are often on his lips, but, in defiance of much contemporary feeling, he absolutely denied an afterlife. So "gather ye rosebuds while ye may" is an ever recurrent theme, though Horace insists on a Golden Mean of moderation—deploring excess and always refusing, deprecating, dissuading.

STRABO

(b. 64/63 BCE, Amaseia, Pontus [now Amasya, Tur.]—d. 23 CE?)

The Greek geographer and historian Strabo is notable for having written the *Geography*, the only extant work covering the whole range of peoples and countries known to both Greeks and Romans during the reign of Augustus (27 BCE–14 CE). Its numerous quotations from technical literature, moreover, provide a remarkable account of the state of Greek geographical science, as well as of the history of the countries it surveys.

Life

Strabo belonged on his mother's side to a famous family, whose members had held important offices under Mithradates V (around 150–120 BCE), as well as under Mithradates the Great, the opponent of Rome (132–63 BCE). His first teacher was the master of rhetoric Aristodemus, a former tutor of the sons of Pompey (106–48 BCE) in Nysa (now Sultanhisar in Turkey) on the Maeander. He moved to Rome in 44 BCE to study with Tyrannion, the former tutor of Cicero, and with Xenarchus, both of whom were members of the Aristotelian school of philosophy. Under the influence of Athenodorus, former tutor of Octavius, who probably introduced him into the future emperor's circle, he turned toward Stoical philosophy, the precepts of which included the view that one unique principle ceaselessly pervading the whole universe causes all phenomena.

It was in Rome, where he stayed at least until 31 BCE, that he wrote his first major works, his 47-book *Historical Sketches,* published about 20 BCE, of which but a few quotations survive. A vast and eclectic compilation, it was meant as a continuation of Polybius's *Histories.* The *Historical Sketches* covered the history of the known world from 145 BCE—that is, from the conquest of Greece by the Romans—to the Battle of Actium (31 BCE), or to the beginnings of the principate of the Roman emperor Augustus (27 BCE).

In 29 BCE, Strabo visited the island of Gyaros (today known as Yiáros, or Nisós) in the Aegean Sea, on his way to Corinth, Greece, where Augustus was staying. In 25 or 24, together with Aelius Gallus, prefect of Egypt, who had been sent on a military mission to Arabia, he sailed up the Nile as far as Philae. There are then no further references to him until 17 CE, when he attended the triumph of the Roman general Germanicus Caesar (15 BCE to 19 CE) in Rome. He died after having devoted his last years to compiling his second important work, his *Geographical Sketches*. Judging by the date when he wrote his personal notes, he must have worked on the book after his stay in Egypt and then have put it aside from 2(?) BCE to 14 CE, when he started the final edition, which he brought to an end in 23 CE.

The Geography

The first two books, in effect, provide a definition of the aims and methods of geography by criticizing earlier works and authors. Strabo found fault with the map designing of the Greek scholar Eratosthenes, who lived from *c.* 276 to *c.* 194 BCE. Eratosthenes had combined astronomical data with coast and road measurements, but Strabo found his work lacking in precision. Although Strabo closely followed the treatise against Eratosthenes of the Greek astronomer Hipparchus, who had lived in the 2nd century BCE, he blamed Hipparchus for neglecting the description of the Earth. On the other hand, he appreciated Polybius, who, in addition to his historical works, had written two books on European geography that Strabo admired for their descriptions of places and peoples. Although he praised Posidonius, the Greek historian and philosopher who lived from about 135 to 51 BCE, for his knowledge of physical geography and ethnography, he rejected Posidonius's theory of climatic zones and particularly his hypothesis that the equatorial zone was habitable. This critical study led him logically to decide in favour of a descriptive type of geography, based on a map with an orthogonal (perpendicular) projection. The problem of projecting the sphere on a flat surface is not dealt with at any length, for his work, as he said, was not designed for mathematicians but for statesmen who must know countries, natural resources, and customs.

In Books III to VI, Strabo described successively Iberia, Gaul, and Italy, for which his main sources were Polybius and Posidonius, both of whom had visited these countries; in addition, Artemidorus, a Greek geographer born around 140 BCE and author of a book describing a voyage around the inhabited Earth, provided him with a description of the coasts and thus of the shape and size of countries. Book VII was based on the same authorities and described the Danube Basin and the European coasts of the Black Sea. Writing about Greece, in Books VIII to X, he still relied upon Artemidorus, but the bulk of his information was taken from two commentators of Homer—Apollodorus of Athens (2nd century BCE) and Demetrius of Scepsis (born around 205 BCE)—for Strabo placed great emphasis on identifying the cities named in the Greek epic the *Iliad*. Books XI to XIV describe the Asian shores of the Black Sea, the Caucasus, northern Iran, and Asia Minor. Here Strabo made the greatest use of his own observations, though he often quoted historians who dealt with the wars fought in these regions and cited Demetrius on problems of Homeric topography in the region about ancient Troy. India and Persia (Book XV) were described according to information given by the historians of the campaigns of Alexander the Great (356 to 323 BCE), whereas his descriptions of Mesopotamia, Syria, Palestine, and the Red Sea (Book XVI) were based on the accounts of the expeditions sent out by Mark Antony (about 83 to 30 BCE) and by the emperor Augustus, as well as on chapters on ethnography in Posidonius and on the book of a Red Sea voyage taken by the Greek historian and geographer Agatharchides (2nd century BCE). Strabo's own memories of Egypt, supplemented by the writings of Posidonius and Artemidorus, provided material for the substance of Book XVII, which dealt with the African shores of the Mediterranean Sea and with Mauretania.

Obviously, personal travel notes formed only a small part of the material used in this considerable work, although Strabo prided himself on having travelled westward from Armenia as far as the regions of Tuscany opposite Sardinia, and southward from the Black Sea as far as the frontiers of Ethiopia. Even on the subject of Italy, where he lived for a long time, Strabo did not himself contribute more than a few scattered impressions. His material, accordingly, mostly dates from the time of the sources he used, although the reader is not made aware of this. The value of firsthand observations, chosen from the sources with care, compensates, however, for his lack of originality and contemporaneousness. Strabo showed himself equally competent in selecting useful information—giving distances from city to city and mentioning the frontiers between countries or provinces as well as the main agricultural and industrial activities, political statutes, ethnographic peculiarities, and religious practices. He also took interest in the histories of cities and states, and—when he knew them—mentioned the circumstances under which they were founded, related myths or legends, wars they had instigated or endured, their expansion or recession, and their celebrities. Geological phenomena were reported when they were in some way unusual or when they furnished an explanation for other phenomena—such as the Atlantic tides in Iberia, the volcanic landscapes to be seen in southern Italy and Sicily, the fountains of naphtha occurring near the Euphrates River, and the rise and fall of the Nile waters. Paradoxically, although the description of Greece fills three whole books, such elements are virtually neglected in them. In this part, indeed, Strabo was more attracted by the problem of identifying the localities mentioned in Homer's works than in the geographical realities. These books, however, illustrate another side of his thought, based on the conviction that Homer was perfectly acquainted with the geography of the Mediterranean area and that the correct critical interpretation would reveal his vast learning. This classical thesis is abundantly defended in Strabo's introduction, which attacks the skepticism of Eratosthenes; moreover, it represents, in Strabo's work, the specific contribution to learning of the Greek cultural tradition.

Livy

(b. 59/64 BCE, Patavium, Venetia, Italy—d. 17 CE, Patavium)

Titus Livius (Livy), together with Sallust and Tacitus, is one of the three great Roman historians. His history of Rome became a classic in his own lifetime and exercised a profound influence on the style and philosophy of historical writing down to the 18th century.

Little is known about Livy's life and nothing about his family background. Patavium, a rich city, famous for its strict morals, suffered severely in the civil wars of the 40s. The wars and the unsettled condition of the Roman world after the death of Caesar in 44 BCE probably prevented Livy from studying in Greece, as most educated Romans did. Although widely read in Greek literature, he made mistakes of translation that would be unnatural if he had

Statue of the Roman historian Livy near the entrance of Austria's parliment building. The top of the Athena fountain, which also stands in front of the structure, can be seen to the statue's left. Renata Sedmakova/Shutterstock.com

spent any length of time in Greece and had acquired the command of Greek normal among his contemporaries. His education was based on the study of rhetoric and philosophy, and he wrote some philosophical dialogues that do not survive. There is no evidence about early career. His family apparently did not belong to the senatorial class, however distinguished it may have been in Patavium itself, and Livy does not seem to have embarked on a political or forensic profession.

Livy is first heard of in Rome after Octavian (later known as the emperor Augustus) had restored stability and peace to the empire by his decisive naval victory at Actium in 31 BCE. Internal evidence from the work itself shows that Livy had conceived the plan of writing the history of Rome in or shortly before 29 BCE, and for this purpose he must have already moved to Rome, because only there were the records and information available. It is significant that another historian, the Greek Dionysius of Halicarnassus, who was to cover much the same ground as Livy, settled in Rome in 30 BCE. A more secure age had dawned.

Most of his life must have been spent at Rome, and at an early stage he attracted the interest of Augustus and was even invited to supervise the literary activities of the young Claudius (the future emperor), presumably about 8 CE. But he never became closely involved with the literary world of Rome—the poets Horace, Virgil, and Ovid, as well as the patron of the arts, Maecenas, and others. He is never referred to in connection with these men. He must have possessed sufficient private means not to be dependent on official patronage. Indeed, in one of the few recorded anecdotes about him, Augustus called him a "Pompeian," implying an outspoken and independent turn of mind. His lifework was the composition of his history.

Livy's History of Rome

Livy began by composing and publishing in units of five books, the length of which was determined by the size of the ancient papyrus roll. As his material became more complex, however, he abandoned this symmetrical pattern and wrote 142 books. So far as it can be reconstructed, the shape of the history is as follows (Books 11–20 and 46–142 have been lost):

- 1–5 From the foundation of the city until the sack of Rome by the Gauls (386 BCE)
- 6–10 The Samnite wars
- 11–15 The conquest of Italy
- 16–20 The First Punic (Carthaginian) War
- 21–30 The Second Punic War (until 201 BCE)
- 31–45 Events until the end of the war with Perseus (167 BCE)
- 46–70 Events until the Social War (91 BCE)
- 71–80 Civil wars until the death of Marius (86 BCE)
- 81–90 Civil wars until the death of Sulla (78 BCE)
- 91–103 Events until the triumph of Pompey in 62 BCE
- 104–108 The last years of the republic
- 109–116 The Civil War until the murder of Caesar (44 BCE)
- 117–133 From the death of Caesar to the Battle of Actium
- 134–142 From 29 to 9 BCE

Apart from fragments, quoted by grammarians and others, and a short section dealing with the death of the orator and politician Cicero from Book 120, the later books after Book 45 are known only from summaries. These were made from the 1st century CE onward, because the size of the complete work made it unmanageable. There were anthologies of the speeches and also concise summaries, two of which survive in part, a 3rd-century papyrus from Egypt (containing summaries of Books 37–40 and 48–55) and a 4th-century summary of contents (known as the *Periochae*) of the whole work. A note in the *Periochae* of Book 121 records that that book (and presumably those that followed) was published after Augustus's death in 14 CE. The implication is that the last 20 books dealing with the events from the Battle of Actium until 9 BCE were an afterthought to the original plan and were also too politically explosive to be published with impunity in Augustus's lifetime.

The sheer scope of the undertaking was formidable. It presupposed the composition of three books a year on average. Two stories reflect the magnitude of the task. In his letters the statesman Pliny the Younger records that Livy was tempted to abandon the enterprise but found that the task had become too fascinating to give it up; he also mentions a citizen of Cádiz who came all the way to Rome for the sole satisfaction of gazing at the great historian.

Livy's Historical Approach

The project of writing the history of Rome down to the present day was not a new one. Historical research and writing had flourished at Rome for 200 years, since the first Roman historian Quintus Fabius Pictor. There had been two main inspirations behind it—antiquarian interest and political motivation. Particularly after 100 BCE, there developed a widespread interest in ancient ceremonies, family genealogies, religious customs, and the like. This interest found expression in a number of scholarly works: Titus Pomponius Atticus, Cicero's friend and correspondent, wrote on chronology and on Trojan families; others compiled lengthy volumes on Etruscan religion; Marcus Terentius Varro, the greatest scholar of his age, published the encyclopaedic work *Divine and Human Antiquities*. The standard of scholarship was not always high, and there could be political pressures, as in the attempt to derive the Julian family to which Julius Caesar belonged from the legendary Aeneas and the Trojans; but the Romans were very conscious and proud of their past, and an enthusiasm for antiquities was widespread.

Previous historians had been public figures and men of affairs. Fabius Pictor had been a praetor, the elder Cato had been consul and censor, and Sallust was a praetor. So, too, many prominent statesmen such as Sulla and Caesar occupied their leisure with writing history. For some it was an exercise in political self-justification (hence, Caesar's *Gallic War* and *Civil War*); for others it was a civilized pastime. But all shared a common outlook and background. History was a political study through which one might hope to explain or excuse the present.

Livy was unique among Roman historians in that he played no part in politics. This was a disadvantage in that his exclusion from the Senate and the magistracies meant that he had no personal experience of how the Roman government worked, and this ignorance shows itself from time to time in his work. It also deprived him of firsthand access to much material (minutes of Senate meetings, texts of treaties, laws, etc.) that was preserved in official quarters. So, too, if he had been a priest or an augur, he would have acquired inside information of great historical value and been able to consult the copious documents and records of the priestly colleges. But the chief effect is that Livy did not seek historical explanations in political terms. The novelty and impact of his history lay in the fact that he saw history in personal and moral terms. The purpose is clearly set out in his preface:

> *I invite the reader's attention to the much more serious consideration of the kind of lives our ancestors lived, of who were the men and what the means, both in politics and war, by which Rome's power was first acquired and subsequently expanded, I would then have him trace the process of our moral decline, to watch first the sinking of the foundations of morality as the old teaching was allowed to lapse, then the final collapse of the whole edifice, and the dark dawning of our modern day when we can neither endure our vices nor face the remedies needed to cure them.*

> *What chiefly makes the study of history wholesome and profitable is this, that in history you have a record of the infinite variety of human experience plainly set out for all to see, and in that record you can find for yourself and your country both examples and warnings.*

Although Sallust and earlier historians had also adopted the outlook that morality was in steady decline and had argued that people do the sort of things they do because they are the sort of people they are, for Livy these beliefs were a matter of passionate concern. He saw history in terms of human personalities and representative individuals rather than of partisan politics. And his own experience, going back perhaps to his youth in Patavium, made him feel the moral evils of his time with peculiar intensity. He punctuates his history with revealing comments:

> *Fortunately in those days authority, both religious and secular, was still a guide to conduct and there was as yet no sign of our modern scepticism which interprets solemn*

compacts to suit its own convenience (3.20.5). Where would you find nowadays in a single individual that modesty, fairness and nobility of mind which in those days belonged to a whole people? (4.6.12).

In looking at history from a moral standpoint, Livy was at one with other thinking Romans of his day. Augustus attempted by legislation and propaganda to inculcate moral ideals. Horace and Virgil in their poetry stressed the same message—that it was moral qualities that had made and could keep Rome great.

The preoccupation with character and the desire to write history that would reveal the effects of character outweighed for Livy the need for scholarly accuracy. He showed little if any awareness of the antiquarian research of his own and earlier generations; nor did he seriously compare and criticize the different histories and their discrepancies that were available to him. For the most part he is content to take an earlier version (from Polybius or a similar author) and to reshape it so as to construct moral episodes that bring out the character of the leading figures. Livy's descriptions of the capture of Veii and the expulsion of the Gauls from Rome in the 4th century BCE by Marcus Furius Camillus are designed to illustrate his piety; the crossing of the Alps shows up the resourceful intrepidity of Hannibal. Unfortunately, it is not known how Livy dealt with the much greater complexity of contemporary history, but the account of Cicero's death contains the same emphasis on character displayed by surviving books.

It would be misplaced criticism to draw attention to his technical shortcomings, his credulity, or his lack of antiquarian curiosity. He reshaped history for his generation so that it was alive and meaningful. It is recorded that the audiences who went to his recitations were impressed by his nobility of character and his eloquence. It is this eloquence that is Livy's second claim to distinction.

Together with Cicero and Tacitus, Livy set new standards of literary style. The earliest Roman historians had written in Greek, the language of culture. Their successors had felt that their own history should be written in Latin, but Latin possessed no ready-made style that could be used for the purpose: for Latin prose had to develop artificial styles to suit the different genres. Sallust had attempted to reproduce the Greek style of Thucydides in Latin by a tortured use of syntax and a vocabulary incorporating a number of archaic and unusual words, but the result, although effective, was harsh and unsuitable for a work of any size. Livy evolved a varied and flexible style that the ancient critic Quintilian characterized as a "milky richness." At one moment he will set the scene in long, periodic clauses; at another a few terse, abrupt sentences will mirror the rapidity of the action. Bare notices of archival fact will be reported in correspondingly dry and formal language, whereas a battle will evoke poetical and dramatic vocabulary, and a speech will be constructed either in the spirit of a contemporary orator such as Cicero or in dramatically realistic tones, designed to recapture the atmosphere of antiquity. "When I write of ancient deeds my mind somehow becomes antique," he wrote.

The work of a candid man and an individualistic thinker, Livy's history was deeply rooted in the Augustan revival and owed its success in large measure to its moral seriousness. But the detached attempt to understand the course of history through character (which was to influence later historians from Tacitus to Lord Clarendon) represents Livy's great achievement.

SEXTUS PROPERTIUS

(b. 55–43 BCE, Assisi, Umbria [Italy] — d. after 16 BCE, Rome)

Very few details of the life of Sextus Propertius are known. His father died when he was still a boy, but he was given a good education by his mother. Part of the family estate was confiscated (*c.* 40 BCE) to satisfy the resettlement needs of the veteran troops of Octavian, later the emperor Augustus, after the civil wars. Propertius's income was thus severely diminished, though he was never really poor. With his mother, he left Umbria for Rome, and there (*c.* 34 BCE) he assumed the dress of manhood. Some of his friends were poets (including Ovid and Bassus), and he had no interest in politics, the law, or army life. His first love affair was with an older woman, Lycinna, but this was only a passing fancy when set beside his subsequent serious attachment to the famous "Cynthia" of his poems.

The first of Propertius's four books of elegies (the second of which is divided by some editors into two) was published in 29 BCE, the year in which he first met "Cynthia," its heroine. It was known as the *Cynthia* and also as the *Monobiblos* because it was for a long time afterward sold separately from his other three books. Complete editions of all four books were also available. *Cynthia* seems to have had an immediate success, for the influential literary patron Maecenas invited Propertius to his house, where he doubtless met the other prominent literary figures who formed Maecenas's circle. These included the poets Virgil (whom Propertius admired) and Horace (whom he never mentions). The influence of both, especially that of Horace in Book III, is manifest in his work.

Cynthia's real name, according to the 2nd-century writer Apuleius, was Hostia. It is often said that she was a courtesan, but elegy 16 in Book I seems to suggest that she belonged to a distinguished family. It is likely that she was married, though Propertius only mentions her other lovers, never her husband. From the poems she emerges as beautiful, passionate, and uninhibited. She was intensely jealous of Propertius's own infidelities and is painted as a woman terrible in her fury, irresistible in her gentler moods. Propertius makes it clear that, even when seeking pleasures apart from his mistress, he still loved her deeply, returning to her full of remorse, and happy when she reasserted her dominion over him.

After many violent scenes, it appears that Propertius finally broke off his tempestuous affair with her in 24 BCE, though inferring dates from the poems' internal evidence cannot be undertaken with real confidence, as this kind of personal poetry often interweaves fact with fancy. He was to look back on his liaison with her as a period of disgrace and humiliation. This may be more than a mere literary pose, although after Cynthia's death (she does not seem to have lived for long after their break) he regretted the brusqueness of their separation and was ashamed that he had not even attended her funeral. In a most beautiful and moving elegy (IV:7), he conjures up her ghost and with it re-creates the whole glamour and shabbiness of the affair. While he makes no attempt to brush over the disagreeable side of her nature, he also makes it clear that he loves her beyond the grave.

Propertius's poetic powers matured with experience. The poetry of Book II is far more ambitious in scope than that of Book I and shows a richer orchestration. His reputation grew, and the emperor Augustus himself seems to have taken notice of him, for, in Books III and IV, the poet laments the premature death of Marcellus, Augustus's nephew and heir apparent (III:18), and he composed a magnificent funeral elegy (IV:11) in praise of Cornelia,

Augustus's stepdaughter—the "Queen of Elegies" as it is sometimes called.

As his poetic powers developed, so also did Propertius's character and interests. In his earliest elegies, love is not only his main theme but is almost his religion and philosophy. It is still the principal theme of Book II, but he now seems a little embarrassed by the popular success of Book I and is anxious not to be thought of simply as a gifted scoundrel who is constantly in love and can write of nothing else. In Book II he considers writing an epic, is preoccupied with the thought of death, and attacks (in the manner of later satirists, such as Juvenal) the coarse materialism of his time. He still loves to go to parties and feels perfectly at ease in the big city with its crowded streets, its temples, theatres, and porticoes, and its disreputable quarters. In a way, he is a conservative snob, in general sympathy with Roman imperialism and Augustan rule; but he is open to the beauties of nature and is genuinely interested in works of art. Though he disapproves of ostentatious luxury, he also appreciates contemporary fashions.

Some of his contemporaries accused him of leading a life of idleness and complained that he contributed nothing to society. But Propertius felt it his duty to support the right of the artist to lead his own life, and he demanded that poetry, and art in general, should not be regarded simply as a civilized way of passing the time. In elegy 3 of Book III he gives deep meaning to the process of artistic creation and emphasizes the importance of the creative artist.

In Books III and IV Propertius demonstrates his command over various literary forms, including the diatribe and the hymn. Many of his poems show the influence of such Alexandrian poets as Callimachus and Philetas. Propertius acknowledges this debt, and his claim to be the "Roman Callimachus," treating Italian themes in the baroque Alexandrian manner, is perhaps best shown in a series of elegies in Book IV that deal with aspects of Roman mythology and history and were to inspire Ovid to write his *Fasti*, a calendar of the Roman religious year. These poems are a compromise between the elegy and the epic. Book IV also contains some grotesque, realistic pieces, two unusual funeral elegies, and a poetic letter.

Two of the lasting merits of Propertius seem to have impressed the ancients themselves. The first they called *blanditia*, a vague but expressive word by which they meant softness of outline, warmth of colouring, a fine and almost voluptuous feeling for beauty of every kind, and a pleading and melancholy tenderness; this is most obvious in his descriptive passages and in his portrayal of emotion. His second and even more remarkable quality is poetic *facundia*, or command of striking and appropriate language. Not only is his vocabulary extensive but his employment of it is extraordinarily bold and unconventional: poetic and colloquial Latinity alternate abruptly, and in his quest for the striking expression he frequently seems to strain the language to the breaking point.

Propertius's handling of the elegiac couplet, and particularly of the pentameter, deserves especial recognition. It is vigorous, varied, and picturesque. In the matter of the rhythms, caesuras, and elisions that it allows, the metrical treatment is more severe than that of Catullus but noticeably freer than that of Ovid, to whose stricter usage, however, Propertius increasingly tended (particularly in his preference for a disyllabic word at the end of the pentameter). An elaborate symmetry is observable in the construction of many of his elegies, and this has tempted critics to divide a number of them into strophes.

As Propertius had borrowed from his predecessors, so his successors, Ovid above all, borrowed from him; and graffiti on the walls of Pompeii attest his popularity in the 1st century CE. In the Middle Ages he was virtually forgotten, and since the Renaissance he has been studied by professional scholars more than he has been enjoyed by the general public. To the modern reader acquainted with psychology, the self-revelations of his passionate, fitful, brooding spirit are of particular interest.

Almost nothing is known about Propertius's life after his love affair with Cynthia was over. It is possible that he married her successor in his affections (perhaps in order to qualify for the financial benefits offered to married men by the *leges Juliae* of 18 BCE) and had a child, for an inscription in Assisi and two passages in the letters of the younger Pliny (61/62–c. 113 CE) indicate that Propertius had a descendant called Gaius Passennus Paulus Propertius, who was also a poet. During his later years he lived in an elegant residential area in Rome on the Esquiline Hill. The date of his death is not certain, though he was still alive in 16 BCE, for two events of that year are mentioned in his fourth book, which was perhaps edited posthumously.

ALBIUS TIBULLUS

(b. *c.* 55 BCE — d. *c.* 19 BCE)

The Roman poet Albius Tibullus was one of the great Latin writers of elegiacs. Apart from his own poems, the only sources for the life of Tibullus are a few references in ancient writers and an extremely short *Vita* of doubtful authority. He was of equestrian rank (according to the *Vita*) and inherited an estate but seems to have lost most of it in 41 BCE, when Mark Antony and Octavian confiscated land for their soldiers. As a young man, however, Tibullus won the friendship and patronage of Marcus Valerius Messalla Corvinus, the statesman, soldier, and man of letters, and became a prominent member of Messalla's literary circle. This circle, unlike that of Gaius Maecenas, kept itself aloof from the court of Augustus, whom Tibullus does not even mention in his poems. Tibullus seems to have divided his time between Rome and his country estate, strongly preferring the latter.

Tibullus's first important love affair, the main subject of Book I of his poems, was with the woman whom he calls Delia. Sometimes he presents her as unmarried, sometimes as having a husband (unless the term *conjunx* is meant to signify "protector"). It is clear, however, that Tibullus took advantage of the "husband's" absence on military service in Cilicia to establish his relationship with Delia and that this relationship was carried on clandestinely after the soldier's return. Tibullus ultimately discovered that Delia was receiving other lovers as well as himself; then, after fruitless protests, he ceased to pursue her.

In Book II of his poems, Delia's place is taken by Nemesis (also a fictitious name), who was a courtesan of the higher class, with several lovers. Though he complains bitterly of her rapacity and hardheartedness, Tibullus seems to have remained subjugated to her for the rest of his life. He is known to have died young, very shortly after Virgil (19 BCE). Ovid commemorated his death in his *Amores*.

The character of Tibullus, as reflected in his poems, is an amiable one. He was a man of generous impulses and a gentle, unselfish disposition. He was not attracted to an active life. His ideal was a quiet retirement in the countryside with a loved one at his side. Tibullus was loyal to his friends and more constant to his mistresses than they would seem to have deserved. His tenderness toward women is enhanced by a refinement and delicacy rare among the ancients.

For idyllic simplicity, grace, tenderness, and exquisiteness of feeling and expression, Tibullus stands alone among the Roman elegists. In many of his poems, moreover, a symmetry of composition can be discerned, though they are never forced into any fixed or inelastic scheme. His clear and unaffected style, which made him a great favourite among Roman readers, is far more polished than that of his rival Propertius and far less loaded with Alexandrian learning, but in range of imagination and in richness and variety of poetical treatment, Propertius is the superior. In his handling of metre, Tibullus is likewise smooth and musical, whereas Propertius, with occasional harshness, is vigorous and varied.

The works of Tibullus, as they have survived, form part of what is generally known as the *Corpus Tibullianum*, a collection of poetry that seems most probably to have been deliberately put together to represent the work of Messalla's circle. The first two of the four books in the *Corpus* are undoubtedly by Tibullus. In its entirety the collection forms a unique and charming document for the literary life of Augustan Rome.

OVID

(b. March 20, 43 BCE, Sulmo, Roman Empire [now Sulmona, Italy]—d. 17 CE, Tomis, Moesia [now Constanța, Romania])

The Roman poet Publius Ovidius Naso (Ovid) is noted especially for his *Ars amatoria* and *Metamorphoses*. Like most Roman men of letters, Ovid was a provincial. He was born at Sulmo, a small town about 90 miles (140 km) east of Rome. The main events of his life are described in an autobiographical poem in the *Tristia* (*Sorrows*).

Life

His family was old and respectable, and sufficiently well-to-do for his father to be able to send him and his elder brother to Rome to be educated. At Rome he embarked, under the best teachers of the day, on the study of rhetoric. Ovid was thought to have the makings of a good orator, but in spite of his father's admonitions he neglected his studies for the verse-writing that came so naturally to him.

As a member of the Roman knightly class (whose rank lay between the commons and the Senate) Ovid was marked by his position, and intended by his father, for an official career. First, however, he spent some time at Athens (then a favourite finishing school for young men of the upper classes) and traveled in Asia Minor and Sicily. Afterward he dutifully held some minor judicial posts, the first steps on the official ladder, but he soon decided that public life did not suit him. From then on he abandoned his official career to cultivate poetry and the society of poets.

Ovid's first work, the *Amores* (*The Loves*), had an immediate success and was followed, in rapid succession, by the *Epistolae Heroidum*, or *Heroides* (*Epistles of the Heroines*), the *Medicamina faciei* ("Cosmetics"; Eng. trans. *The Art of Beauty*), the *Ars amatoria* (*The Art of Love*), and the *Remedia amoris* (*Remedies for Love*), all reflecting the brilliant, sophisticated, pleasure-seeking society in which he moved. The common theme of these early poems is love and amorous intrigue, but it is unlikely that they mirror Ovid's own life very closely. Of his three marriages the first two were short-lived, but his third wife, of whom he speaks with respect and affection, remained constant to him until his death. At Rome Ovid enjoyed the friendship and encouragement of Marcus Valerius Messalla, the patron of a circle which included Tibullus, whom Ovid knew only for a short time before his untimely death. Ovid's other friends included Horace, Sextus Propertius, and the grammarian Hyginus.

Having won an assured position among the poets of the day, Ovid turned to more ambitious projects, the *Metamorphoses* and the *Fasti* ("Calendar"). The former was nearly complete, the latter half finished, when his life was shattered by his sudden banishment to Tomis (or Tomi; near modern Constanța, Romania) on the Black Sea. The

Portrait of Ovid, the Classical Roman poet best known for his work Metamorphoses. Hulton Archive/Getty Images

reasons for Ovid's exile will never be fully known. Ovid specifies two, his *Ars amatoria* and an offense which he does not describe beyond insisting that it was an indiscretion (*error*), not a crime (*scelus*). Of the many explanations that have been offered of this mysterious indiscretion, the most probable is that he had become an involuntary accomplice in the adultery of Augustus's granddaughter, the younger Julia, who also was banished at the same time. In 2 BCE her mother, the elder Julia, had similarly been banished for immorality, and the *Ars amatoria* had appeared while this scandal was still fresh in the public mind. These coincidences, together with the tone of Ovid's reference to his offense, suggest that he behaved in some way that was damaging both to Augustus's program of moral reform and to the honour of the imperial family. Since his punishment, which was the milder form of banishment called relegation, did not entail confiscation of property or loss of citizenship, his wife, who was well-connected, remained in Rome to protect his interests and to intercede for him.

Exile at Tomis, a half-Greek, half-barbarian port on the extreme confines of the Roman Empire, was a cruel punishment for a man of Ovid's temperament and habits. He never ceased to hope, if not for pardon, at least for mitigation of sentence, keeping up in the *Tristia* and the *Epistulae ex Ponto* ("Letters from the Black Sea") a ceaseless stream of pathetic pleas, chiefly through his wife and friends, to the emperor. But neither Augustus nor his successor Tiberius relented, and there are hints in the later poems that Ovid was even becoming reconciled to his fate when death released him.

Works

Ovid's extant poems are all written in elegiac couplets except for the *Metamorphoses*. His first poems, the *Amores*, were published at intervals, beginning about 20 BCE, in five books. They form a series of short poems depicting the various phases of a love affair with a woman called Corinna. Their keynote is not passion but the witty and rhetorical exploitation of erotic commonplace; they chronicle not a real relationship between Ovid and Corinna (who is a literary construct rather than a real woman) but all the vicissitudes of a typical affair with a woman of the demimonde.

In the *Epistles of the Heroines* Ovid developed an idea already used by Propertius into something like a new literary genre. The first 15 of these letters are purportedly from legendary ladies such as Penelope, Dido, and Ariadne to absent husbands or lovers. The letters are really dramatic monologues, in which the lessons of Ovid's rhetorical education, particularly the exercises called *ethopoiea* ("character drawing"), are brilliantly exploited. The inherent monotony of subject and treatment, which all Ovid's skill could not completely disguise, is adroitly transcended in the six later epistles. These form three pairs, the lover addressing and being answered by the lady. In them, Ovid's treatment of his literary sources is particularly ingenious; the correspondence of Paris and Helen is one of antiquity's minor masterpieces.

Turning next to didactic poetry, Ovid composed the *Medicamina faciei*, a witty exercise of which only 100 lines survive. This frivolous but harmless poem was followed in 1 BCE by the notorious *Ars amatoria*, a manual of seduction and intrigue for the man about town. The lover's quarry, in this work, is ostensibly to be sought in the demimonde (i.e., among women on the fringes of respectable society who are supported by wealthy lovers), and Ovid explicitly disclaims the intention of teaching adultery; but all of his teaching could in fact be applied to the seduction of married women. Such a work constituted a challenge, no less effective for being flippant, to Augustus's cherished moral reforms, and it included a number of references, in this context tactless if not indeed provocative, to symbols of the emperor's personal prestige. The first two books, addressed to men, were the original extent of the work; a third, in response to popular demand, was added for women. For many modern readers the *Ars amatoria* is Ovid's masterpiece, a brilliant medley of social and personal satire, vignettes of Roman life and manners, and charming mythological digressions. It was followed by a mock recantation, the *Remedia amoris*, also a burlesque of an established genre, which can have done little to make amends for the *Ars*. The possibilities for exploiting love-elegy were now effectively exhausted, and Ovid turned to new types of poetry in which he could use his supreme narrative and descriptive gifts.

Ovid's *Fasti* is an account of the Roman year and its religious festivals, consisting of 12 books, one to each month, of which the first six survive. The various festivals are described as they occur and are traced to their legendary origins. The *Fasti* was a national poem, intended to take its place in the Augustan literary program and perhaps designed to rehabilitate its author in the eyes of the ruling dynasty. It contains a good deal of flattery of the imperial family and much patriotism, for which the undoubted brilliance of the narrative passages does not altogether atone.

Ovid's next work, the *Metamorphoses*, must also be interpreted against its contemporary literary background, particularly in regard to Virgil's *Aeneid*. The unique character of Virgil's poem, which had been canonized as the national epic, posed a problem for his successors, since after the *Aeneid* a straightforward historical or mythological epic would represent an anticlimax. Ovid was warned against this pitfall alike by his instincts and his intelligence; he chose, as Virgil had done, to write an epic on a new plan, unique and individual to himself.

The *Metamorphoses* is a long poem in 15 books written in hexameter verse and totaling nearly 12,000 lines. It is a collection of mythological and legendary stories in which metamorphosis (transformation) plays some part, however minor. The stories are told in chronological order from the creation of the universe (the first metamorphosis, of chaos into order) to the death and deification of Julius Caesar (the culminating metamorphosis, again of chaos—that is, the civil wars—into order—that is, the Augustan Peace). In many of the stories, mythical characters are used to illustrate examples of obedience or disobedience toward the gods, and for their actions are either rewarded or punished by a final transformation into some animal, vegetable, or astronomical form. The importance of metamorphosis is more apparent than real, however; the essential theme of the poem is passion (*pathos*), and this gives it more unity than all the ingenious linking and framing devices the poet uses.

The erotic emphasis that had dominated Ovid's earlier poetry is broadened and deepened into an exploration of nearly every variety of human emotion—for his gods are nothing if not human. This undertaking brought out, as his earlier work had not, Ovid's full powers: his wit and rhetorical brilliance, his mythological learning, and the peculiar qualities of his fertile imagination. The vast quantities of verse in both Greek and Latin that Ovid had read and assimilated are transformed, through a process of creative adaptation, into original and unforeseen guises. By his genius for narrative and vivid description, Ovid gave to scores of Greek legends, some of them little known before, their definitive form for subsequent generations. No single work of literature has done more to transmit the riches of the Greek imagination to posterity. By 8 CE the *Metamorphoses* was complete, if not yet formally published; and it was at that moment, when Ovid seemed securely placed on a pinnacle of successful achievement, that he was banished to Tomis by the emperor.

Ovid arrived at his place of exile in the spring of 9 CE. Tomis was a semi-Hellenized port exposed to periodic attacks by the surrounding barbarian tribes. Books and civilized society were lacking; little Latin was spoken; and the climate was severe. In his solitude and depression, Ovid turned again to poetry, now of a more personal and introspective sort. The *Tristia* and *Epistulae ex Ponto* were written and sent to Rome at the rate of about a book a year from 9 CE on. They consist of letters to the emperor and to Ovid's wife and friends describing his miseries and appealing for clemency. For all his depression and self-pity, Ovid never retreats from the one position with which his self-respect was identified—his status as a poet. This is particularly evident in his ironical defense of the *Ars* in Book II of the *Tristia*.

That Ovid's poetical powers were not as yet seriously impaired is shown by his poem *Ibis*. This, written not long after his arrival at Tomis, is a long and elaborate curse directed at an anonymous enemy. It is a tour de force of abstruse mythological learning, composed largely without the aid of books. But in the absence of any sign of encouragement from home, Ovid lacked the heart to continue to write the sort of poetry that had made him famous, and the later letters make melancholy reading.

The loss of Ovid's tragedy *Medea*, which he wrote while still in Rome, is particularly to be deplored. It was praised by the critic Quintilian and the historian Tacitus and can hardly have failed to influence Seneca's play on the same theme.

Ovid's Legacy

Judged strictly by his gift for fantasy, Ovid is one of the great poets of all time. In the *Metamorphoses* he created a

Nabokovian caricature of the actual world, the setting for a cosmic comedy of manners in which the endless flux and reflux of the universe itself is reflected in the often paradoxical and always arbitrary fate of the characters, human and divine. Pathos, humour, beauty, and cruelty are mingled in a unique individual vision.

Ovid's immense popularity during his lifetime continued after his death and was little affected by the action of Augustus, who banned his works from the public libraries. From about 1100 onward Ovid's fame, which during late antiquity and the early Middle Ages had been to some extent eclipsed, began to rival and even at times to surpass Virgil's. The 12th and 13th centuries have with some justice been called "the age of Ovid." Indeed, he was esteemed in this period not only as entertaining but also as instructive, and his works were read in schools. His poetry is full of epigrammatic maxims and sententious utterances which, lifted from their contexts, made a respectable appearance in the excerpts in which medieval readers often studied their classics. Ovid's popularity was part, however, of a general secularization and awakening to the beauties of profane literature. He was the poet of the wandering scholars as well as of the vernacular poets, the troubadours and minnesingers; and when the concept of romantic love, in its new chivalrous or "courtly" guise, was developed in France, it was Ovid's influence that dominated the book in which its philosophy was expounded, the *Roman de la rose*.

Ovid's popularity grew during the Renaissance, particularly among humanists who were striving to re-create ancient modes of thought and feeling, and printed editions of his works followed each other in an unending stream from 1471. A knowledge of his verse came to be expected of an educated person, and in the 15th–17th centuries it would be difficult to name a poet or painter of note who was not in some degree indebted to him. The *Metamorphoses*, in particular, offered one of the most accessible and attractive avenues to the riches of Greek mythology. But Ovid's chief appeal stems from the humanity of his writing: its gaiety, its sympathy, its exuberance, its pictorial and sensuous quality. It is these things that have recommended him, down the ages.

SENECA THE YOUNGER

(b. *c.* 4 BCE, Corduba [now Córdoba, Spain]—d. 65 CE, Rome)

Lucius Annaeus Seneca was the second son of a wealthy family. His father, also named Lucius Annaeus Seneca (Seneca the Elder), had been famous in Rome as a teacher of rhetoric; his mother, Helvia, was of excellent character and education; his older brother was Gallio, who met St. Paul the Apostle in Achaea in 52 CE; his younger brother was the father of the poet Lucan. An aunt took the younger Seneca as a boy to Rome; there he was trained as an orator and educated in philosophy in the school of the Sextii, which blended Stoicism with an ascetic Neo-Pythagoreanism. Seneca's health suffered, and he went to recuperate in Egypt, where his aunt lived with her husband, the prefect, Gaius Galerius. Returning to Rome about the year 31, he began a career in politics and law. Soon he fell foul of the emperor Caligula, who was deterred from killing him only by the argument that his life was sure to be short.

In 41 the emperor Claudius banished Seneca to Corsica on a charge of adultery with the princess Julia Livilla, the emperor's niece. In that uncongenial milieu he studied natural science and philosophy and wrote the three treatises entitled *Consolationes* (*Consolations*). The influence of Julia Agrippina, the emperor's wife, had him recalled to Rome in 49. He became praetor in 50, married Pompeia Paulina, a wealthy woman, built up a powerful group of friends, including the new prefect of the guard, Sextus Afranius Burrus, and became tutor to the future emperor Nero.

The murder of Claudius in 54 pushed Seneca and Burrus to the top. Their friends held the great army commands on the German and Parthian frontiers. Nero's first public speech, drafted by Seneca, promised liberty for the Senate and an end to the influence of freedmen and women. Agrippina, Nero's mother, was resolved that her influence should continue, and there were other powerful enemies. But Seneca and Burrus, although provincials from Spain and Gaul, understood the problems of the Roman world. They introduced fiscal and judicial reforms and fostered a more humane attitude toward slaves. Their nominee Corbulo defeated the Parthians. In Britain a more enlightened administration followed the quashing of Queen Boudicca's rebellion. But, as the historian Tacitus said, "Nothing in human affairs is more unstable and precarious than power unsupported by its own strength." Seneca and Burrus were a tyrant's favourites. In 59 they had to condone—or to contrive—the murder of Agrippina. When Burrus died in 62, Seneca knew that he could not go on. He withdrew from public life, and in his remaining years he wrote some of his best philosophical works. In 65 Seneca's enemies denounced him as having been a party to the conspiracy of Piso to murder Nero. Ordered to commit suicide, he met death with fortitude and composure.

Seneca's *Apocolocyntosis divi Claudii* (*Pumpkinification of the Divine Claudius*) stands apart from the rest of his surviving works. A political skit, witty and unscrupulous, it has as its theme the deification—or "pumpkinification"—of the emperor. The rest divide into philosophical works (which are not treated in this book) and the tragedies. Of the 10 "Senecan" tragedies, *Octavia* is certainly, and *Hercules*

Oetaeus is probably, spurious. The others handle familiar Greek tragic themes, with some originality of detail. Intended for play readings rather than public presentation, the pitch is a high monotone, emphasizing the lurid and the supernatural. There are impressive set speeches and choral passages, but the characters are static, and they rant. The principal representatives of Classical tragedy known to the Renaissance world, these plays had a great influence, notably in England. William Shakespeare's *Titus Andronicus*, John Webster's *The Duchess of Malfi*, and Cyril Tourneur's *Revengers Tragaedie*, with their ghosts, witches, cruel tyrants, and dominant theme of vengeance, are the progeny of Seneca's tragedies.

*M*ARTIAL

(b. March 1, 38–41 CE, Bilbilis, Hispania [Spain] — d. *c.* 103)

The Roman poet Marcus Valerius Martialis (Martial) brought the Latin epigram to perfection and provided in it a picture of Roman society during the early empire that is remarkable both for its completeness and for its accurate portrayal of human foibles.

Life and Career

Martial was born in a Roman colony in Spain along the Salo River. Proudly claiming descent from Celts and Iberians, he was, nevertheless, a freeborn Roman citizen, the son of parents who, though not wealthy, possessed sufficient means to ensure that he received the traditional literary education from a grammarian and rhetorician. In his early 20s, possibly not before 64 CE, since he makes no reference to the burning of Rome that occurred in that year, Martial made his way to the capital of the empire and attached himself as client (a traditional relationship between powerful patron and humbler man with his way to make) to the powerful and talented family of the Senecas, who were Spaniards like himself. To their circle belonged Lucan, the epic poet, and Calpurnius Piso, chief conspirator in the unsuccessful plot against the emperor Nero in 65 CE. After the latter incident and its consequences, Martial had to look around for other patrons. Presumably the Senecas had introduced him to other influential families, whose patronage would enable him to make a living as a poet. Yet precisely how Martial lived between 65 and 80 CE, the year in which he published *Liber Spectaculorum* (*On the Spectacles*), a small volume of poems to celebrate the consecration of the Colosseum, is not known. It is possible that he turned his hand to law, although it is unlikely that he practiced in the courts either successfully or for long.

When he first came to Rome, Martial lived in rather humble circumstances in a garret on the Quirinal Hill (one of the seven hills on which Rome stands). He gradually earned recognition, however, and was able to acquire, in addition to a town house on the Quirinal, a small country estate near Nomentum (about 12 miles [19 km] northeast of Rome), which may have been given to him by Polla, the widow of Lucan. In time Martial gained the notice of the court and received from emperors Titus and Domitian the *ius trium liberorum*, which entailed certain privileges and was customarily granted to fathers of three children in Rome. These privileges included exemption from various charges, such as that of guardianship, and a prior claim to magistracies. They were therefore financially profitable and accelerated a political career. Martial was almost certainly unmarried, yet he received this marital distinction. Moreover, as an additional mark of imperial favour, he was awarded a military tribuneship, which he was permitted to resign after six months' service but which entitled him to the privileges of an *eques* (knight) throughout his life, even though he lacked the required property qualification of an *eques*.

From each of the patrons whom Martial, as client, attended at the morning levee (a reception held when arising from bed), he would regularly receive the "dole" of "100 wretched farthings." Wealthy Romans, who either hoped to gain favourable mention or feared to receive unfavourable, albeit oblique, mention in his epigrams, would supplement the minimum dole by dinner invitations or by gifts. The poverty so often pleaded by the poet is undoubtedly exaggerated; apparently his genius for spending kept pace with his capacity for earning.

Martial's first book, *On the Spectacles* (80 CE), contained 33 undistinguished epigrams celebrating the shows held in the Colosseum, an amphitheatre in the city begun by Vespasian and completed by Titus in 79; these poems are scarcely improved by their gross adulation of the latter emperor. In the year 84 or 85 appeared two undistinguished books (confusingly numbered XIII and XIV in the collection) with Greek titles *Xenia* and *Apophoreta*; these consist almost entirely of couplets describing presents given to guests at the December festival of the Saturnalia. In the next 15 or 16 years, however, appeared the 12 books of epigrams on which his renown deservedly rests. In 86 CE Books I and II of the *Epigrams* were published, and between 86 and 98, when Martial returned to Spain, new books of the *Epigrams* were issued at more or less yearly intervals. After 34 years in Rome, Martial returned to Spain, where his last book (numbered XII) was published, probably in 102 CE. He died not much over a year later in his early 60s.

The chief friends Martial made in Rome—Seneca, Piso, and Lucan—have already been mentioned. As his fame grew, he became acquainted with the literary circles of his day and met such figures as the literary critic Quintilian, the letter writer Pliny the Younger, the satirist Juvenal, and the epic poet Silius Italicus. Whether he knew the historian Tacitus and the poet Valerius Flaccus is not certain.

Poetry

Martial is virtually the creator of the modern epigram, and his myriad admirers throughout the centuries, including many of the world's great poets, have paid him the homage of quotation, translation, and imitation. He wrote 1,561 epigrams in all. Of these, 1,235 are in elegiac couplets, each of which consists of a six-foot line followed by a five-foot line. The remainder are in hendecasyllables (consisting of lines 11 syllables long) and other metres. Though some of the epigrams are devoted to scenic descriptions, most are about people—emperors, public officials, writers, philosophers, lawyers, teachers, doctors, fops, gladiators, slaves, undertakers, gourmets, spongers, senile lovers, and revolting debauchees. Martial made frequent use of the mordant epigram bearing a "sting" in its tail—i.e., a single unexpected word at the poem's end that completes a pun, antithesis, or an ingenious ambiguity. Poems of this sort would later greatly influence the use of the epigram in the literature of England, France, Spain, and Italy. Martial's handling of this type of epigram is illustrated by I:28, where the apparent contradiction of an insult masks an insult far more subtle: "If you think Acerra reeks of yesterday's wine, you are mistaken. He invariably drinks till morning." Puns, parodies, Greek quotations, and clever ambiguities often enliven Martial's epigrams.

Martial has been charged with two gross faults: adulation and obscenity. He certainly indulged in a great deal of obsequious flattery of the emperor Domitian, involving, besides farfetched conceits dragging his epigrams well below their usual level, use of the official title "my Lord and my God." Furthermore, Martial cringed before men of wealth and influence, unashamedly whining for gifts and favours. Yet, however much one despises servility, it is hard to see how a man of letters could have survived long in Rome without considerable compromise. As for the charge of obscenity, Martial introduced few themes not touched on by Catullus and Horace (two poets of the last century BCE) before him. Those epigrams that are obscene constitute perhaps one-tenth of Martial's total output. His references to homosexuality, "oral stimulation," and masturbation are couched in a rich setting of wit, charm, linguistic subtlety, superb literary craftsmanship, evocative description, and deep human sympathy. Martial's poetry is generally redeemed by his affection toward his friends and his freedom from both envy of others and hypocrisy over his own morals. In his emphasis on the simple joys of life—eating, drinking, and conversing with friends—and in his famous recipes for contentment and the happy life, one is reminded continually of the dominant themes of Horace's *Satires, Epistles*, and *Second Epode*.

LUCAN

(b. 39 CE, Corduba [now Córdoba, Spain]—d. 65, Rome [Italy])

The Roman poet and republican patriot Marcus Annaeus Lucanus (Lucan) is celebrated for his historical epic, the *Bellum civile*, better known as the *Pharsalia* because of its vivid account of that battle. It is remarkable as the single major Latin epic poem that eschewed the intervention of the gods.

Lucan was the nephew of the philosopher-statesman known as Seneca the Younger. Trained by the Stoic philosopher Cornutus and later educated in Athens, Lucan attracted the favourable attention of the emperor Nero owing to his early promise as a rhetorician and orator. Shortly, however, Nero became jealous of his ability as a poet and halted further public readings of his poetry. Already disenchanted by Nero's tyranny and embittered by the ban on his recitations, Lucan became one of the leaders in the conspiracy of Piso (Gaius Calpurnius) to assassinate Nero. When the conspiracy was discovered, he was compelled to commit suicide by opening a vein. According to Tacitus, he died repeating a passage from one of his poems describing the death of a wounded soldier.

The *Bellum civile*, his only extant poem, is an account of the war between Julius Caesar and Pompey, carried down to the arrival of Caesar in Egypt after the murder of Pompey, when it stops abruptly in the middle of the 10th book. Lucan was not a great poet, but he was a great rhetorician and had remarkable political and historical insight, though he wrote the poem while still a young man. The work is naturally imitative of Virgil, though not as dramatic. Although the style and vocabulary are usually commonplace and the metre monotonous, the rhetoric is often lifted into real poetry by its energy and flashes of fire and appears at its best in the magnificent funeral speech of Cato on Pompey. Scattered through the poem are noble sayings and telling comments, expressed with vigour and directness. As the poem proceeds, the poet's republicanism becomes more marked, no doubt because as Nero's tyranny grew, along with Lucan's hatred of him, he looked back with longing to the old Roman Republic. It has been said that Cato is the real hero of the epic, and certainly the best of Lucan's own Stoicism appears in the noble courage of his Cato in continuing the hopeless struggle after Pompey had failed.

Lucan's poetry was popular during the Middle Ages. The Elizabethan poet and playwright Christopher Marlowe translated the first book of the *Bellum civile*

(1600), and Samuel Johnson praised Nicholas Rowe's translation (1718) as "one of the greatest productions of English poetry." The English poets Robert Southey and Percy Bysshe Shelley in their earlier years preferred him to Virgil. His work strongly influenced Pierre Corneille and other French classical dramatists of the 17th century.

GAIUS PETRONIUS ARBITER

(d. 66 CE)

The most complete and authentic account of the life of Gaius Petronius Arbiter appears in Tacitus's *Annals*, an account that may be supplemented, with caution, from other sources. It is probable that Petronius's correct name was Titus Petronius Niger. From his high position in Roman society, it may be assumed that he was wealthy; he belonged to a noble family and was therefore, by Roman standards, a man from whom solid achievements might have been expected. Tacitus's account, however, shows that he belonged to a class of pleasure-seekers attacked by the Stoic philosopher Seneca, men who "turned night into day"; where others won reputation by effort, Petronius did so by idleness. On the rare occasions, however, when he was appointed to official positions, he showed himself energetic and fully equal to public responsibilities. He served as governor of the Asian province of Bithynia and later in his career, probably in 62 or 63 CE, held the high office of consul, or first magistrate of Rome.

After his term as consul, Petronius was received by Nero into his most intimate circle as his "director of elegance" (*arbiter elegantiae*), whose word on all matters of taste was law. It is from this title that the epithet

"Arbiter" was attached to his name. Petronius's association with Nero fell within the emperor's later years, when he had embarked on a career of reckless extravagance that shocked public opinion almost more than the actual crimes of which he was guilty. What Petronius thought of his imperial patron may be indicated by his treatment of the rich vulgarian Trimalchio in the *Satyricon*. Trimalchio is a composite figure, but there are detailed correspondences between him and Nero that cannot, given the contemporary nature of the work, be accidental and that strongly suggest that Petronius was sneering at the emperor.

Tacitus records that Nero's friendship ultimately brought on Petronius the enmity of the commander of the emperor's guard, Tigellinus, who in 66 CE denounced him as having been implicated in a conspiracy of the previous year to assassinate Nero and place a rival on the imperial throne. Petronius, though innocent, was arrested at Cumae, about 12 miles (19 km) west of Naples in southern Italy. Petronius did not wait for the inevitable sentence but made his own preparations for death. Slitting his veins and then bandaging them again in order to delay his death, he passed the remaining hours of his life conversing with his friends on trivial topics, listening to light music and poetry, rewarding or punishing his slaves, feasting, and finally sleeping "so that his death, though forced upon him, should seem natural."

The *Satyricon*, or *Satyricon liber* ("Book of Satyrlike Adventures"), is a comic, picaresque novel that is related to several ancient literary genres. In style it ranges between the highly realistic and the self-consciously literary, and its form is episodic. It relates the wanderings and escapades of a disreputable trio of adventurers, the narrator Encolpius ("Embracer"), his friend Ascyltos ("Scot-free"), and the boy Giton ("Neighbour"). The surviving portions of the *Satyricon* (parts of Books XV and XVI) probably represent about one-tenth of the complete work, which was evidently very long. The loose narrative framework encloses a number of independent tales, a classic instance being the famous "Widow of Ephesus" (ch. 111–112). Other features, however, recall the "Menippean" satire; these include the mixture of prose and verse in which the work is composed; and the digressions in which the author airs his own views on various topics having no connection with the plot.

The longest and the best episode in the surviving portions of the *Satyricon* is the *Cena Trimalchionis*, or "Banquet of Trimalchio" (ch. 26–78). This is a description of a dinner party given by Trimalchio, an immensely rich and vulgar freedman (former slave), to a group of friends and hangers-on. This episode's length appears disproportionate even to the presumed original size of the *Satyricon*, and it has little or no apparent connection with the plot. The scene is a Greco-Roman town in Campania, and the guests, mostly freedmen like their host, are drawn from what corresponded to the petit bourgeois class. Trimalchio is the quintessence of the parvenu, a figure familiar enough in ancient satirical literature, but especially so in the 1st century CE, when freedmen as a class were at their most influential.

Two features distinguish Petronius's "Banquet" from other ancient examples: its extraordinary realism and the figure of Trimalchio. It is obvious that the table talk of the guests in the "Banquet" is based on the author's personal observation of provincial societies. The speakers are beautifully and exactly characterized and their dialogue, quite apart from the invaluable evidence for colloquial Latin afforded by the vulgarisms and solecisms in which it abounds, is a humorous masterpiece. Trimalchio himself, with his vast wealth, his tasteless ostentation, his affectation of culture, his superstition, and his maudlin lapses into his natural vulgarity, is more than a typical satirist's figure. As depicted by Petronius he is one of the great comic figures of literature and is fit company for Shakespeare's Falstaff. The development of character for its own sake was hardly known in ancient literature: the emphasis was always on the typical, and the classical rules laid down that character was secondary to more important considerations such as plot. Petronius, in his treatment of Trimalchio, transcended this almost universal limitation in a way that irresistibly recalls Charles Dickens, and much else in the "Banquet" is Dickensian—its exuberance, its boisterous humour (rare in ancient literature, where wit predominates), and its loving profusion of detail.

The rest of the *Satyricon* is hardly to be compared to the "Banquet." Insofar as any moral attitude at all is perceptible in the work as a whole, it is a trivial and debased brand of hedonism. The aim of the *Satyricon* was evidently above all to entertain by portraying certain aspects of contemporary society, and when considered as such, the book is of immense value: superficial details of the speech, behaviour, appearance, and surroundings of the characters are exactly observed and vividly communicated. The wealth of specific allusions to persons and events of Nero's time shows that the work was aimed at a contemporary audience, and certain features suggest that the audience in fact consisted of Nero and his courtiers. The realistic descriptions of low life recall the emperor's relish for slumming expeditions; and the combination of literary sophistication with polished obscenity is consistent with the wish to titillate the jaded palates of a debauched court.

If Petronius's book has a message, it is aesthetic rather than moral. The emphasis throughout the account of Trimalchio's dinner party is on the contrast between taste and tastelessness. Stylistically, too, the *Satyricon* is what Tacitus' account of the author would lead one to expect. The language of the narrative and the educated speakers is pure, easy, and elegant, and the wit of the best comic passages is brilliant; but the general impression, even when allowance is made for the fragmentary state of the text, is that of a book written quickly and somewhat carelessly by a writer who would not take the necessary trouble to discipline his astonishing powers of invention. In his book, as in his life, Petronius achieved fame by indolence.

STATIUS

(b. 45 CE, Neapolis [now Naples, Italy] — d. 96, probably Neapolis?)

Publius Papinius Statius is one of the principal Roman epic and lyric poets of the Silver Age of Latin literature (18–133 CE). His occasional poems, collected under the title *Silvae* ("Forests"), apart from their literary merit, are valuable for their description of the lifestyle of a wealthy and fashionable class—the *liberti*—during the reign of the emperor Domitian.

His father was also a poet, and Statius seems to have been trained as one from childhood. Little is known of his life. He lived at Rome and was a court poet under Domitian, who awarded him a prize in 89 or 90. He was, however, unsuccessful in the Capitoline competition at Rome, probably on its third celebration in 94, and shortly afterward returned to Neapolis.

The role of court poet seems to have suited Statius, who used without scruple the flattery that was inevitable under Domitian and exploited it in a way that suited his own nature. He was talented, and his poetic expression, despite its faults, is rich, buoyant, and felicitous.

Statius is at his best in the five books of the *Silvae*. Of the 32 poems, five are devoted to flattery of the emperor and his favourites. Another group gives picturesque descriptions of the villas and gardens of his friends, members of an acquisitive and ostentatious class who surrounded themselves with art works and antiques and patronized the poet in return for his versified praises. There is a striking description of the gifts and amusements provided by the emperor for the Roman populace at the Saturnalia, the festival of the winter solstice, and his birthday ode honouring the poet Lucan has, along with the usual exaggerations, some good lines and shows an appreciation of earlier Latin poets. Also estimable are poems dealing with family affection and personal loss and one poem to sleep.

Statius completed one epic, the 12-book *Thebaid*, but only two books of another, the *Achilleid*. The *Thebaid*, a more ambitious work, describes the struggle of the brothers Polyneices and Eteocles for the throne of the ancient Greek city of Thebes. It has many features borrowed from Virgil, but suffers from overstatement and exaggeration. The work begins and ends, however, with passages that convey an atmosphere of dramatic tension and considerable tragic power. The *Achilleid* gives a charming account of the early education of Achilles, but at the point at which he is taken off to Troy by Odysseus, the poem was evidently interrupted by the poet's death. There is an English-language edition of Statius's works, both the *Silvae* (2003) and a two-volume *Thebiad* (2004) by D.R. Shackleton Bailey, in the Loeb Classical Library.

PLUTARCH

(b. 46 CE, Chaeronea, Boeotia [Greece] — d. after 119)

The biographer and author Plutarch (Greek Plutarchos, Latin Plutarchus) strongly influenced the evolution of the essay, the biography, and historical writing in Europe from the 16th to the 19th century. Among his approximately 227 works, the most important are the *Bioi paralleloi* (*Parallel Lives*), in which he recounts the noble deeds and characters of Greek and Roman soldiers, legislators, orators, and statesmen, and the *Moralia*, or *Ethica*, a series of more than 60 essays on ethical, religious, physical, political, and literary topics.

Life

Plutarch was the son of Aristobulus, himself a biographer and philosopher. In 66–67, Plutarch studied mathematics and philosophy at Athens under the philosopher Ammonius. Public duties later took him several times to Rome, where he lectured on philosophy, made many friends, and perhaps enjoyed the acquaintance of the emperors Trajan and Hadrian. According to the *Suda* lexicon (a Greek dictionary dating from about 1000 CE), Trajan bestowed the high rank of an ex-consul upon him. Although this may be true, a report of a 4th-century church historian, Eusebius, that Hadrian made Plutarch governor of Greece is probably apocryphal. A Delphic

Early 20th-century depiction of the Greek essayist Plutarch. Bob Thomas/Popperfoto/Getty Images

inscription reveals that he possessed Roman citizenship. His *nomen*, or family name, Mestrius, was no doubt adopted from his friend Lucius Mestrius Florus, a Roman consul.

Plutarch traveled widely, visiting central Greece, Sparta, Corinth, Patrae (Patras), Sardis, and Alexandria, but he made his usual residence at Chaeronea (now Khairónia, Greece), where he held the chief magistracy and other municipal posts and directed a school with a wide curriculum in which philosophy, especially ethics, occupied the central place. He maintained close links with the Academy at Athens (he possessed Athenian citizenship) and with Delphi, where, from about 95, he held a priesthood for life; he may have won Trajan's interest and support for the then-renewed vogue of the oracle. The size of Plutarch's family is uncertain. In the *Consolatio* to his wife, Timoxena, on the death of their infant daughter, he mentions four sons; of these at least two survived childhood, and he may have had other children.

Plutarch's literary output was immense. The 227 titles in the so-called catalog of Lamprias, a list of Plutarch's works supposedly made by his son, are not all authentic, but neither do they include all he wrote. The order of composition cannot be determined.

The Lives

Plutarch's popularity rests primarily on his *Parallel Lives*. These, dedicated to Trajan's friend Sosius Senecio, who is mentioned in the lives "Demosthenes," "Theseus," and "Dion," were designed to encourage mutual respect between Greeks and Romans. By exhibiting noble deeds and characters, they were also to provide model patterns of behaviour.

The first pair, "Epaminondas and Scipio," and perhaps an introduction and formal dedication, are lost.

But Plutarch's plan was clearly to publish in successive books biographies of Greek and Roman heroes in pairs, chosen as far as possible for their similarity of character or career, and each followed by a formal comparison. Internal evidence suggests that the *Lives* were composed in Plutarch's later years, but the order of composition can be only partially determined; the present order is a later rearrangement based largely on the chronology of the Greek subjects, who are placed first in each pair. In all, 22 pairs survive (one pair being a double group of "Agis and Cleomenes" and the "Gracchi") and four single biographies, of Artaxerxes, Aratus, Galba, and Otho.

The *Lives* display impressive learning and research. Many sources are quoted, and, though Plutarch probably had not consulted all these at first hand, his investigations were clearly extensive, and compilation must have occupied many years. For the Roman *Lives* he was handicapped by an imperfect knowledge of Latin, which he had learned late in life, for, as he explains in "Demosthenes," political tasks and the teaching of philosophy fully engaged him during his stay in Rome and Italy. The form of the *Lives* represented a new achievement, not closely linked with either previous biography or Hellenistic history. The general scheme was to give the birth, youth and character, achievements, and circumstances of death, interspersed with frequent ethical reflections, but the details varied with both the subject and the available sources, which include anecdote mongers and writers of memoirs as well as historians. Plutarch never claimed to be writing history, which he distinguished from biography. His aim was to delight and edify the reader, and he did not conceal his own sympathies, which were especially evident in his warm admiration for the words and deeds of Spartan kings and generals. His virulent and unfair attack on Herodotus, the Greek historian of the 5th century BCE, probably sprang from his feeling that he had done Athens more and Boeotia less than justice.

The Moralia

Plutarch's surviving writings on ethical, religious, physical, political, and literary topics are collectively known as the *Moralia*, or *Ethica*, and amount to more than 60 essays cast mainly in the form of dialogues or diatribes. The former vary from a collection of set speeches to informal conversation pieces set among members of Plutarch's family circle; the date and dramatic occasion are rarely indicated. The diatribes, which often show the influence of serio-comic writings of the 3rd-century-BCE satirist Menippus, are simple and vigorous. The literary value of both is enhanced by the frequent quotation of Greek poems, especially verses of Euripides and other dramatists.

The treatises dealing with political issues are of especial interest. "Political Precepts" is an enlightening account of political life in contemporary Greece; in "Whether a Man Should Engage in Politics When Old," Plutarch urged his friend Euphanes to continue in public life at Athens; Stoic ideas appear in the short work "To the Unlearned Ruler" and the fragmentary argument that "The Philosopher Should Converse Especially with Princes."

Plutarch's interest in religious history and antiquarian problems can be seen in a group of striking essays, the early "Daemon of Socrates," and three later works concerning Delphi, "On the Failure of the Oracles," in which the decline of the oracle is linked with the decline in the population, "On the E at Delphi," interpreting the word *EI* at the temple entrance, and "On the Pythian Responses," seeking to reestablish belief in the oracle. Contemporary with these is "On Isis and Osiris," with its mystical tones. "Convivial Questions" (nine books) and

"Greek and Roman Questions" assembled a vast collection of antiquarian lore.

Reputation and Influence

Plutarch's later influence has been profound. He was loved and respected in his own time and in later antiquity; his *Lives* inspired a rhetorician, Aristides, and a historian, Arrian, to similar comparisons, and a copy accompanied the emperor Marcus Aurelius when he took the field against the Marcomanni. Gradually, Plutarch's reputation faded in the Latin West, but he continued to influence philosophers and scholars in the Greek East, where his works came to constitute a schoolbook. Proclus, Porphyry, and the emperor Julian all quote him, and the Greek Church Fathers Clement of Alexandria and Basil the Great imitate him without acknowledgment. His works were familiar to all cultivated Byzantines, who set no barrier between the pagan past and the Christian present. It was mainly the *Moralia* that appealed to them; but in the 9th century the Byzantine scholar and patriarch Photius read the *Lives* with his friends.

Plutarch's works were introduced to Italy by Byzantine scholars along with the revival of classical learning in the 15th century, and Italian humanists had already translated them into Latin and Italian before 1509, when the *Moralia*, the first of his works to be printed in the original Greek, appeared at Venice published by the celebrated Aldine Press. The first original Greek text of the *Lives* was printed at Florence in 1517 and by the Aldine Press in 1519. The *Lives* were translated into French in 1559 by Jacques Amyot, a French bishop and classical scholar, who also translated the *Moralia* (1572). The first complete edition of the Greek texts by the French humanist Henri II Estienne in 1572 marked a great improvement in the text.

That François Rabelais knew Plutarch well is proved by the frequency with which he quotes from both the *Lives* and the *Moralia* in his satirical novels. It was Michel de Montaigne, however, who read Plutarch in Amyot's version, who first made his influence widely felt. The style of Montaigne's *Essays* (1580–88) owed much to the *Moralia*, and from the *Lives* he adopted Plutarch's method of revealing character by illustrative anecdote and comment, which he applied to self-revelation. Moreover, the *Essays* made known the ideal, derived from Plutarch's presentation of character and openly expressed opinion, of "high antique virtue and the heroically moral individual" that became the humanist ideal of the Renaissance period.

The *Lives* were translated into English, from Amyot's version, by Sir Thomas North in 1579. His vigorous idiomatic style made his *Lives of the Noble Grecians and Romans* an English classic, and it remained the standard translation for more than a century. Even when superseded by more accurate translations, it continued to be read as an example of Elizabethan prose style. North's translation of Plutarch was William Shakespeare's source for his Roman history plays and influenced the development of his conception of the tragic hero. The literary quality of North's version may be judged from the fact that Shakespeare lifted whole passages from it with only minor changes.

In 1603 the complete *Moralia* was first translated into English directly from the Greek. Its influence can be seen in the 1612 edition of Francis Bacon's *Essays*, which contain counsels of public morality and private virtue recognizably derived from Plutarch. Francis Bacon was more attracted by Plutarch the moralist than by Plutarch the teller of stories or painter of character, but to the Renaissance mind it was the blend of these elements that gave him his particular appeal. His liking for historical gossip, for the anecdote and the moral tale, his portrayal of characters as patterns of virtue or vice (in the manner of the morality play and the character), and his emphasis on the turn of fortune's wheel in causing the downfall of the great, all suited the mood of the age, and from him was derived the Renaissance conception of the heroic and of the "rational" moral philosophy of the ancients.

Historians and biographers in the 16th and 17th centuries followed Plutarch in treating character on ethical principles. The 17th-century English biographer Izaak Walton knew Plutarch well, and his own *Lives* (collected 1670, 1675) imitated Plutarch by dwelling on the strength, rather than the weakness, of his subjects' characters.

Plutarch was read throughout the 17th and 18th centuries. The English poet and dramatist John Dryden edited a new translation of the *Lives* first published in 1683–86, and abridged editions appeared in 1710, 1713, and 1718. The *Moralia* was retranslated in 1683–90 and also frequently reprinted. In France, Amyot's translations were still being reprinted in the early 19th century, and their influence on the development of French classical tragedy equaled that of North's version on Shakespeare. Admiration for those heroes of Plutarch who overthrew tyrants, and respect for his moral values, inspired the leaders of the French Revolution; Charlotte Corday, who assassinated the revolutionary leader Jean-Paul Marat, spent the day before that event in reading Plutarch.

In the German states, the first collected edition of Plutarch's works was published in 1774–82. The *Moralia* was edited by Daniel Wyttenbach in 1796–1834 and was first translated in 1783–1800. The *Lives*, first edited in 1873–75, had already been translated in 1799–1806. The German classical poets—Johann Wolfgang von Goethe, Friedrich von Schiller, and Jean Paul (Johann Paul Richter) especially—were influenced by Plutarch's works, and he was read also by Ludwig van Beethoven and Friedrich Nietzsche.

In the 19th century, Plutarch's direct influence began to decline, in part as a result of the reaction against the French Revolution, in part because the rise of the Romantic movement introduced new values and emphasized the free play of passions rather than their control, and in part because the more critical attitude of scholars to historical accuracy drew attention to the bias of his presentation of fact. He was still admired, however, notably by the American poet, philosopher, and essayist Ralph Waldo Emerson, and, although in the 20th and 21st centuries his direct influence was small, the popular ideas of Greek and Roman history continued to be those derived from his pages.

JUVENAL

(b. 55–60? CE, Aquinum [now Aquino, Italy]—d. probably in or after 127)

Decimus Junius Juvenalis (Juvenal) is the most powerful of all Roman satiric poets. Many of his phrases and epigrams have entered common parlance—for example, "bread and circuses" and "who will guard the guards themselves?"

The one contemporary who ever mentions Juvenal is Martial, who claims to be his friend, calls him eloquent, and describes him as living the life of a poor dependent cadging from rich men. There are a few biographies of him, apparently composed long after his death; these may contain some nuggets of fact, but they are brief, ill-proportioned, and sometimes incredible.

From these sparse sources it can be inferred that Juvenal's family was well-to-do and that he became an officer in the army as a first step to a career in the administrative service of the emperor Domitian (81–96 CE) but failed to obtain promotion and grew embittered. He wrote a satire declaring that court favourites had undue influence in the promotion of officers, and for this he was banished—possibly to the remote frontier town of Syene, now Aswān, in Egypt—and his property was confiscated. In 96, after Domitian's assassination, Juvenal returned to Rome; but, without money or a career, he was reduced to living as a "client" on the grudging charity of the rich. After some years his situation improved, for autobiographical remarks in Satire 11 show him, now elderly, living in modest comfort in Rome and possessing a farm at Tibur (now Tivoli) with servants and livestock. Still pessimistic, the later Satires show a marked change of tone and some touches of human kindness, as though he had found some consolation at last. Though no details of his death exist, he probably died in or after 127.

Juvenal's 16 satiric poems deal mainly with life in Rome under the much-dreaded emperor Domitian and his more humane successors Nerva (96–98), Trajan (98–117), and Hadrian (117–138). They were published at intervals in five separate books. Book One, containing Satires 1–5, views in retrospect the horrors of Domitian's tyrannical reign and was issued between 100 and 110. (The historian Tacitus, a contemporary of Juvenal, was also embittered by the suspicion and fear of that epoch.) Book Two, the single, enormous Satire 6, contains topical references to the year 115. The third Book, with Satires 7, 8, and 9, opens with praise of an emperor—surely Hadrian, who endowed a literary institute to assist deserving authors—whose generosity makes him the sole hope of literature. There is no datable allusion in Book Four, which comprises Satires 10–12. Book Five, made up of Satires 13, 14, 15, and 16, has two clear references to the year 127.

The Satires attack two main themes: the corruption of society in the city of Rome and the follies and brutalities of humankind. In the first Satire, Juvenal declares that vice, crime, and the misuse of wealth have reached such a peak that it is impossible *not* to write satire, but that, since it is dangerous to attack powerful men in their lifetime, he will take his examples from the dead. He does not maintain this principle, for sometimes he mentions living contemporaries; but it provides a useful insurance policy against retaliation, and it implies that Rome has been evil for many generations. Male homosexuals are derided in two poems: passives in Satire 2, actives and passives together in Satire 9. In the third Satire a friend of Juvenal explains why, abandoning the humiliating life of a dependent, he is determined to live in a quiet country town and leave crowded and uncomfortable Rome, which has been ruined by Greeks and other foreign immigrants; while in the fifth Juvenal mocks another such dependent by describing the calculated insults he must endure on the rare occasions when his patron invites him to dinner. The fourth relates how Domitian summoned his cringing Cabinet to consider an absurdly petty problem: how to cook a turbot too large for any ordinary pan.

Satire 6, more than 600 lines long, is a ruthless denunciation of the folly, arrogance, cruelty, and sexual depravity of Roman women. The seventh Satire depicts the poverty and wretchedness of the Roman intellectuals who cannot find decent rewards for their labours. In the eighth, Juvenal attacks the cult of hereditary nobility. One of his grandest poems is the 10th, which examines the ambitions of humankind—wealth, power, glory, long life, and personal beauty—and shows that they all lead to disappointment or danger: what people should pray for is "a sound mind in a sound body, and a brave heart." In Satire 11, Juvenal invites an old friend to dine quietly but comfortably and discourses on the foolishly extravagant banquets of the rich. The 12th is a quiet little poem distinguishing between true and mercenary friendship. In the 13th Juvenal offers sarcastic consolation to a man who has been defrauded of some money by a friend, telling him that such misdeeds are commonplace; while in the 14th he denounces parents who teach their children avarice. Satire 15 tells of a riot in Egypt during which a man was torn to pieces and eaten: a proof that men are crueler than animals. In the 16th Juvenal announces that he will survey the privileges of professional soldiers, an important theme; but the poem breaks off at line 60 in the middle of a sentence: the rest was lost in ancient times.

Technically, Juvenal's poetry is very fine. The structure of the individual Satires is—with a few exceptions—clear and forceful. They are full of skillfully expressive effects in which the sound and rhythm mimic and enhance the sense; and they abound in trenchant phrases and memorable epigrams, many known to people who have never heard of Juvenal: "bread and circuses"; "slow rises worth, by poverty oppressed"; "who will guard the guards themselves?"; "the itch for writing"; "the greatest reverence is due to a child." Vivid, often cruelly frank, remarks appear on almost every page: after describing a rich woman's efforts to preserve her complexion with ointments, tonics, donkey's milk, and poultices, Juvenal asks, "Is that a face, or an ulcer?" He describes striking and disgusting scenes with a clarity that makes them unforgettable: we see the statues of the emperor's discarded favourite melted down to make kitchenware and chamber pots; the husband closing his disgusted eyes while his drunken wife vomits on the marble floor; the emperor Claudius (poisoned by his consort) "going to heaven" with his head trembling and his lips drooling long trains of saliva; the impotent bridegroom whimpering while a paid substitute consoles his wife. Juvenal is not a poet to be relished by soft hearts or optimists, but he has power.

Juvenal's work was forgotten for a time after his death. Later it began to be read and quoted, first by the Christian propagandist Tertullian—who lived and wrote about 200 CE and was as full of passionate indignation as Juvenal— then by other Christian authors and also by pagan students of literature. A commentary on the Satires (which survives) was compiled at some time between 350 and 420, and two editions of the text were produced on the basis of one master copy—apparently the only copy that had been preserved until then. Thenceforward Juvenal has never ceased to be studied and admired, and he has been imitated by many satirists—for instance, by Giovanni Boccaccio, Nicolas Boileau, and Lord Byron. The term *Juvenalian satire* still denotes any criticism of contemporary persons and institutions in Juvenal's manner.

TACITUS

(b. 56 CE—d. *c.* 120)

The Roman orator and public official Publius Cornelius Tacitus (or Gaius Cornelius Tacitus) is probably the greatest historian and one of the greatest prose stylists who wrote in the Latin language. Among his works are the *Germania*, describing the Germanic tribes, the *Historiae* (*Histories*), concerning the Roman Empire from 69 to 96 CE, and the later *Annals*, dealing with the empire in the period from 14 to 68 CE.

Early Life and Career

Tacitus was born perhaps in northern Italy (Cisalpine Gaul) or, more probably, in southern Gaul (Gallia Narbonensis, or present southeastern France). Nothing is known of his parentage. Though Cornelius was the name of a noble Roman family, there is no proof that he was descended from the Roman aristocracy; provincial families often took the name of the governor who had given them Roman citizenship. In any event he grew up in comfortable circumstances, enjoyed a good education, and found the way to start a public career.

Tacitus studied rhetoric, which provided a general literary education including the practice of prose composition. This training was a systematic preparation for administrative office. Tacitus studied to be an advocate at law under two leading orators, Marcus Aper and Julius Secundus; then he began his career with a "vigintivirate" (one of 20 appointments to minor magistracies) and a military tribunate (on the staff of a legion).

In 77 Tacitus married the daughter of Gnaeus Julius Agricola. Agricola had risen in the imperial service to the consulship, in 77 or 78, and he would later enhance his reputation as governor of Britain. Tacitus appears to have made his own mark socially and was making much progress toward public distinction; he would obviously benefit from Agricola's political connections. Moving through the regular stages, he gained the quaestorship (often a responsible provincial post), probably in 81; then in 88 he attained a praetorship (a post with legal jurisdiction) and became a member of the priestly college that kept the Sibylline Books of prophecy and supervised foreign-cult practice. After this it may be assumed that he held a senior provincial post, normally in command of a legion, for four years.

When he returned to Rome, he observed firsthand the last years of the emperor Domitian's oppression of the Roman aristocracy. By 93 Agricola was dead, but by this time Tacitus had achieved distinction on his own. In 97, under the emperor Nerva, he rose to the consulship and delivered the funeral oration for Verginius Rufus, a famous soldier who had refused to compete for power in 68/69 after Nero's death. This distinction not only reflected his reputation as an orator but his moral authority and official dignity as well.

First Literary Works

In 98 Tacitus wrote two works: *De vita Julii Agricolae* and *De origine et situ Germanorum* (the *Germania*), both reflecting his personal interests. The *Agricola* is a biographical account of his father-in-law's career, with special reference to the governorship of Britain (78–84) and the later years under Domitian. It is laudatory yet circumstantial in its description, and it gives a balanced political judgment. The *Germania* is another descriptive piece, this time of the Roman frontier on the Rhine. Tacitus emphasizes the simple virtue as well as the primitive vices of the Germanic tribes, in contrast to the moral laxity of contemporary Rome, and the threat that these tribes, if they acted together, could present to Roman Gaul. Here his writing goes beyond geography to political ethnography. The work gives an administrator's appreciation of the German situation, and to this extent the work serves as a historical introduction to the Germans.

Tacitus still practiced advocacy at law—in 100 he, along with Pliny the Younger, successfully prosecuted Marius Priscus, a proconsul in Africa, for extortion—but he felt that oratory had lost much of its political spirit and its practitioners were deficient in skill. This decline of oratory seems to provide the setting for his *Dialogus de oratoribus*. The work refers back to his youth, introducing his teachers Aper and Secundus. It has been dated as early as about 80, chiefly because it is more Ciceronian in style than his other writing. But its style arises from its form and subject matter and does not point to an early stage of stylistic development. The date lies between 98 and 102; the theme fits this

The writings of Tacitus, whose statue graces the entry corridor to the Austrian parliment building along with figures of other notable statesmen, document the history of the Roman Empire. Renata Sedmakova/Shutterstock.com

period. Tacitus compares oratory with poetry as a way of literary life, marking the decline of oratory in public affairs: the Roman Republic had given scope for true eloquence; the empire limited its inspiration. The work reflects his mood at the time he turned from oratory to history.

There were historians of imperial Rome before Tacitus, notably Aufidius Bassus, who recorded events from the rise of Augustus to the reign of Claudius, and Pliny the Elder, who continued this work (*a fine Aufidii Bassi*) to the time of Vespasian. In taking up history Tacitus joined the line of succession of those who described and interpreted their own period, and he took up the story from the political situation that followed Nero's death to the close of the Flavian dynasty.

The Histories *and the* Annals

The *Historiae* began at January 1, 69, with Galba in power and proceeded to the death of Domitian, in 96. The work contained 12 or 14 books (it is known only that the *Histories* and *Annals*, both now incomplete, totaled 30 books). To judge from the younger Pliny's references, several books were ready by 105, the writing well advanced by 107, and the work finished by 109. Only Books I–IV and part of Book V, for the years 69–70, are extant. They cover the fall of Galba and Piso before Otho (Book I); Vespasian's position in the East and Otho's suicide, making way for Vitellius (Book II); the defeat of Vitellius by the Danubian legions on Vespasian's side (Book III); and the opening of Vespasian's reign (Books IV–V).

This text represents a small part of what must have been a brilliant as well as systematic account of the critical Flavian period in Roman history, especially where Tacitus wrote with firsthand knowledge of provincial conditions in the West and of Domitian's last years in Rome. The narrative as it now exists, with its magnificent introduction, is a powerfully sustained piece of writing that, for all the emphasis and colour of its prose, is perfectly appropriate for describing the closely knit set of events during the civil war of 69.

This was only the first stage of Tacitus's historical work. As he approached the reign of Domitian, he faced a Roman policy that, except in provincial and frontier affairs, was less coherent and predictable. It called for sharper analysis, which he often met with bitterness, anger, and pointed irony. Domitian's later despotism outraged the aristocratic tradition. It is not known, and it is the most serious gap, how Tacitus finally handled in detail Domitian's reputation. Perhaps his picture of the emperor Tiberius in the *Annals* owed something to his exercise on Domitian.

It is necessary to keep the dating of Tacitus's work in mind. He had won distinction under Nerva and enjoyed the effects of liberal policy; at the same time, he had lived through the crisis of imperial policy that occurred when Nerva and Trajan came to the succession. Under Trajan he retained his place in public affairs, and in 112–113 he crowned his administrative career with the proconsulate of Asia, the top provincial governorship. His personal career had revealed to him, at court and in administration, the play of power that lay behind the imperial facade of rule. He was especially familiar with the effect of dynastic control, which tended to corrupt the rulers, as it had in the period from Vespasian to Domitian, and to reduce the supporting nobles to servility, while only military revolt within Rome or from the frontier legions could change the situation—as it had done at the end of Nero's reign.

From what can be reconstructed from his personal career along with the implications of his subsequent historical thought, it is possible to mark an intellectual turning point in his life after which he began to probe deeper into the nature of the Roman Empire. Although in the *Agricola* he had lightly promised to continue his writing from the Flavian years into the new regime, he now moved not forward but backward. He was no longer content to record the present but felt compelled to interpret the political burden of the past from the time when Tiberius consolidated Augustus's policy of imperial government.

The *Annals* (*Cornelii Taciti ab excessu divi Augusti*), following the traditional form of yearly narrative with literary elaboration on the significant events, covered the period of the Julio-Claudian dynasty from the death of Augustus and the accession of Tiberius, in 14, to the end of Nero's reign, in 68. The work contained 18 or 16 books and was probably begun during Trajan's reign and completed early in Hadrian's reign. Only Books I–IV, part of Book V, most of Book VI (treating the years 14–29 and 31–37 under Tiberius), and Books XI–XVI, incomplete (on Claudius from 47 to 51 and Nero from 51 to 66), are extant.

In casting back to the early empire Tacitus did not wish necessarily to supersede his predecessors in the field, whose systematic recording he seemed to respect, judging from the use he made of their subject matter. His prime purpose was to reinterpret critically the Julio-Claudian dynasty, when imperial rule developed a central control that, even after the complex military coup d'état in 68–69, would continue under the Flavians. In effect, the *Annals* represents a diagnosis in narrative form of the decline of Roman political freedom, written to explain the condition of the empire he had already described in the *Histories*. Tacitus viewed the first imperial century as an entity. There was (in his eyes) a comparison to be made, for example, between the personal conduct of Tiberius and that of Domitian, not that they were the same kind of men but that they were corrupted by similar conditions of dynastic power. Yet he did not begin with Augustus, except by cold reference to his memory. The modern world tends to think of Augustus as the founder of the empire. The Romans—one may cite Appian of Alexandria and Publius Annius Florus alongside Tacitus—regarded him, at least during the first part of his career, as the last of the warlords who had dominated the republic.

In opening the *Annals*, Tacitus accepts the necessity of strong, periodic power in Roman government, providing it allowed the rise of fresh talent to take over control. That was the aristocratic attitude toward political freedom, but to secure the continuity of personal authority by dynastic convention, regardless of the qualifications for rule, was to subvert the Roman tradition and corrupt public morality. If Augustus began as a warlord, he ended by establishing a dynasty, but the decisive point toward continuing a tyrannical dynasty was Tiberius's accession.

One may, indeed, believe that Tiberius was prompted to assume imperial power because he was anxious about the military situation on the Roman frontier; but Tacitus had no doubts about the security of the Roman position, and he considered the hesitation that Tiberius displayed on taking power to be hypocritical; hence, the historical irony, in interpretation and style, of his first six books. Here, perhaps, Tacitus had some support for his interpretation. A strong, dour soldier and a suspicious man, Tiberius had little to say in his court circle about public affairs. On his death he was blamed for never saying what he thought nor meaning what he said, and Tacitus elaborated this impression. His criticism of dynastic power also stressed the effect of personality: if Tiberius was false, Claudius was weak, Nero was not only unstable but evil, and the imperial wives were dangerous. With regard to provincial administration, he knew that he could take its regular character for granted, in the earlier period as well as his own.

Sources

For the period from Augustus to Vespasian, Tacitus was able to draw upon earlier histories that contained material from the public records, official reports, and contemporary comment. It has been noted that the work of Aufidius Bassus and its continuation by Pliny the Elder covered these years; both historians also treated the German wars. Among other sources Tacitus consulted Servilius Nonianus (on Tiberius), Cluvius Rufus and Fabius Rusticus (on Nero), and Vipstanus Messalla (on the year 69). He also turned, as far as he felt necessary, to the Senate's records, the official journal, and such firsthand information as a speech of Claudius, the personal memoirs of Agrippina the Younger, and the military memoirs of the general Gnaeus Domitius Corbulo. For Vespasian's later years and the reigns of Titus and Domitian, he must have worked more closely from official records and reports.

In the light of his administrative and political experience, Tacitus in the *Histories* was able to interpret the historical evidence for the Flavian period more or less directly. Yet contemporary writing may lack perspective. He recognized this problem when, in the *Annals*, he revived the study of the Julio-Claudian dynasty. But to go back a century raises additional problems of historical method. Tacitus first had to determine the factual reliability and political attitude of his authorities and then to adjust his own general conception of the empire, in case it was anachronistic, to the earlier conditions. The strength of his conviction limited his judgment at both points. He underplayed the effect of immediate circumstances and overplayed the personal factor, a tendency that influenced his use of the historical sources. In particular Tiberius, who in spite of his political ineptness struggled with real difficulties, suffered in reputation from this treatment. But Tacitus did not spare anyone in power. He controls the performance of his characters; it is magnificent writing, but it is not necessarily strict history.

Style and Importance

Because he was a conscious literary stylist, both his thought and his manner of expression gave life to his work. Greek historiography had defined ways of depicting history: one could analyze events in plain terms, set the scene with personalities, or heighten the dramatic appeal of human action. Each method had its technique, and the greater writer could combine elements from all three. The Roman "annalistic" form, after years of development, allowed this varied play of style in significant episodes. Tacitus knew the techniques and controlled them for his political interpretations; as a model he had studied the early Roman historiographer Sallust.

It is finally his masterly handling of literary Latin that impresses the reader. He wrote in the grand style, helped by the solemn and poetic usage of the Roman tradition, and he exploited the Latin qualities of strength, rhythm, and colour. His style, like his thought, avoids artificial smoothness. His writing is concise, breaking any easy balance of sentences, depending for emphasis on word order and syntactical variation and striking hard where the subject matter calls for a formidable impact. He is most pointed on the theme of Tiberius, but his technique here is only a concentrated form of the stylistic force that can be found throughout his narrative.

Tacitus's work did not provide an easy source for summaries of early imperial history, nor (one may guess) was his political attitude popular in the ruling circles; but he was read and his text copied until in the 4th century Ammianus Marcellinus continued his work and followed his style. In modern scholarship Tacitus's writings are studied seriously—with critical reservation—to reconstruct the early history of the Roman Empire. On the literary side they are appreciated as stylistic masterpieces.

PLINY THE YOUNGER

(b. 61/62 CE—d. c. 113, Bithynia, Asia Minor [now in Turkey])

The Roman author and administrator Gaius Plinius Caecilius Secundus, better known as Pliny the Younger, is known chiefly for his collection of private letters of great literary charm that intimately illustrates public and private life in the heyday of the Roman Empire. Born into a wealthy family and adopted by his uncle, Pliny the Elder (author of the celebrated *Natural History*, an encyclopaedic work on scientific matters), the younger Pliny began to practice law at 18. His reputation in the civil-law courts placed him in demand in the political court that tried provincial officials for extortion. His most notable success (100) was securing condemnation of a governor in Africa and a group of officials from Spain. Meanwhile he had attained the highest administrative posts, becoming praetor (93) and consul (100).

Pliny had financial ability and successively headed the military treasury and the senatorial treasury (94–100). After administering the drainage board of the city of Rome (104–106), he was sent (c. 110) by Emperor Trajan to investigate corruption in the municipal administration of Bithynia, where apparently he died two years later.

Like his contemporary, the historian Tacitus, Pliny was conventional, accepting the Roman Empire, serving under "good" and "bad" emperors, and making the conventional complaints against the latter in his writings. Between 100 and 109 he published nine books of selected, private letters, beginning with those covering events from the death of Emperor Domitian (October 97) to the early part of 100. The 10th book contains addresses to Emperor Trajan on sundry official problems and the emperor's replies.

The private letters are carefully written, occasional letters on diverse topics. Each holds an item of recent social, literary, political, or domestic news, or sometimes an account of an earlier but contemporary historical event, or else initiates moral discussion of a problem. Each has a single subject and is written in a style that mixes, in Pliny's terminology, the historical, the poetical, and the oratorical manner, to fit the theme. The composition of these *litterae curiosius scriptae* ("letters written with special care") was a fashion among the wealthy, and Pliny developed it into a miniature art form. There are letters of advice to young men, notes of greeting and inquiry, and descriptions of scenes of natural beauty or of natural curiosities. Pliny also left a detailed picture of the amateur literary world with its custom of reciting works to seek critical revision from friends. Estate business is a frequent theme, and letters concerned with such matters reveal the abilities for which Trajan chose him to reorganize the municipal finances and local government of Bithynia.

Pliny's letters introduce many of the leading figures of Roman society in the 12 years after the death of Domitian—men of letters, politicians, administrators, generals, and rising young men of rank. They make possible the social reconstruction of an age for which there is otherwise no serious historical record. He was adept at brief character sketches, his works being less satirical, more kindly, and possibly more complete than those of Tacitus. He was also a devotee of literature.

Pliny published his forensic and literary speeches with care, and late in life he took to the contemporary fashion for light verse in the style of Martial. Though fulsome in the praise of contemporary writers, his judgment of the dead Statius was fair: "He was ever writing poems with greater pains than ability." His letters to his fellow advocate Tacitus, then occupied with his first major work, tell the little that is known about the date and circumstances of the composition of the *Historiae,* to which Pliny contributed his famous account of the eruption of Vesuvius. The biographer Suetonius was among his protégés.

A two-volume translation (1969) by Betty Radice of the letters and Pliny's panegyric to Trajan is available from Loeb Classical Library.

SUETONIUS

(b. 69 CE, probably Rome [Italy]—d. after 122)

The Roman biographer and antiquarian Gaius Suetonius Tranquillus (Suetonius) is known for his collection of writings including *De viris illustribus* ("Concerning Illustrious Men"), a collection of short biographies of celebrated Roman literary figures, and *De vita Caesarum* (*Lives of the Caesars*). The latter book, seasoned with bits of gossip and scandal relating to the lives of the first 11 emperors, secured him lasting fame.

Suetonius's family was of the knightly class, or *equites.* A friend and protégé of the government official and letter writer Pliny the Younger, he seems to have studied and then abandoned the law as a career. After Pliny's death Suetonius found another patron, Septicius Clarus, to whom he later dedicated *De vita Caesarum.* Upon the accession of Emperor Hadrian (117), he entered the imperial service, holding, probably simultaneously, the posts of controller of the Roman libraries, keeper of the archives, and adviser to the emperor on cultural matters. Probably around 121 he was promoted to secretary of the imperial correspondence, but in 122 or somewhat later he was dismissed for the neglect of court formality, after which he presumably devoted himself to literary pursuits.

Most of Suetonius's writings were antiquarian, dealing with such subjects as Greek pastimes, the history of Roman spectacles and shows, oaths and imprecations and their origins, terminology of clothing, well-known courtesans, physical defects, and the growth of the civil service. An encyclopaedia called *Prata* ("Meadows"), a work like the *Natural History* of Pliny the Elder, was attributed to him and often quoted in late antiquity.

Suetonius's *De viris illustribus* is divided into short books on Roman poets, orators, historians, grammarians and rhetoricians, and perhaps philosophers. Very nearly all that is known about the lives of Rome's eminent authors stems ultimately from this work, which survives only in the whole of one section and in the preface and five lives from another section. The lives of Horace, Lucan, Terence, and Virgil, for example, are known from writers who derived their facts from Suetonius.

De vita Caesarum, which treats Julius Caesar and the emperors up to Domitian, is largely responsible for that vivid picture of Roman society and its leaders, morally and politically decadent, that dominated historical thought until modified in modern times by the discovery of nonliterary evidence. The biographies are organized not chronologically but by topics: the emperor's family background, career before accession, public actions, private life, appearance, personality, and death. Though free with scandalous gossip, they are largely silent on the growth, administration, and defense of the empire. Suetonius is free from the bias of the senatorial class that distorts much Roman historical writing. His sketches of the habits and appearance of the emperors are invaluable, but, like Plutarch, he used "characteristic anecdote" without exhaustive inquiry into its authenticity.

De vita Caesarum is still exciting reading. Suetonius wrote with firmness and brevity. He loved the *mot juste*, and his use of vocabulary enhanced his pictorial vividness. Above all he was unrhetorical, unpretentious, and capable of molding complex events into lucid expression.

ASHVAGHOSHA

(b. 80 CE?, Ayodhya, India—d. 150?, Peshawar [now in Pakistan])

The philosopher and poet Ashvaghosha (Sanskrit Aśvaghoṣa) is considered India's greatest poet before Kalidasa (5th century) and the father of Sanskrit drama. He popularized the style of Sanskrit poetry known as *kavya*. Ashvaghosha was born a Brahman. Legend obscures the man, but it is known that he was an outspoken opponent of Buddhism until, after a heated debate with a noted Buddhist scholar on the relative merits of Hinduism and Buddhism, he accepted the value of Buddhism and became a disciple of his erstwhile opponent.

While in Varanasi (Benares), where the Buddha had preached his first sermon, Ashvaghosha saw the city conquered by the Kushan (Kushana) emperor Kanishka, a devout Buddhist. A huge war indemnity was demanded, and the ruler of Varanasi handed over instead a symbolic tribute, a begging bowl said to have been used by both the Buddha and Ashvaghosha. Apparently the philosopher rose to the position of spiritual counsellor in Kanishka's court at Peshawar.

A brilliant orator, Ashvaghosha spoke at length on Mahayana (Greater Vehicle) Buddhist doctrine at the fourth Buddhist council, which he helped organize. His fame lay largely in his ability to explain the intricate concepts of Mahayana Buddhism. Among the works attributed to him are the *Mahayana-shraddhotpada-shastra* ("The Awakening of Faith in the Mahayana"); the *Buddhacarita* ("Poetic Discourse on the Acts of the Buddha"), a loving account of the Buddha's life and teachings in verse; the *Mahalankara* ("Book of Glory"); and the *Saundarananda* ("Of Sundari and Nanda"). Ashvaghosha anticipated the style of the Hindu *mahakavya* authors. The *kavya* remains influential in modern Indian languages and literatures.

LUCIAN

(b. 120 CE, Samosata, Commagene, Syria [now Samsat, Turkey] — d. after 180, Athens [Greece])

The sole source of information about Lucian's life is his own writings, but he says little about himself — and not all that he says is to be taken seriously. Moreover, since the chronology of his works is very obscure, the events of his life can be reconstructed only in broad outline, and the order and dating of these events are matters of mere probability.

Life

As a boy Lucian (Greek Lucianos, Latin Lucianus) showed a talent for making clay models and was therefore apprenticed to his uncle, a sculptor. They quarreled, and Lucian soon left home for western Asia Minor, in whose cities he acquired a Greek literary education. He became particularly familiar with the works of Homer, Plato, and the comic poets. So successfully did he master the Greek language (he was raised speaking Aramaic) and culture that he began a career as a public speaker, traveling from city to city giving model speeches and public lectures to display his eloquence and probably also pleading in court. After touring Greece he went to Italy and then to Gaul (modern France). To this period of his life belong many of his surviving declamations on mythological and other stock themes and his rhetorical prologues.

Lucian was evidently successful as a rhetorician, but he seems never to have reached the first rank in his profession. It may have been disillusion with the emptiness of his career that led him to give up his wandering life and settle in Athens in the late '50s of the 2nd century. In Athens he was able to extend his knowledge of Greek literature and thought far beyond anything required of a rhetorician.

In this early Athenian period Lucian gave up public speaking and took to writing critical and satirical essays on the intellectual life of his time, either in the form of Platonic dialogues or, in imitation of Menippus, in a mixture of prose and verse. Lucian's writings apparently sustained the reputation he had won as a public speaker.

Thanks to the patronage of his Roman friends, he obtained a lucrative post in Alexandria as *archistator*, a kind of chief court usher. After some years he returned to Athens and took up public speaking again. The date and circumstances of his death are unknown.

Works

Of the 80 prose works traditionally attributed to Lucian, about 10 are spurious. The writings of Lucian are outstanding for their mordant and malicious wit, embodying a sophisticated and often embittered critique of the shams and follies of the literature, philosophy, and intellectual life of his day. Lucian satirized almost every aspect of human behaviour. One of his favourite topics is the human failure to realize the transience of greatness and wealth. This theme permeates his dialogue *Charon*, while in the *Dialogues of the Dead* and other pieces, the Cynic philosopher Menippus is made to jibe at kings and aristocrats, reminding them how much more they have lost by death than he.

In *Timon* Lucian recounts how Timon, after impoverishing himself by his generosity and becoming a hermit, is restored to wealth, once again to be surrounded by toadies to whom he gives short shrift. Other human frailties Lucian satirized are the folly of bargaining with the gods by sacrifices, crying over spilt milk when bereaved, and the love of telling or listening to strange tales. In *True History*, which starts by warning the reader that its events are completely untrue and impossible, Lucian describes a voyage that starts on the sea, continues in the skies, and includes visits to the belly of a whale and to heaven and hell; the tale is a satirical parody of all those fantastic travelers' tales that strain human credulity. In *Nigrinus* Lucian makes a Platonic philosopher censure the evils of Rome, contrasting the pretentiousness, lack of culture, and avarice of the Romans with the quiet, cultured life of the Athenians.

Lucian is particularly critical of those whom he considers impostors. In *Alexander* Lucian attacks the popular magician and wonder-working charlatan Alexander the Paphlagonian and gives an account of the various hoaxes by which Alexander was amassing wealth as a priest of Asclepius and a seer. Another contemporary personage dubbed by Lucian as an impostor was the Cynic philosopher Peregrinus, who committed public suicide by setting fire to himself on a pyre at the Olympic Games of 165 CE.

Lucian regarded the worst charlatans of all to be those philosophers who failed to practice what they preached. *Banquet* gives an amusing account of an imaginary wedding feast given by a patron of the arts. Among the guests are representatives of every philosophical school, who all behave outrageously and start fighting over delicacies to take home when the party comes to an end. Hypocritical philosophers are also attacked in *Fisher,* in which the founders of the philosophical schools return to life to indict Lucian for writing *The Auction of Lives,*, which was itself a lighthearted work in which Zeno, Epicurus, and others are auctioned by Hermes in the underworld but fetch next to nothing. Lucian's defense is that he was attacking not the founders of the schools but their present unworthy successors. The philosophers acquit Lucian and call to trial their modern disciples, who refuse to have their lives examined until Lucian "fishes" for them from the Acropolis using a bait of gold and figs. He soon has a fine catch of philosophers, who are renounced by the founders of the schools and hurled to their deaths from the Acropolis.

Lucian follows the lead of Xenophanes, Plato, and others also in complaining about the absurd beliefs concerning the Olympian gods. Thus the discreditable love affairs of Zeus with mortal women play a prominent part in *Dialogues of the Gods*, and in *Zeus Confuted* and *Tragic Zeus* the leader of the gods is powerless to intervene on earth and prove his omnipotence to coldly skeptical Cynic and Epicurean philosophers. Lucian's interest in philosophy was basically superficial, however, and his attitude to philosophical studies is best seen in *Banquet*, where, after noting how much worse the philosophers are behaving than the ordinary guests, he cannot help reflecting that book learning is worthless if it does not improve one's conduct.

Lucian's best work in the field of literary criticism is his treatise *How to Write History*. In this work he stresses the impartiality, detachment, and rigorous devotion to truth that characterize the ideal historian. He also comments on the ideal historical style and provides amusing descriptions of contemporary historians who imitate Thucydides by introducing plagues and funeral orations into their narratives.

Lucian's primary literary models for his works were the satires of Menippus, which mocked institutions, ideas, and conventions in a mixture of prose and verse. But Lucian improved on the Menippean satire by creating his own harmonious blend of Platonic dialogue and comic fantasy, and he raised it to the level of art by his broad, fluent, and seemingly effortless command of the Attic Greek language and literary style. The only thing that had real value in his eyes and that provided him with a standard of judgment was Classical Greek literature. In this turning toward a half-imaginary, idealized past, Lucian was at one with his age. His own classicizing style served as a model for writers of the later Roman Empire and for the Byzantine period.

LUCIUS APULEIUS

(b. *c.* 124, Madauros, Numidia [near modern Mdaourouch, Algeria]—d. probably after 170)

The Platonic philosopher, rhetorician, and author Lucius Apuleius is remembered for *The Golden Ass*, a prose narrative that proved influential long after his death. The work, called *Metamorphoses* by its author, narrates the adventures of a young man changed by magic into an ass.

Apuleius, who was educated at Carthage and Athens, traveled in the Mediterranean region and became interested in contemporary religious initiation rites, among them the ceremonies associated with worship of the Egyptian goddess Isis. Intellectually versatile and acquainted with works of both Latin and Greek writers, he taught rhetoric in Rome before returning to Africa to marry a rich widow, Aemilia Pudentilla. To meet her family's charge that he had practiced magic to win her affection, he wrote the *Apologia* ("Defense"), the major source for his biography.

For *The Golden Ass* it is likely that he used material from the lost *Metamorphoses* by Lucius of Patrae, which is cited by some as the source for the brief extant Greek work on a similar theme, *Lucius, or the Ass*, attributed to the Greek rhetorician Lucian. Though Apuleius's novel is fiction, it contains a few definitely autobiographical details, and its hero has been seen as a partial portrait of its author. It is particularly valuable for its description of the ancient religious mysteries, and Lucius's restoration from animal to human shape, with the aid of Isis, and his acceptance into her priesthood suggests that Apuleius himself had been initiated into that cult. Considered a revelation of ancient manners, the work has been praised for its entertaining and at times bawdy episodes that alternate between the dignified, the ludicrous, the voluptuous, and the horrible. Its "Cupid and Psyche" tale (Books 4 through 6) has been frequently imitated by later writers, including the English poets Shakerley Marmion in 1637, Mary Tighe in 1805, William Morris in *The Earthly Paradise* (1868–70), and Robert Bridges in 1885 and 1894, and C.S. Lewis in the novel *Till We Have Faces: A Myth Retold* (1956). Some of Lucius's adventures reappear in *The Decameron* by Giovanni Boccaccio, in *Don Quixote* by Miguel de Cervantes, and in *Gil Blas* by Alain-René Lesage.

Of Apuleius's other literary works his *Florida* is, like *The Golden Ass*, stylistically affected.

More influential than this collection of the author's declamations on various subjects are his philosophical treatises. He wrote three books on Plato (the third is lost): *De Platone et eius dogmate* ("On Plato and His Teaching") and *De Deo Socratis* ("On the God of Socrates"), which expounds the Platonic notion of demons, beneficent creatures intermediate between gods and mortals. His *De mundo* ("On the World") adapts a treatise incorrectly attributed to Aristotle. Apuleius asserts that he wrote a number of poems and works on natural history, but these works are lost. The noted *Asclepius*, a Latin translation of a (now lost) Greek Hermetic dialogue, has been wrongly attributed to him. His collected works were first edited by Joannes Andreas (1469); later editions in Latin include a three-volume collection by Rudolf Helm and Paul Thomas (1905–10) and the *Index Apuleianus* by William Abbott Oldfather, Howard Vernon Canter, and Ben Edwin Perry (1934). In English, *The Golden Ass* was translated by P.G. Walsh in 1994, and other modern editions appear in the Loeb Classical Library series.

CAO ZHI

(b. 192, China—d. 232, Chenjun [now Huaiyang, Henan province])

Cao Zhi (spelled Ts'ao Chih in an earlier transliteration) is one of China's greatest lyric poets and the son of the famous general Cao Cao. He was also called Cao Zijian or Chensiwang (Chinese: "Prince Si of Chen"). Cao Zhi was born at the time his father was assuming command over the northern third of China, later known as the Wei kingdom.

In a family of poets—the verses of Cao Cao and Cao Pi (Cao Zhi's older brother and bitter rival) were also widely known—Cao Zhi's talents quickly surpassed those of his father and brother. Indeed, Cao Cao was so impressed with the poetic skill that Cao Zhi displayed from his earliest years that he once considered making him crown prince instead of Cao Pi. Added to Cao Pi's resentment of Cao Zhi was the fact that as an adolescent Cao Zhi had fallen in love with the Lady Zhen, the woman who later became the consort of his elder brother. Thus, when Cao Pi ascended the throne as Wendi of Wei in 220, he took pains to make his younger brother's life as difficult as possible.

Cao Zhi's resulting frustration and misery is the subject of much of his poetry. Writing in the then-standard five-word line, Cao Zhi extended and strengthened its use to make it a flexible and yet precise vehicle for the expression of his wide-ranging emotions.

RUAN JI

(b. 210, Chenliu, Henan province, China—
d. 263, Luoyang, Henan province)

The eccentric Chinese poet Ruan Ji is the most renowned member of the Seven Sages of the Bamboo Grove, a group of 3rd-century poets and philosophers who sought refuge from worldly pressures in a life of drinking and verse making. His name is spelled Juan Chi in an earlier transliteration system, and he is also called Ruan Bubing.

Born into a prominent family, Ruan Ji was faced with the choice of silent acceptance of the corrupt political maneuverings of the Wei dynasty court (220–265/266) or severe punishment. He found a solution that enabled him to escape both hypocrisy and harm. In a successful effort to avoid commitment to a marriage alliance that he considered dangerous and distasteful, the poet purposely remained drunk for 60 days. When he felt the need to speak out against the ruling class, he did so through poems and essays heavily veiled in allegory. Finally, he retired to a life of pleasure and poetry in the countryside, far from the pressures of the palace.

Despite Ruan Ji's clever tricks at court and his hedonism, his poetry is melancholy and pessimistic and has been praised for its profound view of a troubled time. His best-known collection is *Yonghuaishi* (*Songs of My Heart*).

Lu Ji

(b. 261, Wu [now Suzhou, Zhejiang province], China—d. 303, China)

Lu Ji (also spelled Lu Chi) is a renowned Chinese literary critic and the first important writer to emerge from the kingdom of Wu (222–280). Grandson of the great Lu Xun, one of the founders of the Wu kingdom, and fourth son of Lu Kang, the Wu commander in chief, Lu Ji remained in obscurity for nine years after the Wu kingdom was subjugated by the Jin dynasty (265–317). In 289 Lu traveled to Luoyang, the imperial capital, where he was warmly received by the literary elite and appointed president of the national university. He eventually rose to higher official posts and became a member of the nobility, but he was executed on a false charge of treason.

Although Lu left a considerable body of lyric poetry in imitative style, he is better known as a writer of *fu*, an intricately structured form of poetry mixed with prose. A prime specimen of this form is his *Wenfu* ("On

Literature"; Eng. trans. *The Art of Writing*), a subtle and important work of literary criticism that defines and demonstrates the principles of composition with rare insight and precision.

TAO QIAN

(b. 365, Xunyang [now Jiujiang, Jiangxi province], China—
d. 427, Xunyang)

Tao Qian (spelled Tao Ch'ien in an earlier translit-eration system), also called Tao Yuanming, is one of China's greatest poets and a noted recluse. He was born into an impoverished aristocratic family, and he took a minor official post while in his 20s in order to support his aged parents. After about 10 years at that post and a brief term as county magistrate, he resigned from official life, repelled by its excessive formality and widespread corruption. With his wife and children he retired to a farming village south of the Yangtze River. Despite the hardships of a farmer's life and frequent food shortages, Tao was contented, writing poetry, cultivating the chrysanthemums that became inseparably associated with his poetry, and drinking wine, also a common subject of his verse.

Because the taste of Tao's contemporaries was for an elaborate and artificial style, his simple and straightforward poetry was not fully appreciated until the Tang dynasty (618–907). A master of the five-word line, Tao has been described as the first great poet of *tianyuan* ("fields and gardens"), landscape poetry inspired by pastoral scenes (as opposed to the then-fashionable *shanshui* ["mountains and rivers"] poetry). Essentially a Daoist in his philosophical outlook on life and death, he also freely adopted the elements of Confucianism and Buddhism that most appealed to him.

One of his best-loved poems is the following *gushi* ("ancient style poem"), translated by Arthur Waley. It is one of 12 poems of this type that he wrote under the influence of wine:

> *I built my hut in a zone of human habitation,*
> *Yet near me there sounds no noise of horse or coach.*
> *Would you know how this is possible?*
> *A heart that is distant creates a wilderness round it.*
> *I pluck chrysanthemums under the eastern hedge,*
> *Then gaze long at the distant hills.*
> *The mountain air is fresh at the dusk of day;*
> *The flying birds two by two return.*
> *In these things there lies a deep meaning;*
> *Yet when we would express it, words suddenly fail us.*

XIE LINGYUN

(b. 385, Shining [now Sanjie, Shengzhou], Zhejiang province, China—d. 433, Canton)

The prominent Chinese writer of the Six Dynasties era (220–589 CE) is Xie Lingyun (also spelled Hsieh Ling-yün in an earlier transliteration system), who is known chiefly as a nature poet. The scion of an aristocratic house associated with the displaced southern court, Xie was an official under the Eastern Jin and Liu-Song dynasties, but factional intrigues later disrupted his career, leading to his frequent dismissal and eventual execution in exile.

Xie was knowledgeable about the principles of both Buddhism and Daoism and merged them with Confucianism in his religious works. His literary reputation, however, derived from his poetry, particularly his evocation of a spiritual presence in the wild southern landscape. His refined, imagistic verse set the fashion for his age, prompting early critics to prize his *shanshui* ("mountain and stream") land-scapes above the more pastoral *tianyuan* ("field and garden") scenes depicted by Tao Qian, his countryman and contemporary. Indeed, Xie's poems outnumber those of other Six Dynasties poets in the *Wenxuan* ("Literary Anthology"), the 6th-century canon that defined later Chinese literary tastes.

KALIDASA

(fl. 5th century CE, India)

The Sanskrit poet and dramatist Kalidasa (Sanskrit Kālidāsa) is probably the greatest Indian writer of any epoch. The six works identified as genuine are the dramas *Abhijnanashakuntala* ("The Recognition of Shakuntala"), *Vikramorvashi* ("Urvashi Won by Valour"), and *Malavikagnimitra* ("Malavika and Agnimitra"); the epic poems *Raghuvamsha* ("Dynasty of Raghu") and *Kumarasambhava* ("Birth of the War God"); and the lyric "Meghaduta" ("Cloud Messenger").

As with most classical Indian authors, little is known about Kalidasa's person or his historical relationships. His poems suggest but nowhere declare that he was a Brahman (priest), liberal yet committed to the orthodox Hindu worldview. His name, literally "servant of Kali," presumes that he was a Shaivite (follower of the god Shiva, whose consort was Kali), though occasionally he eulogizes other gods, notably Vishnu.

A Sinhalese tradition says that he died on the island of Sri Lanka during the reign of Kumaradasa, who ascended the throne in 517. A more persistent legend makes Kalidasa one of the "nine gems" at the court of the fabulous king

Vikramaditya of Ujjain. Unfortunately, there are several known Vikramadityas (Sun of Valour—a common royal appellation); likewise, the nine distinguished courtiers could not have been contemporaries. It is certain only that the poet lived sometime between the reign of Agnimitra, the second Shunga king (*c.* 170 BCE) and the hero of one of his dramas, and the Aihole inscription of 634 CE, which lauds Kalidasa. He is apparently imitated, though not named, in the Mandasor inscription of 473. No single hypothesis accounts for all the discordant information and conjecture surrounding this date.

An opinion accepted by many—but not all—scholars is that Kalidasa should be associated with Chandra Gupta II (reigned *c.* 380–*c.* 415). The most convincing but most conjectural rationale for relating Kalidasa to the brilliant Gupta dynasty is simply the character of his work, which appears as both the perfect reflection and the most thorough statement of the cultural values of that serene and sophisticated aristocracy.

Tradition has associated many works with the poet; criticism identifies six as genuine and one more as likely ("Ritusamhara," the "Garland of the Seasons," perhaps a youthful work). Attempts to trace Kalidasa's poetic and intellectual development through these works are frustrated by the impersonality that is characteristic of classical Sanskrit literature. His works are judged by the Indian tradition as realizations of literary qualities inherent in the Sanskrit language and its supporting culture. Kalidasa has become the archetype for Sanskrit literary composition.

In drama, his *Abhijnanashakuntala* is the most famous and is usually judged the best Indian literary effort of any period. Taken from an epic legend, the work tells of the seduction of the nymph Shakuntala by King Dushyanta, his rejection of the girl and his child, and their subsequent reunion in heaven. The epic myth is important because of the child, for he is Bharata, eponymous ancestor of the Indian nation (Bharatavarsha, "Subcontinent of Bharata"). Kalidasa remakes the story into a love idyll whose characters represent a pristine aristocratic ideal: the girl, sentimental, selfless, alive to little but the delicacies of nature, and the king, first servant of the *dharma* (religious and social law and duties), protector of the social order, resolute hero, yet tender and suffering agonies over his lost love. The plot and characters are made believable by a change Kalidasa has wrought in the story: Dushyanta is not responsible for the lovers' separation; he acts only under a delusion caused by a sage's curse. As in all of Kalidasa's works, the beauty of nature is depicted with a precise elegance of metaphor that would be difficult to match in any of the world's literatures.

The second drama, *Vikramorvashi* (possibly a pun on *vikramaditya*), tells a legend as old as the Vedas (earliest Hindu scriptures), though very differently. Its theme is the love of a mortal for a divine maiden; it is well known for the "mad scene" (Act IV) in which the king, grief-stricken, wanders through a lovely forest apostrophizing various flowers and trees as though they were his love. The scene was intended in part to be sung or danced.

The third of Kalidasa's dramas, *Malavikagnimitra*, is of a different stamp—a harem intrigue, comical and playful, but not less accomplished for lacking any high purpose. The play (unique in this respect) contains datable references, the historicity of which have been much discussed.

Kalidasa's efforts in *kavya* (strophic poetry) are of uniform quality and show two different subtypes, epic and lyric. Examples of the epic are the two long poems *Raghuvamsha* and *Kumarasambhava*. The first recounts the legends of the hero Rama's forebears and descendants; the second tells the picaresque story of Shiva's seduction by his consort Parvati, the conflagration of Kama (the god of desire), and the birth of Kumara (Skanda), Shiva's son. These stories are mere pretext for the poet to enchain stanzas, each metrically and grammatically complete, redounding with complex and reposeful imagery. Kalidasa's mastery of Sanskrit as a poetic medium is nowhere more marked.

A lyric poem, the "Meghaduta," contains, interspersed in a message from a lover to his absent beloved, an extraordinary series of unexcelled and knowledgeable vignettes, describing the mountains, rivers, and forests of northern India.

The society reflected in Kalidasa's work is that of a courtly aristocracy sure of its dignity and power. Kalidasa has perhaps done more than any other writer to wed the older, Brahmanic religious tradition, particularly its ritual concern with Sanskrit, to the needs of a new and brilliant secular Hinduism. The fusion, which epitomizes the renaissance of the Gupta period, did not, however, survive its fragile social base; with the disorders following the collapse of the Gupta Empire, Kalidasa became a memory of perfection that neither Sanskrit nor the Indian aristocracy would know again.

VARIOUS: Al-Mu'allaqāt

*A*l-Mu'allaqāt is a collection of seven pre-Islamic Arabic *qaṣīdahs* (odes), each considered to be its author's best piece. Since the authors themselves are among the dozen or so most famous poets of the 6th century, the selection enjoys a unique position in Arabic literature, representing the finest of early Arabic poetry.

Taken together, the poems of the *Mu'allaqāt* provide an excellent picture of Bedouin life, manners, and modes of thought. The idea of grouping together these particular poems is most commonly attributed to Ḥammād

Muslims gather in prayer around the Ka'bah in Mecca, February 2002. Legend has it that scrolls containing the collected odes of the Al-Mu'allaqāt, writ in gold, once hung from this holy Muslim shrine.
© **AP Images**

al-Rāwiyah, who was an 8th-century collector of early poetry. An often-repeated legend that originated in the 10th century states that the poems were written down in golden letters on scrolls of linen that were then hung, or "suspended" (*mu'allaq*), on the walls of the Ka'bah in Mecca. It is by no means clear, however, that Ḥammād himself ever used the name *Mu'allaqāt* in referring to his compilation. Instead, he appears to have referred to it as the "seven renowned ones" (*al-sab' al-mashhūrāt*) or simply as "the renowned ones" (*al-mashhūrāt*). Most probably, the name *Mu'allaqāt* in this context is a derivative of the word '*ilq*, "a precious thing," so that its meaning would be "the poems which are esteemed precious." All that can be said with certainty is that the name *Mu'allaqāt* appeared about 900 to distinguish the seven poems as a subset in a larger compilation of poems.

The precise poems included in the *Mu'allaqāt* present another puzzle. The list usually accepted as standard was recorded by Ibn 'Abd Rabbih and names poems by Imru' al-Qays, Ṭarafah, Zuhayr, Labīd, 'Antarah, 'Amr ibn Kulthum, and al-Ḥārith ibn Ḥilliza. Such authorities as Ibn Qutaybah, however, count 'Abid ibn al-Abras as one of the seven, while Abū 'Ubaydah replaces the last two poets of Ibn 'Abd Rabbih's list with al-Nābighah al-Dhubyānī and al-A'shā.

Of the authors of the *Mu'allaqāt*, the earliest is Imru' al-Qays, who lived in the early part of the 6th century. The others belong to the latter half of that century. Zuhayr and Labīd are said to have survived into the time of Islam, but their poetic output belongs to the pre-Islamic period.

The *Mu'allaqāt* odes are all in the classical *qaṣīdah* pattern, which some Arab scholars believed to have been created by Imru' al-Qays. After a conventional prelude, the *nasib*, in which the poet calls to mind the memory of a former love, most of the rest of the ode consists of a succession of movements that describe the poet's horse or camel, scenes of desert events, and other aspects of Bedouin life and warfare. The main theme of the *qaṣīdah* (the *madīḥ*, or panegyric, the poet's tribute to himself, his tribe, or his patron) is often disguised in these vivid descriptive passages, which are the chief glory of the *Mu'allaqāt*. Their vivid imagery, exact observation, and deep feeling of intimacy with nature in the Arabian Desert contribute to the *Mu'allaqāt*'s standing as a masterpiece of world literature. The lively description of a desert storm at the end of Imru' al-Qays's *qaṣīdah* is a splendid example of such passages.

However, it should not be thought that the poems of the *Mu'allaqāt* are merely naturalistic or romantic descriptions of Bedouin life; their language and imagery embody a complex system of ethical values passed from generation to generation through the poetry.

English translations of *Al-Muʿallaqāt* include *The Seven Golden Odes of Pagan Arabia* (1903) by Lady Anne and Sir Wilfrid Scawen Blunt, *The Seven Odes* (1957, reissued 1983) by A.J. Arberry, *The Seven Poems Suspended in the Temple at Mecca* (1973, originally published in 1893) by Frank E. Johnson, and *The Golden Odes of Love* (1997) by Desmond O'Grady.

ᴀʟ-Kʜᴀɴsā'

(d. after 630)

Tumāḍir bint ʿAmr ibn al-Ḥārith ibn al-Sharīd, better known as al-Khansā' (Arabic: "The Snub-Nosed"), is one of the greatest Arab poets, famous for her elegies. The celebration of the life and courage of a tribal comrade fallen in battle is the occasion for the earliest elegies in Arabic. After an account of the death itself, these elegies include an appreciation of the hero's virtues, thus providing yet another occasion for the community to express its unifying principles.

The deaths of two of al-Khansā''s kinsmen—her brother Muʿāwiyah and her half-brother Ṣakhr, both of whom had been tribal heads and had been killed in tribal raids sometime before the advent of Islam—threw her into deep mourning. Here is one of her verses from an elegy on Ṣakhr:

On that day when I was forever parted from Ṣakhr,
Ḥassan's father,
I bade farewell to all pleasure and converse.
Ah, my grief for him, and my mother's grief!
Is he really consigned to the tomb morning and night?

Al-Khansā"s elegies on her brothers' deaths and that of her father made her the most celebrated poet of her time. When her tribe as a group accepted Islam, she went with them to Medina to meet the Prophet Muhammad, but she persisted in wearing the pre-Islamic mourning dress as an act of devotion to her brothers. When her four sons were slain in the Battle of Qādisīyah (637), the caliph 'Umar is said to have written her a letter congratulating her on their heroism and assigned her a pension.

The collected poetry of al-Khansā', the *Dīwān* (published in an English translation by Arthur Wormhoudt in 1973), reflects the pagan fatalism of the tribes of pre-Islamic Arabia. The poems are generally short and imbued with a strong and traditional sense of despair at the irretrievable loss of life. The elegies of al-Khansā' were highly influential, especially among later elegists.

KAKINOMOTO HITOMARO

(d. 708, Japan)

Kakinomoto Hitomaro was Japan's first great literary figure, and he has been venerated by the Japanese since earliest times. Among his surviving works are poems in the two major Japanese poetic forms of his day—*tanka* and *chōka*. Probably he also wrote *sedōka* ("head-repeated poem," consisting of two three-line verses of 5, 7, 7 syllables), a relatively minor song form that seems to have been first adapted to literary purposes by Hitomaro and to have barely survived him. All of the poems accepted as indisputably authored by Hitomaro (61 *tanka* and 16 *chōka*), as well as a large number of others attributed to him, are to be found in the *Man'yōshū* ("Collection of Ten Thousand

Kakinomoto Hitomaro, multicolour woodblock print by Utagawa Kuniyoshi, 1844–54. Library of Congress, Washington, D.C. (Digital File Number: LC-DIG-jpd-01964)

Leaves"), the first and largest of Japan's anthologies of native poetry. These poems, together with notes by the compilers, are the chief source for information on his life, about which very little is known.

Hitomaro is believed to have been born and reared near Nara. He entered the service of the court in a minor capacity, serving successively two imperial princes; imperial activities are celebrated in some of his most famous poems. Later he became a provincial official, and he is believed to have died in Iwami province (now Shimane prefecture). He seems to have had at least two wives.

Standing on the threshold of Japan's emergence from a preliterate to a literate, civilized society, Hitomaro achieved in his poems a splendid balance between the homely qualities of primitive song and the more sophisticated interests and literary techniques of a new age. He inherited the stiff techniques, plain imagery, and restricted range and subject matter—the traditional "word hoard"— of preliterate song. To that inheritance he added new subjects, modes, and concerns, as well as new rhetorical and other structural techniques (some of which may have been adapted from Chinese poetry), along with a new seriousness and importance of treatment and tone. Many of his longer poems are introduced by a kind of solemn "overture," relating the present with the divine past of the Japanese land and people.

All of Hitomaro's poems are suffused with a deep personal lyricism and with a broad humanity and sense of identity with others. Outstanding among his works are his poem on the ruined capital at Ōmi; his celebration of Prince Karu's journey to the plains of Aki; two poems each on the death of his first wife and on parting from his second; his lament on the death of Prince Takechi; and his poem composed on finding human remains on the island of Samine.

AL-AKHṬAL

(b. *c.* 640, Al-Ḥīrah, Mesopotamia, or the Syrian Desert—d. 710)

Ghiyāth ibn Ghawth ibn al-Ṣalt al-Akhṭal is a poet of the Umayyad period (661–750), esteemed for his perfection of Arabic poetic form in the old Bedouin tradition. Al-Akhṭal ("The Loquacious") was a Christian but did not take the duties of his religion seriously, being addicted to drink and women. He was a favourite panegyrist and friend of the Umayyad caliph Yazīd I and his generals Ziyād ibn Abīhī and al-Ḥajjāj. He continued as court poet to the caliph ʿAbd al-Malik but fell into disfavour under Walīd I. Al-Akhṭal's poetry is highly political; he is known for panegyrics that defended Umayyad policies and for invective that skewered those who opposed them.

Together with the poets Jarīr and al-Farazdaq, al-Akhṭal forms a famous trio in early Arabic literary history. Because they closely resembled one another in style and vocabulary, their relative superiority was disputed. The philologist Abū ʿUbaydah, however, placed al-Akhṭal highest of the three because among his poems there were 10 *qaṣīdahs* (formal odes) regarded as flawless and 10 others as nearly flawless, and this could not be said of the other poets.

AL-FARAZDAQ

(b. *c.* 641, Yamāmah region, Arabia—d. *c.* 728 or 730)

The Arab poet Tammām ibn Ghālib Abū Firās, better known as al-Farazdaq ("The Lump of Dough"), is famous for his satires in a period when poetry was an important political instrument. With his rival Jarīr, he represents the transitional period between Bedouin traditional culture and the new Muslim society that was being forged.

Living in Basra, al-Farazdaq composed satires on the Banū Nashal and Banū Fuqaim tribes, and when Ziyād ibn Abīhi, a member of the latter tribe, became governor of Iraq in 669, he was forced to flee to Medina, where he remained for several years. On the death of Ziyād, he returned to Basra and gained the support of Ziyād's son, ʿUbayd Allāh. When al-Ḥajjāj became governor (694), al-Farazdaq was again out of favour, in spite of the laudatory poems he dedicated to al-Ḥajjāj and members of his family; this was probably a result of the enmity of Jarīr, who had the ear of the governor. Al-Farazdaq became official poet to the caliph al-Walīd (reigned 705–715), to whom he dedicated a number of panegyrics. He also enjoyed the favour of the caliph Sulaymān (715–717) but was eclipsed when ʿUmar II became caliph in 717. He got a chance to recover patronage under Yazīd II (720–724), when an insurrection occurred and he wrote poems excoriating the rebel leader.

Al-Farazdaq was an eccentric of the first order, and his exploits, as well as his verses and his feud with Jarīr, provided subjects for discussion to generations of cultivated persons.

His *Dīwān,* the collection of his poetry, contains several thousand verses, including laudatory and satirical poems and laments. His poems are representative of the nomad poetry at its height. Most of them are characterized by a happy sincerity, but some of his satires are notably obscene.

'UMAR IBN ABĪ RABĪ'AH

(b. November 644, Mecca, Arabia [now in Saudi Arabia]—
d. 712/719, Mecca)

O ne of the great early Arabic poets, 'Umar ibn 'Abd
Allāh ibn Abī Rabī'ah al-Makhzūmī belonged to
the wealthy merchant family of Makhzūm, a member
of the Meccan tribe of Quraysh (of which the Prophet
Muhammad was also a member). 'Umar spent most of
his life in Mecca, also traveling to southern Arabia, Syria,
and Mesopotamia. Little is known about his life, for the
numerous anecdotes related about him are manifestly
literary fabrications. The internal evidence of his poetry,
however, gives a valuable picture of the social life of the
Meccan and Medinan aristocracy of his time.

His poetry centres on his own life and emotions,
eschewing the traditional themes of journeys, battles, and
tribal lore, and celebrates his love affairs with the noble
Arab ladies who came to Mecca on pilgrimage. Although
this genre had been sporadically practiced before his time,
'Umar ibn Abī Rabī'ah was the first to perfect it with a
light metre and an accurate emotional perception.

JARĪR

(b. *c.* 650, Uthayfīyah, Yamāmah region, Arabia [now in Saudi
Arabia]—d. *c.* 729, Yamāmah)

J arīr ibn 'Aṭīyah ibn al-Khaṭafā is one of the great
Arab poets of the Umayyad period, whose career and
poetry show the continued vitality of the pre-Islamic

246

Bedouin tradition. Jarīr's special skill lay in poems insulting personal rivals or the enemies of his patrons. After sharp verbal clashes in Arabia in defense of Kulayb, his tribe, Jarīr moved to Iraq. There he won the favour of the governor, al-Ḥajjāj, and wrote a number of poems in his praise. He also met the poet al-Farazdaq, with whom he had already begun a battle of poems that is said to have lasted 40 years. The results were collected in the following century as *naqā'id* ("slanging-matches on parallel themes"). The governor's goodwill earned Jarīr entry at the Umayyad court in Damascus. Jarīr was not able, however, to dislodge the poet al-Akhṭal from the esteem of the caliph 'Abd al-Malik, and another poetic battle ensued, also producing *naqā'id*. Of the caliphs who succeeded 'Abd al-Malik, only the pious 'Umar II seems to have favoured Jarīr, and much of Jarīr's life was spent away from court in his native Yamāmah.

Many of Jarīr's poems are in the conventional *qaṣīdah* ("ode") form. They typically open with an amatory prelude that is followed by invective and panegyric; the robust style of these later sections is frequently at odds with that of the prelude. Jarīr also wrote elegies, wisdom poetry, and epigrams.

CAEDMON

(fl. 658–680)

Caedmon is the first Old English Christian poet, whose fragmentary hymn to the creation remains a symbol of the adaptation of the aristocratic-heroic Anglo-Saxon verse tradition to the expression of Christian themes. His story is known from Bede the Venerable's *Ecclesiastical History of the English People*, which tells how Caedmon, an illiterate

Noah's Ark takes the form of a Viking ship with dragon prow in an illustration from a 10th-century manuscript of Caedmon. Photos .com/Jupiterimages

herdsman, retired from company one night in shame because he could not comply with the demand made of each guest to sing. Then in a dream a stranger appeared commanding him to sing of "the beginning of things," and the herdsman found himself uttering "verses which he had never heard." When Caedmon awoke he related his dream to the farm bailiff under whom he worked and was conducted by him to the monastery at Streaneshalch (now called Whitby). The abbess St. Hilda believed that Caedmon was divinely inspired and, to test his powers, proposed that he should render into verse a portion of sacred history, which the monks explained. By the following morning he had fulfilled the task. At the request of the abbess he became an inmate of the monastery.

Throughout the remainder of his life his more learned brethren expounded Scripture to him, and all that he heard he reproduced in vernacular poetry. All of his poetry was on sacred themes, and its unvarying aim was to turn men from sin to righteousness. In spite of all the poetic renderings that Caedmon supposedly made, however, it is only the original dream hymn of nine historically precious, but poetically uninspired, lines that can be attributed to him with confidence. The hymn—extant in 17 manuscripts, some in the poet's Northumbrian dialect, some in other Old English dialects—set the pattern for almost the whole art of Anglo-Saxon verse.

BANA

(fl. 7th century CE)

B ana, also called Banabhatta, is one of the great masters of Sanskrit prose, famed principally for his chronicle, *Harshacharita* (c. 640; "The Life of Harsha"), depicting the court and times of the Buddhist emperor Harsha (reigned *c.* 606–647) of northern India.

Bana gives some autobiographical account of himself in the early chapters of the *Harshacharita.* He was born into an illustrious family of Brahmans; his mother died when he was a small child, and he was raised by his father with loving care. His father died, however, when Bana was 14, and for some years he traveled adventurously, visiting various courts and universities with a colourful group of friends—including his two half brothers by a lower-caste woman, a snake doctor, a goldsmith, a gambler, and a musician. At last he returned home and married; then one day he was called to the court of Harsha. Treated coolly at first by the emperor, perhaps because of some gossip about his wayward youth, in time he won the emperor's high regard.

Bana's biography of Harsha provides valuable information about the period, though with some obvious exaggeration in the emperor's favour. Written in the ornate *kavya* style, involving extremely lengthy constructions, elaborate descriptions, and poetic devices, the work has great vitality and a wealth of keenly observed detail. His second great work, the prose romance *Kadambari*, is named for the heroine of the novel. The book describes the affairs of two sets of lovers through a series of incarnations. Both works were left unfinished; the second was completed by the author's son, Bhusanabhatta.

YAMANOUE OKURA

(b. *c.* 660 – d. *c.* 733)

O ne of the most individualistic of Japan's classical poets was Yamanoue Okura. He lived and wrote in an age of bold experimentation when native Japanese poetry was developing rapidly under the stimulus of Chinese literature. His poems are characterized by a Confucian-inspired moral emphasis unique in Japanese poetry. The stern logic of Confucian morality, however, is often tempered with a Buddhist resignation more in keeping with the typical Japanese view of the world.

Relatively little is known of Okura's early life. From 726 to 732 he was governor of the province of Chikuzen, in Kyushu. There he was responsible to the governor-general of the island, Ōtomo Tabito, himself a major poet and patron of letters, and the two formed a close literary relationship that both influenced and encouraged Okura. All of Okura's extant work is contained in the 8th-century anthology *Man'yōshū*. The most famous of his poems is the "Hinkyū mondō" ("Dialogue on Poverty"), which treats the sufferings of poverty in the form of an exchange between a poor man and a destitute man. Also outstanding are poems expressing love for his children and laments on the death of his son, on the instability of human life, and on his own sickness and old age.

*A*NONYMOUS: The Book of the Dun Cow

The work known to English-speaking readers as *The Book of the Dun Cow* (Irish *Lebor na h-Uidre* or *Leabhar na h-Uidhri*) is the oldest surviving miscellaneous manuscript in Irish literature. It is so called because the original vellum upon which it was written was supposedly taken from the hide of the famous cow of St. Ciarán of Clonmacnoise. Compiled about 1100 by learned Irish monks at the monastery of Clonmacnoise from older manuscripts and oral tradition, the book is a collection of factual material and legends that date mainly from the 8th and 9th centuries, interspersed with religious texts. It contains a partial text of *The Cattle Raid of Cooley* (*Táin Bó Cuailnge*), the longest tale of the Old Irish Ulster cycle and the one that most nearly approaches epic stature, as well as other descriptions of the conflict between Ulster and Connaught. The book also includes a poem praising St. Columba, credited to Dallán Forgaill; a poem on winter, ascribed to Finn MacCumhail, the legendary hero of the Fenian cycle; historical accounts of Mongan, an Ulster king of the 7th century, and of the Battle of Cnucha; and the story of the court of Dá Derga, an Irish romantic saga.

BEDE THE VENERABLE

(b. 672/673, traditionally Monkton in Jarrow, Northumbria—
d. May 25, 735, Jarrow)

The Anglo-Saxon theologian, historian, and chronologist Bede (Baeda, Beda) the Venerable is best known today for his *Historia ecclesiastica gentis Anglorum* ("Ecclesiastical History of the English People"), a source vital to the history of the conversion to Christianity of the Anglo-Saxon tribes. During his lifetime and throughout the Middle Ages Bede's reputation was based mainly on his scriptural commentaries, copies of which found their way to many of the monastic libraries of western Europe. His method of dating events from the time of the incarnation, or Christ's birth—i.e., AD (a reckoning, incidentally, which is also present, though not stated in the abbreviation CE)—came into general use through the popularity of the *Historia ecclesiastica* and the two works on chronology.

Bede's influence was perpetuated at home through the school founded at York by his pupil Archbishop Egbert of York and was transmitted to the Continent by Alcuin, who studied there before becoming master of Charlemagne's palace school at Aachen.

Nothing is known of Bede's parentage. At the age of seven he was taken to the Monastery of St. Peter, founded at Wearmouth (near Sunderland, Durham) by Abbot St. Benedict Biscop, to whose care he was entrusted. By 685 he was moved to Biscop's newer Monastery of St. Paul at

Portrait of the Anglo-Saxon historian Bede the Venerable, whose most noteworthy work, Historia ecclesiastica, *recorded events in Britain from the raids by Julius Caesar to the arrival in Kent of St. Augustine.* **Hulton Archive/Getty Images**

Jarrow. Bede was ordained deacon when 19 years old and priest when 30. Apart from visits to Lindisfarne and York, he seems never to have left Wearmouth–Jarrow. Buried at Jarrow, his remains were removed to Durham and are now entombed in the Galilee Chapel of Durham Cathedral.

Bede's works fall into three groups: grammatical and "scientific," scriptural commentary, and historical and biographical. His earliest works include treatises on spelling, hymns, figures of speech, verse, and epigrams. His first treatise on chronology, *De temporibus* ("On Times"), with a brief chronicle attached, was written in 703. In 725 he completed a greatly amplified version, *De temporum ratione* ("On the Reckoning of Time"), with a much longer chronicle. Both these books were mainly concerned with the reckoning of Easter. His earliest biblical commentary was probably that on the Revelation to John (703?–709); in this and many similar works, his aim was to transmit and explain relevant passages from the Fathers of the Church. Although his interpretations were mainly allegorical, treating much of the biblical text as symbolic of deeper meanings, he used some critical judgment and attempted to rationalize discrepancies. Among his most notable are his verse (705–716) and prose (before 721) lives of St. Cuthbert, bishop of Lindisfarne. These works are uncritical and abound with accounts of miracles; a more exclusively historical work is *Historia abbatum* (*c.* 725; "Lives of the Abbots").

In 731/732 Bede completed his *Historia ecclesiastica*. Divided into five books, it recorded events in Britain from the raids by Julius Caesar (55–54 BCE) to the arrival in Kent (597 CE) of St. Augustine. For his sources he claimed the authority of ancient letters, the "traditions of our forefathers," and his own knowledge of contemporary events. Bede's *Historia ecclesiastica* leaves gaps tantalizing to secular historians. Although overloaded with the miraculous, it is the work of a scholar anxious to assess the accuracy of his sources and to record only what he regarded as trustworthy evidence. It remains an indispensable source for some of the facts and much of the feel of early Anglo-Saxon history. Bede was canonized by the Roman Catholic Church in 1899. His feast day is the date of his death, May 25.

BHAVABHUTI

(fl. 700)

The Indian dramatist and poet Bhavabhuti is known for a group of dramas, written in Sanskrit and noted for their suspense and vivid characterization, which rival the outstanding plays of the better-known playwright Kalidasa.

A Brahman of Vidarbha (the part of central India later called Berar), Bhavabhuti passed his literary life chiefly at the court of Yashovarman of Kannauj (Kanauj). Bhavabhuti is best known as the author of three plays: *Mahaviracharita* ("Exploits of the Great Hero"), which gives in seven acts the main incidents in the *Ramayana* up to the defeat of Ravana and the coronation of Rama; *Malatimadhava* ("Malati and Madhava"), a complex original love intrigue (complete with sorcery, human sacrifice, and Tantric practice) in 10 acts abounding in stirring, though sometimes improbable, incidents; and *Uttararamacharita* ("The Later Deeds of Rama"), which continues the story of Rama from his coronation to the banishment of Sita and their final reunion. This last play bears some resemblance to Shakespeare's *The Winter's Tale*. Though it contains far less action than the two earlier plays, it shows Bhavabhuti at the height of his power in characterization and in presenting suspense and climax. Bhavabhuti is considered to be a master of the *kavya* form, a literary style that is dominated by elaborate figures of speech, particularly metaphors and similes.

WANG WEI

(b. 701, Qi county, Shanxi province, China—d. 761, Chang'an [now Xi'an], Shaanxi province)

Wang Wei, also called Wang Youcheng, was one of the most famous men of arts and letters during the Tang dynasty, one of the golden ages of Chinese cultural history. Wang is popularly known as a model of humanistic education as expressed in poetry, music, and painting. In the 17th century the writer on art Dong Qichang established Wang as the founder of the revered Southern school of painter-poets, whom Dong characterized as more concerned with personal expression than surface representation.

Wang was born and brought up during the Tang dynasty (618–907) when the capital, Chang'an, was a truly cosmopolitan city that enjoyed both wealth and security. He received the prestigious *jinshi* ("advanced scholar") degree in the imperial civil-service examination system in 721—probably more for his musical talents than anything else, although he is said to have revealed his literary talents as early as age nine. He rose to high office but was soon demoted and given an unimportant position in Jizhou, before being recalled to the capital in 734 and given a post in the censorate. In 756, when Chang'an was occupied by the troops of the rebellious general An Lushan, Wang was captured and taken to the rebel capital at Luoyang, where he was forced to accept a post in the administration. After Chang'an and Luoyang had been recaptured by the imperial forces in 758, Wang was saved from disgrace because of the loyal sentiments expressed in a poem he had composed while a prisoner of the rebels and because of the intercession of his brother Wang Jin, an imperial high official. Toward the end of his life Wang Wei became disillusioned; further saddened by the deaths of his wife and mother, he withdrew into the study of Buddhism at his country villa at the Wang River, where many of his best poems were inspired by the local landscape.

Wang's art can only be reconstructed theoretically on the basis of contemporary records and surviving copies of his paintings. He undoubtedly painted a variety of subjects and employed various styles, but he is particularly renowned for being among the first to develop the art of landscape painting. He is best known for ink monochrome (*shuimo*) landscapes, especially snowscapes. The latter demanded the use of *pomo* ("breaking the ink"), a broader ink-wash technique with which he is typically associated.

Wang Wei's paintings were both innovative and traditional, but certainly it was his combination of masterful painting and poetic skills that brought about his almost mythical status in later ages. Virtually every anthology of Chinese poetry includes his works, and he is mentioned alongside Li Bai and Du Fu as one of the great poets of the Tang dynasty.

*L*I *B*AI

(b. 701, Jiangyou, Sichuan province, China—
d. 762, Dangtu, Anhui province)

Li Bai (also spelled Li Pai or Li Bo) rivals Du Fu for the title of China's greatest poet. Li Bai liked to regard himself as belonging to the imperial family, but he actually

Statue showing the revered Chinese poet Li Bai reclining in a peaceful setting in his hometown of Jiangyou, Sichuan province. **The Washington Post/Getty Images**

belonged to a less exalted family of the same surname. At age 24 he left home for a period of wandering, after which he married and lived with his wife's family in Anlu (now in Hubei province). He had already begun to write poetry, some of which he showed to various officials in the vain hope of becoming employed as a secretary. After another nomadic period, in 742 he arrived at Chang'an, the Tang dynasty capital, no doubt hoping to be given a post at court. No official post was forthcoming, but he was accepted into a group of distinguished court poets. In the autumn of 744 he began his wanderings again.

In 756 Li Bai became unofficial poet laureate to the military expedition of Prince Lin, the emperor's 16th son. The prince was soon accused of intending to establish an independent kingdom and was executed; Li Bai was arrested and imprisoned at Jiujiang. In the summer of 758 he was banished to Yelang; before he arrived there, he benefited from a general amnesty. He returned to eastern China, where he died in a relative's house, though popular legend says that he drowned when, sitting drunk in a boat, he tried to seize the moon's reflection in the water.

Li Bai was a romantic in his view of life and in his verse. One of the most famous wine drinkers in China's long tradition of imbibers, Li Bai frequently celebrated the joy of drinking. He also wrote of friendship, solitude, the passage of time, and the joys of nature with brilliance and great freshness of imagination.

Du Fu

(b. 712, Gongxian, Henan province, China—d. 770, on a riverboat between Danzhou [now Changsha] and Yueyang, Hunan province)

The Chinese poet Du Fu (also spelled Tu Fu, also called Du Gongbu or Du Shaoling) is considered by many literary critics to be the greatest Chinese poet of all time. Born into a scholarly family, Du Fu received a traditional Confucian education but failed in the imperial examinations of 735. As a result, he spent much of his youth traveling. During his travels he won renown as a poet and met other poets of the period, including the great Li Bai. After a brief flirtation with Daoism while traveling with Li Bai, Du Fu returned to the capital and to the conventional Confucianism of his youth. He never again met Li Bai, despite his strong admiration for his older, freewheeling contemporary.

During the 740s Du Fu was a well-regarded member of a group of high officials, even though he was without money and official position himself and failed a second time in an imperial examination. He married, probably in 741. Between 751 and 755 he tried to attract imperial attention by submitting a succession of literary products that were couched in a language of ornamental flattery, a device that eventually resulted in a nominal position at court. In 755 during An Lushan's rebellion, Du Fu experienced extreme personal hardships. He escaped, however, and in 757 joined the exiled court, being given the position of censor. His memoranda to the emperor do not appear to have been particularly welcome; he was eventually relieved of his post and endured another period of poverty and hunger. Wandering about until the mid-760s, he briefly served a local warlord, a position that enabled him to acquire some land and to become a gentleman farmer, but in 768 he again started traveling aimlessly toward the south. Popular legend attributes his death (on a riverboat on the Xiang River) to overindulgence in food and wine after a 10-day fast.

Du Fu's early poetry celebrated the beauty of the natural world and bemoaned the passage of time. He soon began to write bitingly of war—as in *Bingqu xing* (*The Ballad of the Army Carts*), a poem about conscription—and with hidden satire—as in *Liren xing* (*The Beautiful Woman*), which speaks of the conspicuous luxury of the court. As he matured, and especially during the tumultuous period of 755 to 759, his verse began to sound a note of profound compassion for humanity caught in the grip of senseless war.

Du Fu's paramount position in the history of Chinese literature rests on his superb classicism. He was highly erudite, and his intimate acquaintance with the literary tradition of the past was equaled only by his complete ease in handling the rules of prosody. His dense, compressed language makes use of all the connotative overtones of a phrase and of all the intonational potentials of the individual word, qualities that no translation can ever reveal. He was an expert in all poetic genres current in his day, but his mastery was at its height in the *lüshi*, or "regulated verse," which he refined to a point of glowing intensity. (The *lüshi* form consists of eight lines of five or seven syllables, each line set down in accordance with strict tonal patterns.)

CEN SHEN

(b. 715, Jiangling [now in Hubei province], China—
d. 770, Chengdu, Sichuan province)

Cen Shen (spelled Ts'en Shen in an earlier transliteration system; also called Cen Jiazhou [Ts'en Chia-chou]) is one of the celebrated poets of the Tang dynasty (618–907) of China. Because of the decline of his aristocratic family, Cen had to rely upon his literary skill to secure government appointment through the examination system. During the 750s he held several assignments in the Central Asian outposts of the far-flung Tang empire until the eruption of An Lushan's rebellion of 755 forced his return to China. Having supported the loyalist cause, he succeeded to a number of provincial posts under the restoration until his retirement in 768.

A member of the second generation of High Tang poets, which included such masters as Li Bai and Du Fu, Cen participated in the effort to reinvigorate the *lüshi*, or "regulated poem," through innovations in diction and metre. His contemporaries praised him for his stylistic craftsmanship, particularly his skill at creating unconventional metaphors and imaginative phrases. He came to be best known as a "frontier poet" because he so frequently set his poems in exotic Central Asia.

ŌTOMO YAKAMOCHI

(b. 718?, Nara, Japan—d. Oct. 5, 785, Michinoku, northern Honshū)

The Japanese poet Ōtomo Yakamochi, noted for his compilation of the *Man'yōshū*, was born into a family known for having supplied personal guards to the imperial family. Yakamochi became in 745 the governor of Etchū province, on the coast of the Sea of Japan (East Sea). Although he had been composing poetry throughout his life, he was intensely productive during his five years in Etchū and produced some of his best work there. His last datable poem is from 759; no works can be dated to the last 26 years of his life, a period during which he was likely preoccupied with compiling the *Man'yōshū*, the greatest imperial anthology of Japanese poetry. He contributed some 10 percent of the poems in the *Man'yōshū*.

Yakamochi's poetry is often compared with that of Kakinomoto Hitomaro and Yamanoue Okura, two of the major poets whose work also appears in the *Man'yōshū*, although Yakamochi is rarely thought to match either. His poetry's subject matter ranges widely from the personal to the public and is throughout tinged with melancholy.

ABŪ NUWĀS

(b. *c.* 747–762, Ahvāz, Iran—d. *c.* 813–815, Baghdad, Iraq)

Abū Nuwās al-Ḥasan ibn Hāni' al-Ḥakamī is an important poet of the early ʿAbbāsid period (750–835).

Abū Nuwās (Abū Nuʿās), of mixed Arab and Persian heritage, studied in Basra and al-Kūfah, first under the poet Wālibah ibn al-Ḥubāb, later under Khalaf al-Aḥmar. He also studied the Qur'ān (Islamic sacred scripture), Hadith (traditions relating to the life and utterances of the Prophet), and grammar and is said to have spent a year with the Bedouins in the desert to acquire their traditional purity of language.

Abū Nuwās's initial appearance at the 'Abbāsid court in Baghdad met with little success; his alliance with the Barmakids, the 'Abbāsid viziers, forced him to seek refuge in Egypt when the Barmakid dynasty collapsed. On his return to Baghdad, however, his panegyrics earned the favour of the caliphs Hārūn al-Rashīd and al-Amīn, and he enjoyed great success in the 'Abbāsid court until his death.

The language of Abū Nuwās's formal odes (*qaṣīdah*s) is grammatically sound and based on the old Arab traditions. His themes, however, are drawn from urban life, not the desert. He is particularly renowned for his poems on wine and pederasty. His verse is laced with humour and irony, reflecting the genial yet cynical outlook of the poet, who spent much of his life in pursuit of pleasure.

ABŪ AL-'ATĀHIYAH

(b. 748, Al-Kūfah or 'Ayn al-Tamr, Iraq—d. 825/826, Baghdad, Iraq)

Abū Isḥāq Ismā'īl ibn al-Qāsim ibn Suwayd ibn Kaysān, who came to be known as Abū al-'Atāhiyah ("Father of Craziness"), was the first Arab poet of note to break with the conventions established by the pre-Islamic poets of the desert and to adopt a simpler and freer language of the village. He came from a family of *mawlā*s, poor non-Arabs who were clients of the 'Anaza Arab tribe. The family's poverty prevented Abū al-'Atāhiyah from receiving a formal education, which may account for his subsequently original and untraditional poetic style. He began to write *ghazal*s (lyrics) in his early years in Al-Kūfah; they later gained him notoriety as well as the favour of the 'Abbāsid caliph Hārūn al-Rashīd. Abū al-'Atāhiyah's fame, however, rested on the ascetic poems of his later years, the *Zuhdīyāt* (Ger. trans. by O. Rescher, 1928), collected in 1071 by the Spanish scholar Ibn 'Abd al-Barr. The *Zuhdīyāt* depicts the leveling of the rich and powerful by the horrors of death. These poems found an enthusiastic following among the masses, as well as being popular at court, and were frequently set to music.

Anonymous: Beowulf

Written in the period 700–750 CE, the heroic poem *Beowulf* is considered to be the highest achievement of Old English literature and is the earliest European vernacular epic. Preserved in a single manuscript (Cotton Vitellius A XV) from *c.* 1000, it deals with events of the early 6th century and is believed to have been composed between 700 and 750. It did not appear in print until 1815. Although originally untitled, it was later named after the Scandinavian hero Beowulf, whose exploits and character provide its connecting theme. There is no evidence of a historical Beowulf, but some characters, sites, and events in the poem can be historically verified.

The poem falls into two parts. It opens in Denmark, where King Hrothgar's splendid mead hall, Heorot, has been ravaged for 12 years by nightly visits from an evil monster, Grendel, who carries off Hrothgar's warriors and devours them. Unexpectedly, young Beowulf, a prince of the Geats of southern Sweden, arrives with a small band of retainers and offers to cleanse Heorot of its monster. The king is astonished at the little-known hero's daring but welcomes him, and after an evening of feasting, much courtesy, and some discourtesy, the king retires, leaving

Beowulf in charge. During the night Grendel comes from the moors, tears open the heavy doors, and devours one of the sleeping Geats. He then grapples with Beowulf, whose powerful grip he cannot escape. He wrenches himself free, tearing off his arm, and leaves, mortally wounded.

The next day is one of rejoicing in Heorot. But at night as the warriors sleep, Grendel's mother comes to avenge her son, killing one of Hrothgar's men. In the morning Beowulf seeks her out in her cave at the bottom of a mere and kills her. He cuts the head from Grendel's corpse and returns to Heorot. The Danes rejoice once more. Hrothgar makes a farewell speech about the character of the true hero, as Beowulf, enriched with honours and princely gifts, returns home to King Hygelac of the Geats.

The second part passes rapidly over King Hygelac's subsequent death in a battle (of historical record), the death of his son, and Beowulf's succession to the kingship and his peaceful rule of 50 years. But now a fire-breathing dragon ravages his land and the doughty but aging Beowulf engages it. The fight is long and terrible and a painful contrast to the battles of his youth. Painful, too, is the desertion of his retainers except for his young kinsman Wiglaf. Beowulf kills the dragon but is mortally wounded. The poem ends with his funeral rites and a lament.

Beowulf belongs metrically, stylistically, and thematically to the inherited Germanic heroic tradition. Many incidents, such as Beowulf's tearing off the monster's arm and his descent into the mere, are familiar motifs from folklore. The ethical values are manifestly the Germanic code of loyalty to chief and tribe and vengeance to enemies. Yet the poem is so infused with a Christian spirit that it lacks the grim fatality of many of the Eddic lays or the Icelandic sagas. Beowulf himself seems more altruistic than other Germanic heroes or the heroes of the *Iliad*.

It is significant that his three battles are not against men, which would entail the retaliation of the blood feud, but against evil monsters, enemies of the whole community and of civilization itself. Many critics have seen the poem as a Christian allegory, with Beowulf the champion of goodness and light against the forces of evil and darkness. His sacrificial death is not seen as tragic but as the fitting end of a good (some would say "too good") hero's life.

That is not to say that *Beowulf* is an optimistic poem. The English writer and critic J.R.R. Tolkien suggests that its total effect is more like a long, lyrical elegy than an epic. Even the earlier, happier section in Denmark is filled with ominous allusions that were well understood by contemporary audiences. Thus, after Grendel's death, King Hrothgar speaks sanguinely of the future, which the audience knows will end with the destruction of his line and the burning of Heorot. In the second part the movement is slow and funereal; scenes from Beowulf's youth are replayed in a minor key as a counterpoint to his last battle, and the mood becomes increasingly sombre as the *wyrd* (fate) that comes to all men closes in on him. John Gardner's *Grendel* (1971) is a retelling of the story from the point of view of the monster. In 1999 Irish Nobel Prize–winning poet Seamus Heaney produced a memorable translation of *Beowulf*.

HAN YU

(b. 768, Heyang [now Mengxian], Henan province, China— d. 824, Chang'an [now Xi'an], Shaanxi province)

Han Yu (Han Yü) was a master of Chinese prose, an outstanding poet, and the first proponent of what later came to be known as Neo-Confucianism, which had wide influence in China and Japan. He was also called Han Changli or Han Wengong.

An orphan, Han initially failed his civil service exams because the examiners refused to accept his unconventional prose style, but he eventually entered the bureaucracy and served in several high government posts. At a time when the popularity of Confucian doctrine had greatly declined, Han began a defense of it. He attacked Daoism and Buddhism, which were then at the height of their influence. So outspoken was he that he castigated the emperor for paying respect to the supposed finger bone of the Buddha; this act of criticism almost cost Han his life and caused him to be banished to South China for a year. In defending Confucianism, Han quoted extensively from the *Mencius*, the *Daxue* ("Great Learning"), the *Zhongyong* ("Doctrine of the Mean"), and the *Yijing* ("Classic of Changes"; known to many as *I-Ching*), works that hitherto had been somewhat neglected by Confucians. In so doing, he laid the foundations for later Neo-Confucianists who took their basic ideas from these books.

Han advocated the adoption of *guwen*, the free, simple prose of these early Zhou philosophers and early Han writers as models for prose writing. Their style was unencumbered by the mannerisms and elaborate verselike regularity of the *pianwen* ("parallel prose") style that was prevalent in Han's time. Han Yu boldly advocated the use of Zhou philosophers and early Han writers as models for prose writing. This seemingly conservative reform had, in fact, a liberalizing effect, for the sentence unit in prose writing was now given perfect freedom to seek its own length and structural pattern as logic and content might dictate, instead of slavishly conforming to the rules of *pianwen*. His own essays (e.g., *On the Way, On Man,* and *On Spirits*) are among the most beautiful ever written in Chinese, and they became the most famous models of the prose style he espoused. In his poetry also, Han tried to break out of the existing literary forms, but many of his efforts at literary reform failed. He is considered the first of the renowned Eight Masters of the Tang and Song. At his death the title of president of the ministry of rites was conferred upon him, as well as the epithet "Master of Letters," both great honours.

BAI JUYI

(b. 772, Xinzheng, Henan province, China—
d. 846, Luoyang, Henan province)

Bai Juyi (Bo Juyi) is a Chinese poet of the Tang dynasty (618–907) who used his elegantly simple verse to protest the social evils of his day, including corruption and militarism. His name is spelled Pai Chü-i or Po Chü-i in an earlier transliteration system.

Bai Juyi began composing poetry at age five. Because of his father's death in 794 and difficult family circumstances, Bai did not take the official examinations for the bureaucracy until the late age of 28. He passed them and also did extremely well at another examination he took two years later. As a result, he was given a minor post at the palace library, as was another successful examination candidate and poet, Yuan Zhen. They shared views on the need for both literary and political reform, and their lifelong friendship became perhaps the most famous in Chinese history. In 807 Bai became a member of the prestigious Hanlin Academy in Chang'an, the capital, and he rose steadily in official life, except for his banishment in 814 to a minor post at Jiujiang, which arose from the slander of rival courtiers.

He assumed the important posts of governor of Zhongzhou (818), Hangzhou (822), and, later, Suzhou. In 829 he became mayor of Luoyang, the eastern capital, but he retired from that post in 842 because of illness.

Bai was the informal leader of a group of poets who rejected the courtly style of the time and emphasized the didactic function of literature, believing that every literary work should contain a fitting moral and a well-defined social purpose. He considered his most important contributions to be his satirical and allegorical ballads and his "new *yuefu*," which usually took the form of free verse based on old folk ballads. The most prolific of the Tang poets, Bai aimed for simplicity in his writing, and—like Du Fu, a great Tang poet of the preceding generation whom Bai greatly admired—he was deeply concerned with the social problems of the time; he deplored the dissolute and decadent lifestyles of corrupt officials and sympathized with the sufferings of the poor. Many of Bai's poems are quoted in the Japanese classic *The Tale of Genji*.

LIU ZONGYUAN

(b. 773, Hedong [now Yongji], Shanxi province, China—
d. 819, Liuzhou, Guangxi province)

The Chinese poet and prose writer Liu Zongyuan (Liu Tsung-yüan) supported the movement to liberate writers from the highly formalized *pianwen*, the parallel prose style cultivated by the Chinese literati for nearly 1,000 years. *Pianwen* had become so burdened with restrictive rules as to make forthright expression virtually impossible.

A talented writer from his youth, Liu Zongyuan served as a government official for most of his life, acting with integrity and courage despite his politically motivated exile to minor positions in isolated regions of China. Liu joined the writer and poet Han Yu in condemning the artificialities and restrictions of the *pianwen* style and in urging a return to the simple and flexible classical prose style. In pursuit of this goal, Liu Zongyuan produced many examples of clear and charming prose, notably travel and landscape pieces. Like Han Yu, Liu Zongyuan was reputed as one of the renowned Eight Masters of Tang and Song.

YUAN ZHEN

(b. 779, Luoyang, Henan province, China—
d. 831, Wuchang, Hubei province)

Yuan Zhen (Yüan Chen) is a key literary figure of the middle Tang dynasty of China, influential in the *guwen* ("ancient-style prose") revival, which employed the styles of the early classical Chinese writers.

Yuan entered state service through the examination system and briefly held ministerial rank. While in office he became a member of the literary circle of the poet-official Bai Juyi. Deeming literature an instrument of ethical and social improvement, the group rejected the courtly trends of the time and called for a revival of the moral themes and the straightforward style of ancient literature. Yuan thus joined Bai in reviving an old ballad tradition associated with social protest. Though famed for these *xinyuefu*, or "new music bureau," ballads, as well as for his more conventional poetry, Yuan was best known for his short fiction. Using contemporary settings, figures, and themes, he adapted the traditional *chuanqi*, or "marvel tale," to serious moral and social purposes. Works such as his semiautobiographical *Yingyingzhuan* ("Story of Yingying") thus set a new standard for the genre of the tale in Chinese literature.

ABŪ TAMMĀM

(b. 804, near Damascus [now in Syria]—d. *c.* 845, Mosul, Iraq)

Abū Tammām Ḥabīb ibn Aws was a poet and the editor of an anthology of early Arabic poems known as the *Ḥamāsah*. The volume takes its title from the title of its first book, which contains poems descriptive of fortitude in battle, patient endurance of calamity, steadfastness in seeking vengeance, and constancy under reproach and in temptation—in a word, the attribute of *ḥamāsah*.

Abū Tammām changed his Christian father's name of Thādhūs to Aws and invented for himself an Arab genealogy. In his youth he worked in Damascus as a weaver's assistant but on going to Egypt began to study poetry. It is not certain when he began to write verse, but by the time of the caliph al-Muʿtaṣim (reigned 833–842) he had established a small reputation. This was greatly enlarged through his association with al-Muʿtaṣim's court, where he became the most acclaimed panegyrist of his day. He traveled to Armenia and Nīshāpūr, Iran, and on his return from Iran stopped in Hamadan, where he began compiling his *Ḥamāsah*.

Abū Tammām's *divan*, or collection of poems, generally deals with contemporary events of historical significance. In his own day it was variously judged by the Arab critics; while his command and purity of language were generally recognized, many deprecated his excessive use of tortuous poetical devices.

WEN TINGYUN

(b. 812, Qi county, Shanxi province, China—d. 866, China)

Wen Tingyun (Wen T'ing-yün), born Wen Qi, is a Chinese lyric poet of the late Tang dynasty who helped to establish a new style of versification associated with the *ci* form, which flourished in the subsequent Song dynasty (960–1279).

Derived from ballads performed by professional female singers in the wineshops and brothels of the day, *ci* borrowed metres from existing musical scores and were themselves sung to instrumental accompaniment. Wen, whose aristocratic birth allowed him a life of leisure, frequented the urban amusement quarters to collect ballads as models for his own love lyrics. Admired for the delicate sensuality of his verse and his skill at evoking feminine sensibility, Wen was chosen as the lead poet in the first major anthology of *ci* poetry, the *Huajianji* (*Among the Flowers*), compiled by Zhao Chongzuo in 940 to popularize the new genre.

LI SHANGYIN

(b. 813, Henei [now Qinyang], Henan province, China—
d. 858, Zhengzhou, Henan province)

The Chinese poet Li Shangyin (Li Shang-yin) is remembered for his elegance and obscurity. A member of a family of minor officials, he pursued a generally unsuccessful career as a government official, composing poetry during and between his various posts. Until the second half of the 20th century little of his poetry had been studied seriously by Western critics, despite the fact that Chinese scholars since the Song dynasty (960–1279) had paid close attention to his work.

To Chinese critics he has been one of the most controversial, difficult, and complex of poets because of his use of exotic imagery, abstruse allusions, political allegory, and personal satire involving both historical and contemporary events and figures. These qualities also make his poetry difficult to translate. His works reflect the social and political conditions of his time, and, although few of his contemporaries recognized his genius, he greatly influenced early Song dynasty poets. One hundred of his poems are translated and collected in James J.Y. Liu's *The Poetry of Li Shang-yin* (1969).

AL-BUḤTURĪ

(b. 821, Manbij, Syria—d. 897, Manbij)

Abū ʿUbādah al-Walīd ibn ʿUbayd Allāh al-Buḥturī was an outstanding poet of the ʿAbbāsid period (750–1258). He devoted his early poetry, written between the ages of 16 and 19, to his tribe, the Ṭayyiʾ. Sometime after 840 he came to the attention of the prominent poet Abū Tammām, who encouraged his panegyrics and brought him to the caliphal capital of Baghdad. Al-Buḥturī met with little success there and returned to Syria in 844. On his second visit to Baghdad, *c.* 848, he was introduced to the caliph, al-Mutawakkil, and thus launched a court career; he enjoyed the patronage of successive caliphs, through the reign of al-Muʿtaḍid. In 892 al-Buḥturī went to Egypt as court poet to its governor and finally returned to his birthplace, where he died in 897.

The majority of al-Buḥturī's poems, produced during his years as court poet, are panegyrics, famed for their finely conceived and detailed descriptions and their musicality of tone. Those written during the early part of his career are historically valuable for the allusions they make to contemporary events. Like his mentor Abū Tammām, al-Buḥturī compiled a *ḥamāsah*, an anthology of early Arabic verse, but it was only mildly successful. Al-Buḥturī is often praised for his "natural" style, which is contrasted with Abū Tammām's "artificial," mannered exploitation of rhetorical devices.

IBN QUTAYBAH

(b. 828, Al-Kūfah, Iraq—d. 889, Baghdad)

Abū Muḥammad ʿAbd Allāh ibn Muslim ibn Qutaybah al-Dīnawarī is noted as a writer of *adab* literature—that is, of literature exhibiting wide secular erudition—and also of theology, philology, and literary criticism. He introduced an Arabic prose style outstanding for its simplicity and ease, or "modern" flavour.

Little is known of Ibn Qutaybah's life. Of Khorāsānian stock, he was *qāḍī* (religious judge) of Dinawar (*c.* 851–870). From *c.* 871 until his death he taught at Baghdad.

The 14 surviving works definitively ascribed to Ibn Qutaybah include the *Kitāb adab al-kātib* ("Secretary's Guide"), a compendium of Arabic usage and vocabulary; *Kitāb al-ʿArab* ("Book of the Arabs"), a defense of Arab rather than Iranian cultural preeminence; *Kitāb al-maʿārif* ("Book of Knowledge"), a handbook of history; *Kitāb al-shiʿr wa al-shuʿarāʾ* ("Book of Poetry and Poets"), a chronological anthology of early Arabic poetry, with an introduction that presented Ibn Qutaybah's canons of literary criticism; and *Kitāb ʿuyūn al-akhbar* ("Book of

Choice Narratives"), a collection of *adab* studies dealing with the authority of the overlord, the conduct of war, nobility, character, eloquence, and friendship, valued for its wealth of examples from history, poetry, and proverbs.

SUGAWARA MICHIZANE

(b. 845, Japan—d. March 26, 903, Dazaifu, Japan)

Sugawara Michizane is a Japanese political figure and scholar of Chinese literature of the Heian period, who was later deified as Tenjin, the patron of scholarship and literature. Sugawara was born into a family of scholars, and as a boy he began studying the Chinese classics. After passing the civil-service examination in 870 he entered the Japanese court as a scholar and poet. In 886 he was appointed governor of Sanuki Province (modern Kagawa prefecture) on the island of Shikoku.

Sugawara returned to Kyōto in 890. He was promoted to a succession of important posts by the emperor Uda, who sought to use him to counterbalance the influence of the powerful Fujiwara family. By 899 he was made minister of the right (*udaijin*), the second most important ministerial position, by Uda's son, the emperor Daigo. But Daigo favoured the Fujiwara, and in 901 Fujiwara Tokihira, Sugawara's rival, convinced the emperor that Sugawara was plotting treason. Sugawara was banished from the capital by being appointed to an administrative post on the island of Kyushu.

Following Sugawara's death there two years later, a series of calamities—storms, fires, and violent deaths—were attributed to his vengeful spirit. To placate the spirit, Sugawara was posthumously reinstated to high rank and later was deified. His writings include a history of Japan and two volumes of Chinese poetry.

A major festival honouring Tenjin is held annually on July 25 at the Temman Shrine in Ōsaka. There are also numerous local shrines throughout Japan at which schoolchildren buy amulets for luck during the period of school entrance examinations in the spring.

RŪDAKĪ

(b. *c.* 859, Rudak, Khorāsān — d. 940/941, Rudak?)

Abū ʿAbdollāh Jaʿfar ibn Moḥammad, better known by his byname Rūdakī, was the first poet of note to compose poems in the "New Persian," written in Arabic alphabet. He is widely regarded as the father of Persian poetry.

A talented singer and instrumentalist, Rūdakī served as a court poet to the Sāmānid ruler Naṣr II (914–943) in Bukhara until he fell out of favour in 937. He ended his life in wretched poverty. Approximately 100,000 couplets are attributed to Rūdakī, but of that enormous output, fewer than 1,000 have survived, and these are scattered among many anthologies and biographical works. His poems are written in a simple style, characterized by optimism and charm and, toward the end of his life, by a touching melancholy. In addition to parts of his divan (collection of poems), one of his most important contributions to literature is his translation from Arabic to New Persian of *Kalī lah wa Dimnah* ("Kalīlah and Dinmah"), a collection of fables of Indian origin. Later retellings of these fables owe much to this lost translation of Rūdakī, which further ensured his fame in Perso-Islamic literature.

CYNEWULF

(fl. 9th century CE, Northumbria or Mercia [now in England])

Cynewulf (also spelled Cynwulf or Kynewulf) was the author of four Old English poems. *Elene* and *The Fates of the Apostles* are in the Vercelli Book, a manuscript in Old English written in the 10th century CE, and *The Ascension* (which forms the second part of a trilogy, *Christ*, and is also called *Christ II*) and *Juliana* are in the Exeter Book, the largest extant collection of Old English poetry, copied about 975 CE. An epilogue to each poem, asking for prayers for the author, contains runic characters representing the letters *c, y, n, (e), w, u, l, f,* which are thought to spell his name. A rhymed passage in the *Elene* shows that Cynewulf wrote in the Northumbrian or Mercian dialect. Nothing is known of him outside his poems, as there is no reason to identify him with any of the recorded persons bearing this common name. He may have been a learned cleric since all of the poems are based on Latin sources.

Elene, a poem of 1,321 lines, is an account of the finding of the True Cross by St. Helena.

The Fates of the Apostles, 122 lines, is a versified martyrology describing the mission and death of each of the Twelve Apostles.

Christ II (*The Ascension*) is a lyrical version of a homily on the Ascension written by Pope Gregory I the Great. It is part of a trilogy on Christ by different authors. *Juliana*, a poem of 731 lines, is a retelling of a Latin prose life of St. Juliana, a maiden who rejected the courtship of a Roman prefect, Eleusius, because of her faith and consequently was made to suffer numerous torments.

Although the poems do not have great power or originality, they are more than mere paraphrases. Imagery
from everyday Old English life and from the Germanic
epic tradition enlivens descriptions of battles and sea
voyages. At the same time, the poet, a careful and skillful craftsman, consciously applies the principles of Latin
rhetoric to achieve a clarity and orderly narrative progress
that is quite unlike the confusion and circumlocution of
the native English style.

ANONYMOUS: The Thousand and One Nights

B elieved to have been written sometime in the 9th century CE, the work known variously in English as *The
Thousand and One Nights* or *The Arabian Nights* (Arabic *Alf
laylah wa laylah*) is a collection of Middle Eastern stories
of uncertain date and authorship whose tales of Aladdin,
Ali Baba, and Sindbad the Sailor have become part of
Western folklore. As in much medieval European literature, the stories—fairy tales, romances, legends, fables,
parables, anecdotes, and exotic or realistic adventures—
are set within a frame story. Its scene is Central Asia or
"the islands or peninsulae of India and China," where
King Shahryar, after discovering that during his absences
his wife has been regularly unfaithful, kills her and those
with whom she has betrayed him. Then, loathing all wom-
ankind, he marries and kills a new wife each day until no
more candidates can be found. His vizier, however, has two
daughters, Shahrazad (Scheherazade) and Dunyazad; and
the elder, Shahrazad, having devised a scheme to save herself and others, insists that her father give her in marriage

Illustration titled "Aladdin's Wonderful Lamp," by Karl Offterdinger,
from a 19th-century edition of The Thousand and One Nights.
Kharbine-Tapabor/The Art Archive at Art Resource, NY

to the king. Each evening she tells a story, leaving it incomplete and promising to finish it the following night. The stories are so entertaining, and the king so eager to hear the end, that he puts off her execution from day to day and finally abandons his cruel plan.

Though the names of its chief characters are Iranian, the frame story is probably Indian, and the largest proportion of names is Arabic. The tales' variety and geographical range of origin—India, Iran, Iraq, Egypt, Turkey, and possibly Greece—make single authorship unlikely; this view is supported by internal evidence—the style, mainly unstudied and unaffected, contains colloquialisms and even grammatical errors such as no professional Arabic writer would allow.

The first known reference to the *Nights* is a 9th-century fragment. It is next mentioned in 947 by al-Mas'ūdī in a discussion of legendary stories from Iran, India, and Greece, as the Persian *Hazār afsāna*, "A Thousand Tales," "called by the people 'A Thousand Nights'." In 987 Ibn al-Nadīm adds that Abū 'Abd Allāh ibn 'Abdūs al-Jashiyārī began a collection of 1,000 popular Arabic, Iranian, Greek, and other tales but died (942) when only 480 were written.

It is clear that the expressions "A Thousand Tales" and "A Thousand and One..." were intended merely to indicate a large number and were taken literally only later, when stories were added to make up the number.

By the 20th century, Western scholars had agreed that the *Nights* is a composite work consisting of popular stories originally transmitted orally and developed during several centuries, with material added somewhat haphazardly at different periods and places. Several layers in the work, including one originating in Baghdad and one larger and later, written in Egypt, were distinguished in 1887 by the

German Arabist August Müller. By the mid-20th century, six successive forms had been identified: two 8th-century Arabic translations of the Persian *Hazār afsāna*, called *Alf khurafah* and *Alf laylah*; a 9th-century version based on *Alf laylah* but including other stories then current; the 10th-century work by al-Jahshiyārī; a 12th-century collection, including Egyptian tales; and the final version, extending to the 16th century and consisting of the earlier material with the addition of stories of the Islamic Counter-Crusades and tales taken to the Middle East by the Mongols. Most of the tales best known in the West—primarily those of Aladdin, Ali Baba, and Sindbad—were much later additions to the original corpus.

The first European translation of the *Nights*, which was also the first published edition, was made by Antoine Galland as *Les Mille et Une Nuits, contes arabes traduits en français*, 12 vol. (vol. I to vol. X, 1704–12; vol. XI and XII, 1717). Galland's main text was a four-volume Syrian manuscript, but the later volumes contain many stories from oral and other sources. His translation remained standard until the mid-19th century, parts even being retranslated into Arabic. The Arabic text was first published in full at Calcutta (now Kolkata), 4 vol. (1839–42). The source for most later translations, however, was the so-called Vulgate text, an Egyptian recension published at Bulaq, Cairo, in 1835, and several times reprinted.

Meanwhile, French and English continuations, versions, or editions of Galland had added stories from oral and manuscript sources, collected, with others, in the Breslau edition, 5 vol. (1825–43) by Maximilian Habicht. Later translations followed the Bulaq text with varying fullness and accuracy. Among the best-known of the 19th-century translations into English is that of scholar and explorer Sir Richard Burton, who used John Payne's little-known full English translation, 13 vol. (9 vol., 1882–84; 3 supplementary vol., 1884; vol. xiii, 1889), to produce his unexpurgated *The Thousand Nights and a Night*, 16 vol. (10 vol., 1885; 6 supplementary vol., 1886–88).

Al-Mas'ūdī

(b. before 893, Baghdad, Iraq—
d. September 956, Al-Fusṭāṭ, Egypt [now part of Cairo])

The historian and traveler Abū al-Ḥasan ʿAlī ibn al-Ḥusayn al-Masʿūdī is known as the "Herodotus of the Arabs." He was the first Arab to combine history and scientific geography in a large-scale work, *Murūj al-dhahab wa maʿ ādin al-jawāhir* ("The Meadows of Gold and Mines of Gems"), a world history.

As a child, al-Masʿūdī showed an extraordinary love of learning, an excellent memory, a capacity to write quickly, and a boundless curiosity that led him to study a wide variety of subjects, ranging from history and geography—his main interests—to comparative religion and science. He was not content to learn merely from books and teachers but traveled widely to gain firsthand knowledge of the countries about which he wrote. His travels extended to Syria, Iran, Armenia, the shores of the Caspian Sea, the Indus valley, Sri Lanka, Oman, and the east coast of Africa as far south as Zanzibar, at least, and, possibly, to Madagascar.

The titles of more than 20 books attributed to him are known, including several about Islamic beliefs and sects and even one about poisons, but most of his writings have been lost. His major work was *Akhbār al-zamān* ("The History of Time") in 30 volumes. This seems to have been an encyclopaedic world history, taking in not only political history but also many facets of human knowledge and activity. A manuscript of one volume of this work is said to be preserved in Vienna; if this manuscript is genuine, it is all that remains of the work. Al-Mas'ūdī followed it with *Kitāb al-awsaṭ* ("Book of the Middle"), variously described as a supplement to or an abridgment of the *Akhbār al-zamān*. The *Kitāb* is undoubtedly a chronological history. A manuscript in the Bodleian Library, Oxford, may possibly be one volume of it.

Neither of these works had much effect on scholars — in the case of *Akhbār al-zamān*, possibly because of its daunting length. So al-Mas'ūdī rewrote the two combined works in less detail in a single book, to which he gave the fanciful title of *Murūj al-dhahab wa ma'ādin al-jawāhir*. This book quickly became famous and established the author's reputation as a leading historian. Ibn Khaldūn, the great 14th-century Arab philosopher of history, describes al-Mas'ūdī as an imam ("leader," or "example") for historians. Though an abridgment, *Murūj al-dhahab* is still a substantial work. In his introduction, al-Mas'ūdī lists more than 80 historical works known to him, but he also stresses the importance of his travels to "learn the peculiarities of various nations and parts of the world." He claims that, in the book, he has dealt with every subject that may be useful or interesting.

The work is in 132 chapters. The second half is a straightforward history of Islam, beginning with the Prophet Muhammad and then dealing with the caliphs down to al-Mas'ūdī's own time, one by one. While it often makes interesting reading because of its vivid descriptions and entertaining anecdotes, this part of the book is superficial. It is seldom read now, as much better accounts can be found elsewhere, particularly in the writings of al-Ṭabarī.

The first half, in contrast, is of great value, though somewhat sprawling and confused in its design. It starts with the creation of the world and Jewish history. Then it intersperses chapters describing the history, geography, social life, and religious customs of non-Islamic lands, such as India, Greece, and Rome, with accounts of the oceans, the calendars of various nations, climate, the solar system, and great temples. Among particularly interesting sections are those on pearl diving in the Persian Gulf, amber found in East Africa, Hindu burial customs, the land route to China, and navigation, with its various hazards, such as storms and waterspouts. The relative positions and characteristics of the seas are also explained.

Al-Masʿūdī's approach to his task was original: he gave as much weight to social, economic, religious, and cultural matters as to politics. Moreover, he utilized information obtained from sources not previously regarded as reliable. He retailed what he learned from merchants, local writers (including non-Muslims), and others he met on his travels. He displayed interest in all religions, including Hinduism and Zoroastrianism as well as Judaism and Christianity. But he tended to reproduce uncritically what he had heard; thus, his explanations of natural phenomena are often incorrect. Yet he was no worse, in this respect, than medieval European travelers such as Marco Polo and Sir John Mandeville.

Al-Masʿūdī had no settled abode for most of his adult life. In 945 he settled in Damascus. Two years later he left there for Al-Fusṭāṭ ("Old Cairo"), where he remained until his death in 956. It was there, in the last year of his life, that he wrote *Kitāb al-tanbīh wa al-ishrāf* ("The Book of Notification and Verification"), in which he summarized, corrected, and brought up to date the contents of his former writings, especially the three historical works.

MINAMOTO SHITAGŌ

(b. 911, Japan — d. 983, Japan)

The middle-Heian-period Japanese poet Minamoto Shitagō was a descendant of the emperor Saga and was a member of the powerful Minamoto clan. Despite this ancestry, Shitagō was barred from high political position because he did not belong to the Fujiwara family, which controlled the government. Instead he devoted himself to scholarly and literary pursuits and became recognized as one of the outstanding poets of ancient Japan. He helped compile the second official anthology of poetry, *Gosen-shū* and, as one of the poets later known as the Nashitsubo Go'nin ("Five Men of the Pear Garden"), also engaged in the interpretation of the first official anthology, the *Man'yōshū*. *Minamoto Shitagō shū*, a collection of his works, revealed his discontent and frustration over his lack of success in official life. He frequently participated in poetry contests. During the Shōhei era (931–938) he compiled the *Wamyō ruijūshō*, a dictionary of Japanese and Chinese words by categories, which was the first dictionary in Japan. He is also thought to have written many other works, including (some research suggests) the *Utsubo monogatari* ("The Tale of the Hollow Tree"), written between 956 and 983.

AL-MUTANABBĪ

(b. 915, Kūfah, Iraq — d. Sept. 23, 965, near Dayr al-ʿĀqūl)

Abū al-Ṭayyib Aḥmad ibn Ḥusayn al-Mutanabbī was the son of a water carrier who claimed noble and ancient southern Arabian descent. Because of his poetic talent, al-Mutanabbī received an education. When Shīʿite Qarmatians sacked Kūfah in 924, he joined them and lived among the Bedouin, learning their doctrines and the Arabic language. Claiming to be a prophet—hence the name al-Mutanabbī ("The Would-Be Prophet")—he led a Qarmatian revolt in Syria in 932. After its suppression and two years' imprisonment, he recanted in 935 and became a wandering poet.

He began to write panegyrics in the tradition established by the poets Abū Tammām and al-Buḥturī. A panegyric on the military victories of Sayf al-Dawlah, the Ḥamdānid poet-prince of northern Syria, resulted in al-Mutanabbī's attaching himself to the ruler's court in 948. During his time there, al-Mutanabbī lauded his patron in panegyrics that rank as masterpieces of Arabic poetry. Among his lines of praise for Sayf al-Dawlah are ones written after the prince's recovery from illness:

> *Light is now returned to the sun; previously it was extinguished,*
> *As though the lack of it in a body were a kind of disease.*

The latter part of this period was clouded with intrigues and jealousies that culminated in al-Mutanabbī's leaving Syria in 957 for Egypt, then ruled in name by the Ikhshīdids. Al-Mutanabbī attached himself to the regent, the Ethiopian eunuch Abū al-Misk Kāfūr, who had been born a slave. But he offended Kāfūr by lampooning him in scurrilous satirical poems and fled Egypt about 960. After further travels—including to Baghdad, where he was unable to secure patronage, and to Kūfah, where he again defended the city from attack by the Qarmatians— al-Mutanabbī lived in Shīrāz, Iran, under the protection of the emir ʿAḍud al-Dawlah of the Būyid dynasty until

965, when he returned to Iraq and was killed by bandits near Baghdad.

Al-Mutanabbī's pride and arrogance set the tone for much of his verse, which is ornately rhetorical yet crafted with consummate skill and artistry. He gave to the traditional *qaṣīdah*, or ode, a freer and more personal development, writing in what can be called a neoclassical style that combined some elements of Iraqi and Syrian stylistics with classical features. Many regard him as the greatest poet of the Arabic language.

FERDOWSĪ

(b. *c.* 935, near Ṭūs, Iran—d. *c.* 1020–26, Ṭūs)

The Persian poet Ferdowsī (also spelled Firdawsī, Firdusi, or Firdousi) was born Abū al-Qasem Manṣūr, in a village on the outskirts of the ancient city of Ṭūs. In the course of the centuries many legends have been woven around the poet's name but very little is known about the real facts of his life. The only reliable source is given by Neẓāmī-ye ʿArūẓī, a 12th-century poet who visited Ferdowsī's tomb in 1116 or 1117 and collected the traditions that were current in his birthplace less than a century after his death.

According to Neẓāmī-ye ʿArūẓī, Ferdowsī was a *dehqān* ("landowner"), deriving a comfortable income from his estates. He had only one child, a daughter, and it was to provide her with a dowry that he set his hand to the task that was to occupy him for 35 years. The *Shāh-nāmeh* of Ferdowsī, a poem of nearly 60,000 couplets, is based mainly on a prose work of the same name compiled in the poet's early manhood in his native Ṭūs. This prose *Shāh-nāmeh* was in turn and for the most part the translation of a Pahlavi (Middle Persian) work, the *Khvatāy-nāmak*, a history of the kings of Persia from mythical times down to the reign of Khosrow II (590–628), but that work also contained additional material continuing the story to the overthrow of the Sāsānians by the Arabs in the middle of the 7th century. The first to undertake the versification of this chronicle of pre-Islamic and legendary Persia was Daqīqī, a poet at the court of the Sāmānids, who came to a violent end after completing only 1,000 verses. These verses, which deal with the rise of the prophet Zoroaster, were afterward incorporated by Ferdowsī, with due acknowledgements, into his own poem.

The *Shāh-nāmeh*, finally completed in 1010, was presented to the celebrated sultan Maḥmūd of Ghazna, who by that time had made himself master of Ferdowsī's homeland, Khorāsān. Information on the relations between poet and patron is largely legendary. According to Neẓāmī-ye ʿArūẓī, Ferdowsī went to Ghazna in person and through the good offices of the minister Aḥmad ebn Ḥasan Meymandī was able to secure the sultan's acceptance of the poem. When Maḥmūd consulted certain enemies of the minister as to the amount of the poet's reward they suggested that Ferdowsī should be given 50,000 dirhams, and even this, they said, was too much, in view of his heretical Shīʿite tenets. Maḥmūd, a confirmed Sunni, was influenced by their words, and in the end Ferdowsī received only 20,000 dirhams. Bitterly disappointed, he went to the bath and, on coming out, bought a draft of *foqāʿ* (a kind of beer) and divided the whole of the money between the bath attendant and the seller of *foqāʿ*.

Fearing the sultan's wrath, he fled first to Herāt, where he was in hiding for six months, and then, by way of his native Ṭūs, to Māzanderān, where he found refuge at the court of the Sepahbād Shahreyār, whose family claimed descent from the last of the Sāsānians. There Ferdowsī composed a satire of 100 verses on Sultan Maḥmūd that he inserted in the preface of the *Shāh-nā meh* and read it to Shahreyār, at the same time offering to dedicate the poem to him, as a descendant of the ancient

Ferdowsi (lower left corner) *with three poets in a garden, miniature from a Persian manuscript,* 17th century; *in the* British Library. Courtesy of the trustees of the British Library

kings of Persia, instead of to Maḥmūd. Shahreyār, how-ever, persuaded him to leave the dedication to Maḥmūd, bought the satire from him for 1,000 dirhams a verse, and had it expunged from the poem. The whole text of this satire, bearing every mark of authenticity, has sur-vived to the present.

It was long supposed that in his old age the poet had spent some time in western Persia or even in Baghdad under the protection of the Būyids, but this assumption was based upon his presumed authorship of *Yūsofo-Zalīkhā*, an epic poem on the subject of Joseph and Potiphar's wife, which, it later became known, was composed more than 100 years after Ferdowsī's death. According to the narrative of Neẓāmī-ye ʿArūẓī, Ferdowsī died inoppor-tunely just as Sultan Maḥmūd had determined to make amends for his shabby treatment of the poet by sending him 60,000 dinars' worth of indigo. But the recorder of this information does not mention the date of Ferdowsī's death. The earliest date given by later authorities is 1020 and the latest 1026; it is certain that he lived to be more than 80.

The Persians regard Ferdowsī as the greatest of their poets. For nearly a thousand years they have continued to read and to listen to recitations from his masterwork, the *Shāh-nāmeh*, in which the Persian national epic found its final and enduring form. Though written about 1,000 years ago, this work is as intelligible to the average, mod-ern Iranian as the King James Version of the Bible is to a modern English-speaker. The language, based as the poem is on a Pahlavi original, is pure Persian with only the slight-est admixture of Arabic. European scholars have criticized this enormous poem for what they have regarded as its monotonous metre, its constant repetitions, and its ste-reotyped similes, but Iranians view it as the history of the country's glorious past, preserved for all time in sonorous and majestic verse.

KI TSURAYUKI

(d. *c.* 945)

K i Tsurayuki was a court noble, government official, and noted man of letters in Japan during the Heian period (794–1185). While serving as chief of the Imperial Documents Division, Tsurayuki took a prominent part in the compilation of the first Imperial poetry anthology, *Kokin-shū* (905). In a prose introduction, Tsurayuki discussed the general nature of poetry and the styles of the poets represented. This introduction, which was written in the newly developed cursive *kana* syllabic alphabet, is regarded as one of the early masterpieces of Japanese prose. Tsurayuki was himself a prolific and highly respected writer of Japanese verse (*uta*), and he ranks among the "36 Japanese poets," the most illustrious of the 8th to the 10th century. In 936 he wrote *Tosa nikki* (*The Tosa Diary*), a travel book composed in the phonetic script instead of the Chinese that was normal for men's diaries.

Few details are available about Tsurayuki's life and character. He appears to have devoted his life chiefly to literature. His son, Ki Tokibumi (or Tokifumi), was one of the five poets (later called the Five Men of the Pear-Jar Room) who in 951 compiled the *Gosen-shū*, the second official poetic anthology.

LI YU

(b. 937, Jinling [now Nanjing, Jiangsu province], China—
d. Aug. 15(?), 978, Bianjing [now Kaifeng], Henan province)

T he poet Li Yu (Li Yü; also known as Li Houzhu) was the last ruler of the Nan (Southern) Tang dynasty

(937–975). He succeeded his poet father, Li Jing, as ruler in 961. In 974 his country was invaded by Taizu, founder of the Song dynasty (960–1279). When Li Yu's capital, Jinling, fell the next year, he surrendered and was taken to the Song capital, Bianjing. There he was given a nominal title, but his life was one of misery. After Taizu died in 976, his brother and successor, Taizong, had Li Yu poisoned.

Li Yu was a master of the *ci*, a song form characterized by lines of unequal length with prescribed rhyme schemes and tonal patterns. More than 30 of his lyrics have survived. His earlier poems reflect the gay and luxurious life at his court, though some are tinged with romantic melancholy. His middle poems are those written from the time of his wife's death (964) to his captivity (975). He achieved his greatness, however, in his later poems in which he expressed his grief and despair at the loss of his kingdom. The direct and powerful emotional appeal of these later works has won them lasting popularity. In addition to being a poet, Li Yu was also a painter, calligrapher, collector, and musician.

PAMPA

(fl. 940)

The South Indian poet and literary figure known as Pampa was called *ādikavi* ("first poet") in the Kannada language. He created a style that served as the model for all future works in the Kannada language. Although Pampa's family had been orthodox Hindus for generations, his father, Abhirāmadevarāya, together with his whole family, was converted to Jainism, a religion of India that teaches a path to spiritual purity and enlightenment through a disciplined mode of life founded upon the tradition of *ahimsa*, nonviolence to all living creatures. True to his rearing, Pampa cared little for material possessions and gave freely of what he had. He highly esteemed his guru, Devendramuni, and his royal patron, Arikesari, and lauded both in his writings.

Pampa's great work was the *Adipurana* ("First [or Original] Scriptures"), in which Jain teaching and tenets are expounded. Another epic of his creation is the *Pampa-Bharata* (*c.* 950; Bharata is both the ancient name for India and the name of a famous king), in which Pampa likened his royal master to the mythical hero Arjuna in the *Mahabharata* ("Great Bharata"), one of the two great epic poems of ancient India.

SEI SHŌNAGON

(b. *c.* 966, Japan — d. *c.* 1025, Japan)

The diarist and poet Sei Shōnagon was a witty, learned lady of the court, whose *Pillow Book* (*Makura no sōshi*), apart from its brilliant and original Japanese prose style, is the best modern-day source of information on Japanese court life in the Heian period (784–1185).

Sei Shōnagon was the daughter of the poet Kiyohara Motosuke and was in the service of the empress Sadako at the capital of Heian-kyō (Kyōto) from about 991 to 1000. Her *Pillow Book*, which covers the period of her life at court, consists in part of vividly recounted memoirs of her impressions and observations and in part of categories such as "Annoying Things" or "Things Which Distract in Moments of Boredom" within which she lists and classifies the people, events, and objects around her. The work is notable for Sei Shōnagon's sensitive descriptions of nature and everyday life and for its mingling of appreciative sentiments and the detached, even caustic, value judgments typical of a sophisticated court lady.

Sei Shōnagon was apparently not a beauty, but her ready wit and intelligence secured her place at court. Those qualities, according to the diary of her contemporary Murasaki Shikibu, also won her numerous enemies. Though capable of great tenderness, Sei Shōnagon was often merciless in the display of her wit, and she showed little sympathy for those unfortunates whose ignorance or poverty rendered them ridiculous in her eyes. Her ability to catch allusions or to compose in an instant a verse exactly suited to each occasion is evident in the bedside jottings that are contained in her *Pillow Book*. Legend states that Sei Shōnagon spent her old age in misery and loneliness. English translations of the *Pillow Book* were prepared by Arthur Waley (1929, reissued 1957), Ivan Morris (1967, reissued 1991), and Merdith McKinney (2006).

Al-Hamadhānī

(b. 969, Ecbatana [now in Hamadān, Iran]—
d. 1008, Herāt, Ghaznavid Afghanistan)

Arabic writer Badī' al-Zamān Abū al-Faḍl Aḥmad ibn al-Ḥusayn al-Hamadhānī introduced the *maqāmah* ("assembly") genre. It involves entertaining anecdotes, often about rogues, charlatans, and beggars, written in a combination of rhymed prose *(saj')* and poetry and presented in the dramatic or narrative context most suitable to revealing the author's eloquence, wit, and erudition.

Al-Hamadhānī, often known as Badī' al-Zamān ("Wonder of the Age"), achieved an early success through a public debate with Abū Bakr al-Khwarizmī, a leading savant, in Nīshāpūr. He subsequently traveled throughout the area occupied today by Iran and Afghanistan before settling in Herāt. Al-Hamadhānī is credited with the composition of 400 *maqāmah*s (Arabic plural *maqāmat*), of which some 52 are extant (Eng. trans. by W.J. Prendergast, *The Maqámát of Badíʿ al-Zamán al-Hamadhānī*, 1915). The *maqāmah* of al-Hamadhānī typically relate the encounters of the narrator ʿIsā ibn Hishām with Abūal-Fatḥ al-Iskandarī, a witty orator and talented poet who roams in search of fortune unencumbered by Islamic conventions of honour. A later and better known writer of *maqāmat* was al-Ḥirīrī (1054–1122).

AL-MAʿARRĪ

(b. December 973, Maʿarrat al-Nuʿmān, near Aleppo, Syria—
d. May 1057, Maʿarrat al-Nuʿmān)

The great Arab poet Abū al-ʿAlāʾ Aḥmad ibn ʿAbd Allāh al-Maʿarrī was known for his virtuosity and for the originality and pessimism of his vision. He was a descendant of the Tanūkh tribe, an ancient group that migrated out of Arabia. A childhood disease left him virtually blind. He studied at the Syrian cities of Aleppo, Antioch, and Tripoli and soon began his literary career, supported by a small private income. His early poems were collected in *Saqṭ al-zand* ("The Tinder Spark"), which gained great popularity; it includes a series of poems on armour.

After about two years in Baghdad, al-Maʿarrī returned to northern Syria in 1010, partly because of his mother's ill health. In Baghdad he had been well received at first in prestigious literary salons. When he refused to sell his panegyrics (poems of praise), he was unable to find a dependable patron. He renounced material wealth and retired to a secluded dwelling, living there on a restrictive diet. Al-Maʿarrī enjoyed respect and authority locally, and many students came to study with him. He also maintained an active correspondence.

Al-Maʿarrī wrote a second, more original collection of poetry, *Luzūm mā lam yalzam* ("Unnecessary Necessity"), or *Luzūmīyāt* ("Necessities"), referring to the unnecessary complexity of the rhyme scheme. The skeptical humanism of these poems was also apparent in *Risālat al-ghufrān* (Eng. trans. *The Epistle of Forgiveness: Risalat ul Ghufran, a Divine Comedy*, 1943), in which the poet visits paradise and meets his predecessors, heathen poets who have found forgiveness. These later works aroused Muslim suspicions. *Al-Fuṣūl wa al-ghāyāt* ("Paragraphs and Periods"), a collection of homilies in rhymed prose, has even been called a parody of the Qur'ān. Although he was an advocate of social justice and action, al-Maʿarrī suggested that people should not have children, so that future generations would be spared the pains of life. His writings are also marked by an obsession with philology.

MURASAKI SHIKIBU

(b. *c.* 978, Kyōto, Japan—d. *c.* 1014, Kyōto)

Genji monogatari (*The Tale of Genji*) is generally considered the greatest work of Japanese literature and thought to be the world's oldest full novel. Its author's real name is unknown; it is conjectured that she acquired the sobriquet of Murasaki from the name of the heroine of her novel, and the name Shikibu reflects her father's

Silk-scroll portrait of the Japanese author known as Murasaki Shikibu.
DEA/G. Dagli Orti/De Agostini Picture Library/Getty Images

position at the Bureau of Rites. She was born into a lesser branch of the noble and highly influential Fujiwara family and was well educated, having learned Chinese (generally the exclusive sphere of males). She married a much older distant cousin, Fujiwara Nobutaka, and bore him a daughter, but after two years of marriage he died.

Some critics believe that she wrote the entire *Tale of Genji* between 1001 (the year her husband died) and 1005, the year in which she was summoned to serve at court (for reasons unknown). It is more likely that the composition of her extremely long and complex novel extended over a much greater period. Her new position within what was then a leading literary centre likely enabled her to produce a story that was not finished until about 1010. In any case this work is the main source of knowledge about her life. It possesses considerable interest for the delightful glimpses it affords of life at the court of the empress Jōtō mon'in, whom Murasaki Shikibu served. The author also kept a diary, which—translated by Annie Shepley Ōmori and Kōchi Doi—is included in *Diaries of Court Ladies of Old Japan* (1935).

The Tale of Genji captures the image of a unique society of ultrarefined and elegant aristocrats, whose indispensable accomplishments were skill in poetry, music, calligraphy, and courtship. Much of it is concerned with the loves of Prince Genji and the different women in his life, all of whom are exquisitely delineated. Although the novel does not contain scenes of powerful action, it is permeated with a sensitivity to human emotions and to the beauties of nature hardly paralleled elsewhere. The tone of the novel darkens as it progresses, indicating perhaps a deepening of Murasaki Shikibu's Buddhist conviction of the vanity of the world. Some, however, believe that its last 14 chapters were written by another author.

The translation (1935) of *The Tale of Genji* by Arthur Waley is a classic of English literature. Waley's version is beautiful and inspiring, but the translation itself is very free as well as incomplete. Edward Seidensticker's translation of *The Tale of Genji* (1976) is true to the original in both content and tone, and it set a new standard in scholarship. but its notes and reader aids are sparse. Royall Tyler's translation (2001) provides yet another layer of understanding and is espcially mindful of the contemporary reader.

GLOSSARY

aphoristic Marked by the use of few words to convey much information or meaning.

dithyrambic A literary term used to describe poetry that expresses exhaltation or enthusiasm.

epic poem A long, narrative poem detailing heroic deeds and glorious adventures.

epigram A concise poem dealing pointedly and often satirically with a single thought or event, often ending with an ingenious turn of thought.

epistle A composition written in the form of a letter.

epithet A disparaging or abusive word or phrase used in place of the true name of a person or thing.

fable A narrative work of fiction intended to enforce a useful truth.

lamentation In literature, a work written in such a way that it represents sorrow, mourning, or deep regret on the part of the writer or narrator of a story.

lyric verse A type of poetry characterized by the presentation of the poet's thoughts and feelings, frequently in a songlike structure.

metre The systematically arranged and measured rhythm found in verse.

motif A dominant idea or recurring theme.

pastoral Of or relating to rural or country concerns.

polemic An aggressive attack on or refutation of the opinions or principles of another.

prologue The preface or introduction to a literary work.

rhapsodic Characterized by extreme, ecstatic emotion.

rhetoric The art of writing or speaking effectively, especially as a means of persuasion.

satyr play A genre of ancient Greek drama that preserve the structure and characters of tragedy while adopting a happy atmosphere and a rural background.

spurious Having a false or deceitful nature.

strophic A stanza or rhythmic system of poetry composed of two or more lines repeated as a unit.

BIBLIOGRAPHY

Each of the various individuals discussed in this volume belongs to a specific tradition. Books on the ancient traditions of the main literatures treated are offered for additional reading and consultation.

Greek Literature

Among many surveys of Greek literature, the best are P.E. Easterling and B.M.W. Knox, *The Cambridge History of Classical Literature*, vol. 1, *Greek Literature* (1985); Jacqueline De Romilly, *A Short History of Greek Literature* (1985; originally published in French, 1980), with an excellent bibliography; K.J. Dover (ed.), *Ancient Greek Literature* (1980); Albin Lesky, *A History of Greek Literature* (1966; originally published in German, 2nd ed., 1963); Oliver Taplin (ed.), *Literature in the Greek World* (2001); and Gregory Nagy (ed.), *Greek Literature*, 9 vol. (2001), an exhaustive reference.

Aspects of poetry are treated in C.M. Bowra, *Greek Lyric Poetry from Alcman to Simonides* (1961, reprinted 1967); J.C.B. Petropoulos, *Eroticism in Ancient and Medieval Greek Poetry* (2003); and Ellen Greene (ed.), *Women Poets in Ancient Greece and Rome* (2005). C.A. Trypanis, *Greek Poetry: From Homer to Seferis* (1981), covers the entire Greek poetic tradition.

Latin Literature

Helpful surveys of Latin literature include Gian Biagio Conte, *Latin Literature: A History* (1994; originally published in Italian, 1987); and Laurie J. Churchill, Phyllis R. Brown and Jane E. Jeffrey (eds.), *Women Writing Latin: From Roman*

Antiquity to Early Modern Europe, 3 vol. (2002). Detailed and documented accounts include E.J. Kenney and W.V. Clausen (eds.), *The Cambridge History of Classical Literature*, vol. 2, *Latin Literature* (1982); and Michael von Albrecht, *A History of Roman Literature: From Livius Andronicus to Boethius: With Special Regard to Its Influence on World Literature*, rev. by Gareth Schmeling and Michael von Albrecht, 2 vol. (1997; originally published in German, 1992).

Other general surveys of the literature include Ward W. Briggs (ed.), *Ancient Roman Writers* (1999). Examinations of poetry include Ellen Greene (ed.), *Women Poets in Ancient Greece and Rome* (2005); and Kirk Freudenburg (ed.), *The Cambridge Companion to Roman Satire* (2005). The posthumous influence of various authors is traced in Gilbert Highet, *The Classical Tradition: Greek and Roman Influences on Western Literature* (1949, reissued 1985).

Arabic Literature

Comprehensive overviews of Arabic literature include Roger Allen, *The Arabic Literary Heritage: The Development of Its Genres and Literary Criticism* (1998), and *An Introduction to Arabic Literature* (2000); Pierre Cachia, *Arabic Literature: An Overview* (2002); Julie Scott Meisami and Paul Starkey (eds.), *Encyclopedia of Arabic Literature*, 2 vol. (1998); A.F.L. Beeston et al. (eds.), *Arabic Literature to the End of the Umayyad Period* (1983); Julie Ashtiany et al. (eds.), *Abbasid Belles-Lettres* (1990); Gregor Schoeler, *The Oral and the Written in Early Islam*, trans. by Uwe Vagelpohl, ed. by James E. Montgomery (2006; originally published in French, 2002); and Reynold A. Nicholson, *A Literary History of the Arabs* (1907, reissued 1998). An authoritative collection of essays in the series *The Cambridge History of Arabic Literature* (1983–2006) is Maria Rosa Menocal, Raymond P. Scheindlin, and Michael Sells (eds.), *The Literature of Al-Andalus* (2000).

Anthologies containing English-language translations of works of Arabic literature can be found in W.A. Clouston (ed.), *Arabian Poetry for English Readers* (1881, reissued 1986); Alan Jones (ed. and trans.), *Early Arabic Poetry*, 2 vol. (1992–96); James Kritzeck (ed.), *Anthology of Islamic Literature: From the Rise of Islam to Modern Times* (1964, reissued 1975); Ilse Lichtenstadter, *Introduction to Classical Arabic Literature* (1974); Robert Irwin (ed.), *Night and Horses and the Desert: An Anthology of Classical Arabic Literature* (2000); Reynold A. Nicholson (ed.), *Translations of Eastern Poetry and Prose* (1922, reissued 1987); Alqamah ibn ʿAbadah, *Desert Tracings*, trans. by Michael Sells (1989); and Stefan Sperl and C. Shackle (eds.), *Eulogy's Bounty, Meaning's Abundance*, vol. 2 of *Qasida Poetry in Islamic Asia and Africa* (1996).

Chinese Literature

General works on classical Chinese literature include John Minford and Joseph S.M. Lau, *Classical Chinese Literature* (2000–); Victor H. Mair, *The Columbia Anthology of Traditional Chinese Literature* (1994); Wu-Chi Liu, *An Introduction to Chinese Literature* (1966); Yuanjun Feng, *An Outline History of Classical Chinese Literature*, trans. by Xianyi Yang and Gladys Yang (1983); Burton Watson, *Early Chinese Literature* (1962); Patrick Hanan, *The Chinese Vernacular Story* (1981); C.T. Hsia, *The Classic Chinese Novel: A Critical Introduction* (1968, reissued 1980); and William H. Nienhauser, Jr. (ed.), *Indiana Companion to Traditional Chinese Literature* (1985), containing essays and entries with extensive bibliographies on all aspects of traditional Chinese literature.

Also of use to the general reader are Wu-Chi Liu and Irving Yucheng Lo (eds.), *Sunflower Splendor: Three Thousand Years of Chinese Poetry* (1975), one of the most extensive collections of translations. Also useful are Tingyun Wen et al., *Ten Thousand Miles of Mountains and Rivers: Translations of Chinese Poetry* (1998); and Ian Johnston (trans.), *Singing of Scented Grass: Verses from the Chinese* (2003).

Japanese Literature

General works on Japanese classical literature include Donald Keene, *Seeds in the Heart* (1993), which covers works from the earliest to those of the late 16th century. Jin'ichi Konishi, *A History of Japanese Literature*, trans. from Japanese, ed. by Earl Miner, 3 vol. (1984–91), includes a volume on ancient literature. Haruo Shirane and Tomi Suzuki (eds.), *Inventing the Classics* (2000), consists of a series of essays on the establishment of major works of Japanese literature as classics. David Pollack, *The Fracture of Meaning: Japan's Synthesis of China from the Eighth Through the Eighteenth Centuries* (1986), is a valuable survey of the Chinese component of Japanese literature. Hiroaki Sato and Burton Watson (eds. and trans.), *From the Country of Eight Islands* (1981), includes poetry from all periods. Ivan Morris, *The World of the Shining Prince* (1964, reissued 1994), is a general introduction to the Heian court. Diaries by court ladies include Michitsuna no Haha, *The Gossamer Years*, trans. by Edward Seidensticker (1964, reissued 2001); Izumi Shikibu, *The Izumi Shikibu Diary*, trans. by Edwin A. Cranston (1969); Sugawara no Takasue no Musume, *As I Crossed a Bridge of Dreams*, trans. by Ivan Morris (1971, reissued 1983); and Murasaki Shikibu, *Murasaki Shikibu, Her Diary and Poetic Memoirs*, trans. by Richard Bowring (1982).

INDEX